The
South
Atlantic
Quarterly
Fall 1995
Volume 94
Number 4

The *South Atlantic Quarterly* (ISSN 0038-2876) is published quarterly, at $66.00 for libraries and institutions
and $26.00 for individuals, by Duke University Press,
905 W. Main St., 18-B, Durham, NC 27701. Second-class
postage paid at Durham, NC. POSTMASTER: Send address
changes to *South Atlantic Quarterly*, Box 90660, Duke
University, Durham, NC 27708-0660.

The *South Atlantic Quarterly* is indexed in *Abstracts
of English Studies*, *Academic Abstracts*, *America: History and Life*, *American Humanities Index*, *Arts and
Humanities Citation Index*, *Book Review Index*, *Current
Contents*, *Humanities Index*, *Index to Book Reviews in
the Humanities*, and *Social Science Source*. This journal is a member of the Council of Editors of Learned
Journals.

ISSN 0038-2876

ISBN for this issue: 0-8223-6428-X

The
South
Atlantic
Quarterly
Fall 1995
Volume 94
Number 4

Nations, Identities, Cultures

SPECIAL ISSUE EDITOR: V. Y. MUDIMBE

V. Y. Mudimbe

Introduction

Nations, Identities, Cultures. Three apparently transparent concepts. But are they really transparent? In 1993, I decided to face them and organized a semester-long international seminar that focused on these concepts and their relation to exile, to the ethnicization of the political, and to the recess of the social in our contemporary world. The historical background for our reflections was the nineteenth century and the progressive transformation of such paradigms as *nation*, *nationality*, *class*, and *civil society*. Twenty-five scholars participated as faculty in this seminar. They included five Duke professors, two professors from UNC–Chapel Hill, and seven from other U. S. institutions. The other participants were from Canada, England, France, Germany, Ireland, Israel, and Sweden.

Each faculty member presented an original paper to the seminar participants and then led a general discussion. All the papers addressed, pro or con, a general argument that I had prepared in collaboration with

The *South Atlantic Quarterly* 94:4, Fall 1995.
Copyright © 1995 by Duke University Press.
CCC 0038-2876/95/$1.50.

Bogumil Jewsiewicki of Laval University. They also addressed each other by focusing on theory or on a completed case study, such as of Quebec, Israel's national borders, the Mediterranean basin, Eastern Europe, gender in rural Zaire, Kongo nationalism, the women of Lebanon, the Danish/Swedish border, or Rwanda. The theoretical perspectives dealt with such issues as the identity of memory and the memory of identity; popular cultures, race or ethnic origins, and internationality; civil society and the contradictions of liberalism; dialectical identity in Hegel; or utopia and postmodernity.

Twenty-three graduate students from Duke and UNC–Chapel Hill were registered in the seminar; however, the average weekly attendance was fifty participants. The seminar took place in thirteen weekly sessions of two and one-half hours. Each session was introduced by myself, followed by the presentation of the first speaker's paper and a discussion period. After a break, the second part of the session, again introduced by me, consisted of the presentation of the second speaker's paper and its discussion. The presentation of each paper was videotaped and broadcast by Satellite Communication of Languages (SCOLA) to more than 4,000 colleges and universities in the United States, Russia, and China.

The general argument of this collective reflection is that the concepts of exile, the ethnicization of the political, and the recess of the social, as well as their sociopolitical actualizations, go along with the apparent triumph of liberalism, the "end of history" described by Francis Fukuyama, and indeed, in some way, the end of a millennium. One might think that they could also mean the eclipse of the twentieth century, which could be seen as simply the continuation of a long nineteenth century. With the exception of Heidegger, most twentieth-century thinkers do belong to the nineteenth century in the same way that the concepts and realities of the *state/nation*, the *bourgeoisie*, and the *proletariat*, as well as *colonization, revolution*, and *modernity*, are nineteenth-century products. Postmodernity might be understood as a fashionable name for post–nineteenth century, indicating that the twentieth century has been living on the ideals and ideas of the nineteenth.

On that account, our contemporary thought seems to be a thought of exile, a thought hiding behind nostalgia for a recent past, a thought speaking from spaces and cultures that no longer exist and were dead before the death of the long nineteenth century. Concrete illustrations in today's literature might be Emmanuel Levinas's exegesis of European margins, Edward Said's of Palestine, Jacques Derrida's of Algeria, and Tadeusz Konwicki's or Andrzej Wadja's of Poland's borders. Our thought is haunted by the fear that the space from which it speaks might be its own contrivance. In order to avoid speaking about the Other, without whom the Self could not be constituted in its present shape, contemporary thought delights itself in an "ego massage," cultivating narcissism.

It seems possible to distinguish three main periods articulating three paradigms of subordination of the social to the political in a framework defined as secular. All three paradigms existed before the nineteenth century, but they became indispensable then for the description and management of the state and its secularized society. One could hypothesize that the French Revolution initiated a representation of the *political society* as essentially *national*, and thus the promotion of the concept of *nationality*. Next, the October Revolution in Russia articulated a new conception of the political society as essentially a *class society*, thus the promotion of the concept of *class*. Finally, the recent implosion of the Soviet bloc was paralleled by a representation of the political society as a *civil society*. During each period, the dominant paradigm (nationality, class, or civil society) organized an intellectual configuration and a way of *thinking the political* by interpreting and reinterpreting the notions of social conflict, on the one hand, and of a community of interests, on the other. The hegemonic role of the *nation* as a political subject expelled legitimate conflicts from the *state*; and the state, in order to be legitimated in its own right, had to become a nation–state. The hegemonic role of class as a political subject situated the conflict in the heart of the nation; and, finally, the hegemonic role of civil society-as-political subject organized the conflict between nation and state. Thus we get an ethnicization of the nation, and, paradoxically, the *ethnic* is affirmed as a political subject looking for a sovereignty. One can link these mutations of the legitimate political subject to other transformations, such as those concerning the notion of the *people*. This highly abstract notion (the basis of state sovereignty), which implies an original and primitive body, corresponded first to the primitive nation, and, in this sense, *popular* culture was what nurtured *national* culture. From this perspective, the invention of the *primitive*, with nineteenth-century colonial expansion, tolled the death knell of this perception of the popular, and the notion of the people became transmuted into that of the class society. Under the hegemony of the notion of class, the people (assimilated largely to both the notion and the reality of peasantry) were no longer the basis of national sovereignty, which then fused with a historical mission in the same way that a revolutionary party will fuse with the state. In this context, the popular is a legacy of the past, testifying to a reality condemned by history. Yet one should note that in practice, and because the proletariat has an international dimension, it is the popular which nurtures representations of a national culture that the state is always trying in vain to destroy. Finally, the hegemony of the civil society (one made actual by virtue of a multitude of associations and institutions) easily fuses the popular with everyday life and tends to bring together popular culture and *mass* culture. The popular actualizes itself, then, as a common denominator of the multitude constituting civil society and thus tends to transform popular culture into a *universal* culture which is seen as transcending national boundaries.

This is the basic argument that the contributors to the seminar discuss here in an interdisciplinary framework.

≡≡≡≡

For their support, I thank especially the heads of my three Duke University departments: Fredric Jameson, Director of the Program in Literature; Jean-Jacques Thomas, then Chair, and Walter Mignolo, now Chair, of the Department of Romance Studies; and Naomi Quinn, Chair of the Department of Cultural Anthropology.

I am also grateful to my staff. Priscilla Lane administered the seminar from its inception to its conclusion, assisted by Kathryn Shaffer. Dan Pillay, my research assistant, was generous with his time and his savoir faire. Lee Lubers, Director of SCOLA, and Pegge Abrams, Coordinator of Learning Services, programmed the SCOLA project, and Tim Searles filmed and edited all of the sessions. I thank them, as well as the Duke Student Development Program, for their involvement in the seminar. My thanks also go to Ben Ward and Frank McNutt, who were tremendously helpful in managing the presenters' on-campus stay and in arranging undergraduate meetings.

I am especially grateful to Richard White, Dean of Trinity College and Vice-Provost for Undergraduate Education, and former Vice-Provost Margaret Bates; Dr. Josefina Tiryakian, Senior Coordinator of the Center for International Studies; Patrice Leclerc, Administrative Coordinator of the Canadian Studies Center; and Lee Lubers, who supported the project from the beginning and sustained it at various stages of its promotion.

The seminar was sponsored or generously supported by the following Duke University centers, departments, offices, and programs, to all of which I am very grateful: African-American Studies Program; Canadian Studies Center; Center for International Studies; Center for Slavic, Eurasian and East European Studies; Departments of Classical Studies, Cultural Anthropology, Philosophy, Romance Studies, Slavic Languages and Literatures, and Sociology; International House; Offices of the Deans of the Faculty of Arts and Sciences and of Trinity College; Offices of the Provost and of the Vice President; Office of Student Development; Program in German Studies; Program in Literature and The Center for Critical Theory; and Technical Services.

I am also immensely grateful to the following students and colleagues, who played an important part in the seminar's organization by hosting and escorting our visiting faculty: Chris Andre, Katya Azoulay, Leonard Beckum, Dee Blankfard, Nicholas Brown, Peter Burian, Diskin Clay, Sara Danius, Gaurav Desai, Lesley Feracho, Owen Flanagan, Michael Hardt, Carlisle Harvard, Jennifer Hasty, Rod Herrera, Maude Hines, Stefan Jonsson, Samira Kawash, Thomas Lahusen, Kenneth Land, David Lipten, Sangeeta Luthra, Denise McCoskey, Frank McNutt, Charlie Piot, Andre Robinson, James Rolleston, Robert Sikorski, Faith Smith, Philip Stewart, Kenneth Surin, Sandy Swanson, Jing Wang, Tom Whiteside, and George

Wright. Finally, I would like to thank Bogumil Jewsiewicki, Hervé Moulin, Marie Moulin, and Elisabet Mudimbe-Boyi, who were extremely helpful throughout.

Ultimately, the seminar's success was due to its faculty, all of whom I thank wholeheartedly. A number of them have accepted my invitation to revise their papers for this special issue of the *South Atlantic Quarterly*, for which I am also very grateful. Finally, I owe special thanks to Candice Ward, managing editor of *SAQ*, for her help and her exceptional editing.

Martin Bernal

Race, Class, and Gender in the Formation of the Aryan Model of Greek Origins

My work *Black Athena: The Afroasiatic Roots of Classical Civilization* is concerned with the formation of ancient Greece, which I believe is quite rightly seen as the largest single source of European culture.[1] In this project I have found it useful to classify the many different stories of Greek origins according to what I call the Ancient and Aryan models. By "model" I mean a reduced and simplified representation, and I am acutely aware that creating models inevitably distorts the complex contours of the past. As the Italian proverb states, *traduttore traditore* (translator, traitor). Even the translated text has problems; as David Lodge puts it in his novel *Small World*, "Decoding is merely re-encoding." Having said all this, I believe that models, like words, are essential for organized thought and that some codes are better than others—in terms of the accuracy of their representation of "reality" and/or their comprehensibility. Thus it has been helpful to set up these two models of Greek origins.

The *South Atlantic Quarterly* 94:4, Fall 1995.
Copyright © 1995 by Duke University Press.
CCC 0038-2876/95/$1.50.

According to the Aryan model with which I and my contemporaries were brought up, Greek civilization was the result of the conquest of the Aegean basin from the north by the Hellenes, speakers of an Indo-European language, or—as slippage between language and "race" was very easy—"Aryans." Among many other things, the original inhabitants of the region are supposed to have lost their name, so for convenience modern scholars have simply called them "pre-Hellenes." Greek language and society are believed to have emerged from this mixture, and all of the considerable portion of it that could not be related to other Indo-European-speaking cultures was designated "pre-Hellene." By definition, the pre-Hellenes must not have been Indo-European speakers, yet they are seen as Caucasian and definitely unrelated to Africans or Semitic speakers from Southwest Asia. The nineteenth-century creators of the Aryan model saw Greece as fundamentally different from India, where the Aryans had conquered a "dark" people but had eventually been corrupted by them; Greece, by contrast, was seen as racially pure and essentially European, an appropriate cradle for "Western Civilization."

This picture was essentially created in the 1830s and 1840s. Before that, the predominant view of Greek origins was informed by what I call the Ancient model, which was fully articulated in the fifth century B.C., but there is strong evidence to suggest that it had existed much earlier. According to this model, the ancestors of the Greeks had lived around the Aegean in idyllic simplicity until the Phoenicians and rulers from Egypt arrived and acquired territories, built cities, and founded dynasties. The strangers also introduced many of the arts of civilization, notably, irrigation, various types of armaments, writing, and religion. These had later been refined by Greeks studying in Egypt and, to a lesser extent, in Mesopotamia. This image of cultural dependence was not one that made fifth-century Greeks happy, so the Athenians developed a myth whereby the Thebans and Peloponnesians had foreign ancestry, but they themselves were autochthonous sons of the soil. However, the credibility of the Ancient model is increased precisely because it went against the Panhellenic, anti-"barbarian" passions of the time. This point was taken up by the eighteenth- and nineteenth-century scholars who felt obliged to defend the Ancient model against skeptics. Before that, there had been no need for any defense, as it was accepted by all scholars who considered the subject.

My project has two aspects, one historical and the other historiographical. In the historical one I set up a compromise model, the "revised Ancient model." This accepts the arguments behind the Aryan model that it is plausible to postulate a single, ancestral proto-Indo-European language originally spoken somewhere to the north of the Balkans and that Greek is therefore fundamentally an Indo-European language. Thus at some stage the Aegean basin must have been substantially influenced by the north, and this influence could have been the result of migration or conquest. On the other hand, there is no reason to see this northern influence as precluding the possibility of substantial cultural influence from the south and east as well. The fundamental structure of Greek is Indo-European, and the Greek tradition remembered the overseas settlements rather than conquests from the Balkans. It is plausible to suppose that, rather than being the result of a pre-Hellenic substrate, the non-Indo-European elements in the Greek language and culture were largely later Semitic and Egyptian superimpositions on an Indo-European base. Possibly these were the result of conquest and elite settlement around the Aegean, and certainly they came from trade and diplomatic contacts between Egypt and the Levant, on the one hand, and the Aegean, on the other.

When I wrote volume one of *Black Athena* in the late 1970s I had hoped to measure the utility of the revised Ancient model against that of the Aryan model simply by confronting the "evidence" from archaeology, linguistics, religious cults, and so on. In preparing volume two, however, I came to realize that such an approach had two devastating flaws. At a superficial level, it would have been disingenuous for me to claim impartiality toward the two models. More fundamentally, I came to realize that there is no objective evidence above or beyond the models. Even in volume one, I had specifically rejected claims of *certainty* or *proof*, maintaining that the best one could hope for was what I called "competitive plausibility," or the least bad historical narrative. In volume two, I merely set out to show that it was more interesting and satisfying to work with or live in the revised Ancient model than it was to inhabit the Aryan one.

Here, however, I shall not be concerned with reconstructing the history of the origins of ancient Greece, but with trying to understand its historiography. I am particularly interested in the crux of the late eighteenth and early nineteenth centuries, when first the Ancient model was abandoned and then, a little later, the Aryan one was created and adopted by most scholars. Before getting down to this, however, I should like to take an approach formerly used in the history of science: that of seeing two aspects, "internalist" and "externalist," in scientific or scholarly shifts. This approach is unfashionable today because historians of science now believe that, in practice, the two components are not easily distinguished and that, even at a theoretical level, such a distinction is inevitably arbitrary. While recognizing these shortcomings, I am convinced that, as with my two models, such crude distinctions are often helpful and sometimes necessary.

Internalist developments are those that take place within a particular discipline; the historian then tries to determine who made the discovery, who knew the discoverer at the time, who was corresponding with him or her, who read publications on the discovery, and so on. Externalist developments are those forces and concerns throughout society as a whole that have an impact on the scholar and his or her work. A good example of this is Darwin's theory of evolution, which was clearly influenced by the proto-sociologist Malthus, who equally clearly had drawn his theories of the survival of the fittest from observing, and wanting to justify, the ravages of laissez-faire capitalism. Darwinism neatly illustrates that even when a scientific theory or historical interpretation is more or less crudely derived from contemporary concerns and needs, it is not necessarily useless. A dubious origin of this kind, however, does justify a more rigorous scrutiny.

When I separated the fall of the Ancient model from the rise of the Aryan one, above, I needed to distinguish them because the first took place completely without internalist developments: two of the three relevant great discoveries of the nineteenth century—the decipherment of cuneiform and the archaeology of the Bronze Age Aegean—took place after 1850, decades after experts had abandoned the Egyptian component of the Ancient model. The third major discovery—the decipherment of hieroglyphic—took place at about the same time that the model fell, but the decipherment was not accepted by most classicists until the 1850s, and the destroyers of the Ancient model were completely uninterested in Champollion's work. Given this lack of internal factors, the only way to explain the abandonment of the Ancient model is to identify external forces affecting the social and ideological environments of scholars in the late eighteenth and early nineteenth centuries. I have found it useful to classify these external forces or factors under four headings: (1) the establishment of the paradigm of progress; (2) the triumph of Romanticism; (3) the revival of Christianity; and (4) racism.

The rise of the Aryan model some twenty years after the abandonment of the Ancient model can be at least partially explained in internalist terms as the result of an important development in a relevant field: that is, the working out of the Indo-European language family and the recognition of Greek as one of its charter members— hence the need for some massive cultural influence from the north. However, I am convinced that this development, too, was affected by the cultural environment of the mid-nineteenth century, in which the same four factors were still powerful.

The establishment of progress as the normal way in which to view the long-term passage of time became a dominant paradigm in Europe only in the eighteenth century. Before then, it was more common to see periods in terms of decline or as cycles. The new paradigm of progress reversed the relative status of Egypt and Greece. Previously, Egypt had been considered superior precisely because it was older, hence closer to original wisdom and morality. In a progressive world, however, later is better, so the younger Greece had the advantage. The shift was epitomized by a new interpretation of the same story. According to Plato, the Athenian lawgiver and statesman Solon, on a visit to Sais (the Egyptian capital at the time), was granted an interview with some aged priests. When he began to tell them about some Greek myths, they interrupted him—saying, "Pathetic," or words to that effect—and claimed that while they, the Egyptians, had full records of early times, the Greeks had lost what little knowledge they possessed through natural disasters. Thus, said the priests, "You

Greeks are all children—you know nothing, you remember nothing." Before 1700, this statement was considered absolutely damning to the Greeks. With the establishment of the paradigm of progress, however, "Greek childhood" (the period of life with a future) became good, and what had been seen as the wisdom of Egyptian maturity was reconceived as senility and futility. Hence the Ancient model's claim that Egypt was in some way the precursor of Greece *had* to be false.

"Childhood" was not merely seen as the early stage of progress, but also as the age of feeling and passion—which brings us to the second factor behind the overthrow of the Ancient model, the triumph of Romanticism. I define Romanticism crudely as the conviction of the inadequacy of reason and, as such, the counterpoint to the Enlightenment. The gentlemen who upheld the values of the Enlightenment admired large, long-lasting empires, which they perceived as having been ruled by reason, without recourse to revealed religion. Their models were Rome, Egypt, and China. By contrast, the Romantics loved small, "free" communities with tumultuous histories that reflected passion and dynamism. Their ideals were Scotland, Switzerland, and Greece.

Eighteenth-century Romantics also loved the cold. In this they were following and developing an ancient tradition. Many ancient writers maintained that cold climates made people virtuous—rendering men martial and women chaste. However, ancient Greeks and Arabs tended to see these virtues as counterbalanced by the northern peoples' stupidity. As Aristotle put it in *The Politics*:

> The peoples of cold countries generally and particularly of Europe are full of spirit but deficient in skill and intelligence and this is why they continue to remain comparatively free but attain no political development and show no capacity for governing others. The peoples of Asia are endowed with skill and intelligence, but are deficient in spirit and this is why they continue to be peoples of subjects and slaves. The Greek stock, intermediate in geographical position, unites the qualities of both sets of peoples. It possesses both spirit and intelligence[:] the one quality makes it continue free; the other enables it to attain the highest political development and show a capacity for governing other people.[2]

Eighteenth-century Northern Europeans extended the benefits of a harsh climate from morality to a manly intelligence. The Romantic belief that living further north or higher up the mountain made one think better was still very much alive when I was a student at Cambridge. It was explained to me that Cambridge was superior to Oxford because there was no substantial barrier between it and the North Pole. Oxford, however, stuck as it was in a miasmic river valley in the center of England, would naturally produce muddy and muddled thought. Furthermore, as if Cambridge's geographical advantage were not enough, we were encouraged to spend vacations uncomfortably in the Alps or the Lake District, opening our synapses in the bracing air.

Scotland and Switzerland fit the Romantic ideal perfectly, while ancient Greece, despite having the required small communities, creativity, and turbulent history, was flawed by a distressingly comfortable climate. Climatic determinists therefore began to suppose that such an admirable people must have been formed in a more demanding environment further north. Even before the Aryan model had been worked out, there was a widespread inclination to see the ancient Greeks as a northern people who had migrated to the Mediterranean and had somehow retained their vitality.

I shall come to the converse of the belief in the benefits of cold, the ways in which heat was supposed to damage intellectual ability, when discussing racism. Meanwhile, I should like to touch on the third major force behind the abandonment of the Ancient model, that is, the revival of Christianity in the early nineteenth century. During the late seventeenth and eighteenth centuries, the upper classes of Europe and North America had turned decisively away from Christianity. This changed in the 1790s. The reason was suggested by Tocqueville when, with his usual perceptiveness, he noted in *L'Ancien régime et la révolution* that the French aristocracy, which had been the most libertine of classes in thought and deed, suddenly became deeply Catholic in 1792–93 with the trial and execution of Louis XVI.[3] His implication was that while the aristocracy had previously considered the gallows sufficient to keep the lower classes in check, they now appreciated the value of religion to maintain the social hierarchy and order. Furthermore, while the skeptical and cynical gentlemen of the Enlightenment could maintain a twofold philosophy (i.e., philosophy for the elite and superstitious religion for the masses), the new Romantic aristocrats insisted on authenticity. Therefore, if the poor had to believe, then so did they.

In Protestant countries another aspect of the return to Christianity was the perceived need for aristocrats to conform to the norms of an increasingly powerful bourgeoisie, one whose subscription to Christianity had been less shaken by the Enlightenment. The reason why this ideological shift had such an impact on the Ancient model was that an idealized image of ancient Egypt was at the heart of Freemasonry, and Freemasonry was at the heart of the Enlightenment. Freemasons saw themselves as the Egyptian priests of the modern age; chosen for their exceptional intelligence and morality, they would guide the masses and serve their best interests, which the masses were too stupid to perceive for themselves. To get a sense of this outlook, one need only attend Mozart's *Magic Flute*, with its abundant Masonic symbolism. The hero and his party escape from the Queen of the Night, representing both the empress Maria Theresa of Austria and the Catholic Church, and find themselves in the territory of Sarastro, the High Priest of Isis and Osiris. There, after undergoing rites of initiation, they emerge into the bright realm of masculine—and Egyptian—reason.

The importance of ancient Egyptian symbolism to the Masonic founders of the American republic can be seen in the Great Seal of the United States as represented on dollar bills, where there is a pyramid and an eye. Furthermore, the city of Washington is laid out according to the principles of Masonic geometry and is centered on the Washington Monument, the form of which is an Egyptian obelisk and the foundation stone of which was laid by the Grand Master of the Washington Masonic Lodge.

Christian apologists had sniped at the Deist and Masonic uses of symbols from Egyptian antiquity to attack religion since the late seventeenth century. However, hostility toward ancient Egypt rose to a crescendo among reactionaries because of the perceived and actual role played by Freemasonry in the French Revolution and the Bonapartist empire. And, as the reputation of ancient Egypt fell, that of ancient Greece, which had already been elevated by the Romantics, now became transcendent. In the late seventeenth century, when Homer and Pindar were considered the greatest poets of Western civilization, Greece was thought to have surpassed all other nations in poetry, the expression of the childhood of a people. Then, in the 1750s, Johann Winkelmann's new art history established Greek sculpture as the summa of the visual arts, the expression of youth. By the 1780s, German historians of philosophy were claiming—in the teeth of ancient testimony—that the Greeks, not the Egyptians or the "Orientals," had been the first philosophers. Thus the Greeks were also triumphant in the expression of maturity. Having prevailed at every stage of the biography of a race, the Greeks attained a semidivine status well beyond the realm of ordinary humanity.

Although it was only one of four factors behind the fall of the Ancient model, racism later became the major ideological force by which the Aryan model achieved and maintained its dominance from 1850 to 1950. Central to the historiography of *Black Athena*, racism is also directly related to two of the three paradigms described by V. Y. Mudimbe in his introduction to this special issue of *SAQ*. He sees all three paradigms—nationality, class, and civil society—as necessary to "the description and management of the state and its secularized society." Moreover, he contextualizes these paradigms historically, relating nationality to the French Revolution of 1789, class to the Russian Revolution of 1917, and civil society to the implosion of European Communism in 1989, describing the latter as the actualization of "a representation of the political society as a civil society." Although Mudimbe's third paradigm raises many interesting issues, it is not as directly relevant to my own project as the first two—nationality and class—are, especially with the addition of gender. I am sure that Mudimbe does not intend his periodization to function as a straitjacket; I think it useful to see all three paradigms as having been present in the ancient world, for instance, and there is no doubt that all three were central to intellectual life between 1770 and 1840, the period with which the historiographical section of *Black Athena* is primarily concerned.

In addition to their contemporary linkage, I believe that nationality or ethnicity, class or status, and gender were all linked even in antiquity both by their hierarchical nature and by correspondences of inequality. In ancient Mesopotamia, Egypt, Phoenicia, and Greece, there were considerable conceptual and practical overlaps between foreigners and servitude, and an even greater one between women and slaves. The latter association is epitomized by the Sumerian ideogram for "slave," which combines the element "woman" with "mountain," the symbol of foreign lands for people living in flat Mesopotamia. The Chinese character for "slave" merely contains the radical for "woman" with a phonetic sign to indicate its pronunciation. Women, especially those from elsewhere, were more easily coerced than men and were confined not only by the slave owner, but also by the patriarchal society as a whole.

The enslavement of one's own countrymen was always difficult because the male slave could gain sympathy or help from outside; he also needed constant and expensive watching to prevent his running away. Thus all the ancient civilizations of Southwest Asia tended to limit the debt–slavery terms of their own citizens, giving the male slave an incentive to serve out his time. Even the enslavement of foreign men was difficult, however, because of the risk of revolt or escape, hence the tendency to castrate, blind, or at least brand male prisoners both to distinguish them from the rest of the population and to make them as helpless as women in a patriarchal society.

Maritime societies in which slave owners controlled shipping and thus could trap the slaves found the enslavement of adult males easier to maintain as an economically viable system. It is interesting to note that in both the ancient world and early capitalist societies there was a strong correlation between chattel slavery and islands—Crete and Sicily in the first case, and the Canaries, Fernando Po, and the West Indies in the second—from which escape was almost impossible.

The ancient link of ethnicity with servitude was clear in the Greeks' distinction between themselves, who were naturally free, and the barbarians, who were naturally slavish. As Aristotle put it:

> There are some [i.e., the barbarians] who are everywhere and inherently slaves and others [i.e., the Greeks] who are everywhere

and inherently free. The same line of thought is followed in regard to nobility as well as slavery. Greeks regard themselves as
noble not only in their own country, but absolutely and in all
places; but they regard the barbarians as noble only in their own
country—thus assuming there is one sort of nobility and freedom
which is absolute and one which is only relative.[4]

Aristotle, whose political views were apparently typical of the Greek
upper class of his time and whose ideals remained central to Islamic
and European thought until the seventeenth century, saw a clear correlation between ethnicity and social status. However, as mentioned
earlier, he distinguished between the kinds of inferiority associated
with northern and southern barbarians, the latter being more suitable
as slaves.

The identification of foreignness with inferior status was also present in the other great source of "Western" culture, biblical Israel,
with its great stress on Israelite freedom and the unnaturalness of
holding one's own people as slaves and its countervailing tradition of
the justice and normality of Canaanite slavery (e.g., Noah's famous
exclamation, "Cursed be Canaan, slave of slave shall he be to his
brothers" [Gen. 9.25]). Later, those few Canaanites who survived the
Israelite massacres were condemned to be perpetual hewers of wood
and drawers of water (Josh. 9.21). The curse on Canaan was clearly
the etiology of, or at least the justification for, the exploitation of
Canaanites by Israelites. However, the biblical text contains an ambi-
guity in that Canaan was not the brother of Noah's sons Shem and
Japhet, nor was it he who committed the "crime" of seeing his father
drunk and naked; it was *his* father, Ham.

Ham was the eponym of Egypt and was seen as the ancestor of
African peoples. In talmudic times (i.e., the first centuries of our
era), the curse was thought to apply to these peoples, as symbolized by their "blackness." This brings us to the thorny question of
whether "racism" was exclusively a phenomenon of early capitalism.
Frank Snowden, former professor of classics at Howard University,
has devoted his scholarly life to arguing this case; specifically, that
classical Greeks and Romans viewed Africans or Ethiopians no more
negatively than they did Scythians or Northern Europeans, who also

differed from the Mediterranean somatic norm.[5] With considerable sadness, I have come to accept a less idyllic picture of race relations at this time, finding the case made by the great anthropologist and historian St. Clair Drake much more plausible. Drake firmly denies the thesis of Kenneth Gergen and Carl Degler that fear and dislike of the dark, including its manifestation in skin tones, are human universals. He shows that there was no color prejudice in ancient Egypt and no anti-African feeling in ancient Israel or Homeric Greece.[6] (Indeed, Homer saw the Ethiopians as the most virtuous of all peoples.) However, there was at that time a relationship between gender and color. For men working outdoors, dark coloring was a sign of heroism and virility, a tradition that still survives in our "tall, dark, and handsome." Homer described Memnon the Ethiopian as the most handsome man in Troy (*Od.* 11.522). Women, on the other hand, were expected to be confined to the house, so fair skin in them was considered a sign of high status and beauty. By contrast, paleness in men was an indication of femininity or cowardice—still seen in Shakespeare's relatively latter-day term "lily-livered."

Attitudes on color began to shift around the fifth century B.C., a shift that Drake attributes to the rise of the Persian Empire in the sixth century and the rigid dualism of Zoroastrianism, with its perpetual battle between good and evil symbolized by light and dark, or white and black, respectively. In Israel, sins were originally scarlet, but became black in the New Testament. Snowden denies that such abstractions were applied to human skin color. Nevertheless, there is evidence of Africans being seen in both Hellenistic Greece and Rome as bringers of misfortune. This attitude was even more intense in early Christianity, as reflected by Jerome's Latin translation of the bride's line in *Song of Songs*—which the Hebrew and Greek texts render "I am black and beautiful"—as "I am black *but* beautiful."

The talmudic interpretation of the Curse of Canaan as blackness first emerged in Mesopotamian society, which had an increasing number of African slaves. However, fear of and hostility toward blacks in late antiquity did not mean that Africans or other dark-skinned peoples were seen by West Eurasians of the time as they were by eighteenth-century Europeans, that is, as automatically evil or synonymous with slaves. The word "slave" itself derives from "Slav," as these heathen and particularly pale East Europeans constituted a major proportion of the slaves in early medieval Islam and Christendom.

There is no doubt that Snowden is right to claim that something categorically new occurred with the beginnings of the Portuguese, Dutch, and English transatlantic slave trade in the fifteenth and sixteenth centuries, which led to the development during the seventeenth century of a caste racism whereby the best black was seen as worse than the worst white. Aristotle's justifications for slavery and for the existence of "natural slaves" as well as the talmudic interpretation of the Curse of Canaan were both revived in the seventeenth century by Protestants. Skin color and physiognomy became increasingly obsessional issues among Northern Europeans and North Americans. The basic reason for this was the Christians' need to dehumanize the people whom they were treating inhumanely, both in the transatlantic slave trade and in the exploitation of Africa itself.

This brings us back to the fall of the Ancient model of Greek origins. The dehumanization of Africans naturally placed them at the opposite pole to civilization. In this situation, regarding Egypt as the font of world and European civilization presented difficulties due to its awkward placing on the African continent. In the eighteenth century, there were two possible ways out of this dilemma for a society that was becoming increasingly racist. The first path, taken by the Egyptophiles of the Enlightenment, was to deny that Egypt was African; the second, taken by Christian apologists and the Romantics, was to deny that Egypt was civilized.

Later scholars have tended toward a compromise view, holding that Egypt was neither truly African nor truly civilized. All three arguments succeed in placing a categorical barrier between *true* Africans and *true* civilization. Seen in this light, the triumph of Romanticism over the Enlightenment during and after the French Revolution made it ideologically impossible for Greece to have been culturally indebted to African Egypt. The extension of this argument—denying that "Semitic" Phoenicians could have played a central role in the formation of Greek civilization—came with the systematization of racial anti-Semitism in the 1880s and 1890s. In examining this development, we must turn from what could be called *intercontinental racism* to *intracontinental ethnicity*.

≡≡≡

It is generally agreed that "nationalism" is a product of capitalism and the formation of the modern state. I share with Humpty Dumpty, in *Through the Looking-Glass*, the belief that words can be used in any way one wants, although there may be some difficulty in being understood. How, then, should we use the words "nation" and "nationalism"? My colleague Benedict Anderson, who believes that nations are products of the modern age, has called them "imagined communities," that is, societies larger than those with face-to-face relationships and, unlike a "clan" or "tribe," having only the flimsiest claim, if any, to common descent. Members of a nation also have to have—and this is crucial—a sense of *other* peoples who may be inferior but must be recognized as human.[7] Differentiations of self and others as strong as those between Chinese and barbarians, Christians and heathens, Muslims and "kaffirs," or—after 1650, Europeans and non-Europeans—constitute a "world" or "common culture" but not a nation. I believe that entities fulfilling the criteria for nationhood have existed sporadically throughout history, as recorded over the past 5,000 years.

The clearest early examples of nations are those of peoples who were sporadically or partially subdued on the fringes of large empires. The Vietnamese and Koreans, for example, who have always acknowledged that the Chinese are people, feel intense pride in and loyalty toward their own languages and cultures, even though both have been saturated by Chinese influences. Germans felt the same way about the Romans and themselves. One reason that modern scholars are reluctant to recognize such early "nationalism" is the clear attachment of peoples in Mesopotamia, Syro-Palestine, and Greece to their cities and the frequent lack of cohesion among cities of the same culture against outsiders, such as the Phoenician cities' failing to unite against the Assyrians, or the Greek city–states against the Persians. In Greece, as we have seen from Aristotle's distinction between free Hellenes and slavish barbarians and as we know from other sources, notably, Aristophanes' *Lysistrata*, an articulate ideology of Panhellenism argued against internecine squabbles among the Greek city–states in the face of a common enemy like Persia. I think it useful to see this as at least a proto-nationalism in the period before Alexander the Great established a "Greek world."

In any event, one should avoid seeing localism and nationalism as necessarily contradictory. Indeed, the two can often reinforce each other. Texans do not see themselves as less American than those of other, less fortunate states. The most moving segment of Leni von Riefenstahl's Nazi propaganda film *Triumph des Willens* occurs when the young men call out, "Ich bin von Friesland, Ich bin von Bayern," and so on, culminating in "ein Volk ein Führer. . . ."

As for the word "nation" itself, the Romans used *natio, nationis* much as Europeans in America used *nations* to refer to different groups of "Indians." These "nations" were perceived as more or less cohesive collections of primitive *natives*. The idea of oneself as belonging to a "nation" derives from the University of Paris and other early medieval European universities, where students from the same birthplace, speaking the same dialect and having the same tastes in food, lived together in common houses. To this day, student dormitories in some German and Scandinavian universities are still called "nations."

The idea of a "nation–state" came later. While such an entity had existed in Vietnam since the tenth century, the first European nation–states only emerged some 500 years later. In England and France, fifteenth-century figures such as Henry V and Joan of Arc's Dauphin based their legitimacy on the idea of a territorial nation and appealed to the local language and traditions. These politico-cultural entities arose during the Hundred Years War precisely in opposition to the other Western Christian powers. The breakthrough of nationalism came with the Reformation in the 1520s, which gave two major boosts to the nation and the nation–state. First, it meant that in Northern Europe the transcendent ideological and political power of the Roman Catholic Church, the successor to the Roman Empire, was broken, allowing religious and political power to be concentrated in one (secular) ruler. In England and Scandinavia, the king became head of a national church. The German Protestant princes clearly

operated at a subnational level, but German nationalism was delib-
erately consolidated by Martin Luther through his translation of the
Bible into German. The translation of the Bible into the languages of
the Protestant nations made what had been dialects standard forms
with religious, literary, and political authority. A common language
has always been seen as the heart or core of a nation, so this was the
second boost to nationalism provided by the Reformation.

The fact that most of the Protestant nations spoke related Germanic
languages, while the peoples who spoke the Romance ones tended to
remain Catholic, increased the sense of difference between Northern
and Southern Europe. Just before the Reformation, the rediscovery of
the *Germania*, Tacitus's laudatory and idyllic picture of their ancestors, had encouraged Germans to see themselves as poorer but more
virtuous than the degenerate peoples to their south. From the late
sixteenth century on, there was a growing sense that the English,
Dutch, and Germans were all descendants of these independent, martial tribes and that Protestantism was a true expression of this noble,
masculine nature. The implications of a gender distinction between
manly Protestants and the celibate, effeminate, skirt-wearing Catholic priests still resonate in the speeches and sermons of the Ulster
(ultra-)Protestant Ian Paisley as he damns the pope and his minions.

In England, the different images of masculine Protestant Germans
and feminine Catholic Latins were used by radicals during the Civil
War of the seventeenth century, when supporters of the Parliamen-
tarians claimed to be overthrowing the "Norman yoke" imposed by
William the Conqueror over 500 years earlier in 1066. The masculine/
Protestant image became a club with which to beat the aristocratic
descendants of the French invaders. This affection for the manly, independent, nonaristocratic Saxons survived in America, where Thomas
Jefferson—a considerable scholar of Anglo-Saxon—attempted to replace Latin with it as the ancient language to be taught in American universities.[8] In England, the restoration of the very frenchified
Charles II and the return of exiled royalists in 1660 meant that this
subversive Saxonism disappeared or was driven underground until
its revival—in a nonthreatening form but in full force nonetheless—
precisely during the period with which we are concerned, 1820–50.

In Germany, the ravages of the Thirty Years War in the middle of the seventeenth century were followed by a military, political, and cultural threat from the new Rome, the Paris (or rather, the Versailles) of Louis XIV. More books were published in French and Latin than in German during the first half of the eighteenth century. The spoken as well as written language of the court of Frederick the Great was French. German was not considered a cultured language capable of expressing poetry or philosophy. There was a fear among some patriots that German would go the way of the language of the Germanic Franks and be swallowed up by French. It was only by means of major and fully conscious efforts that German poets and intellectuals were able to beat back the Latin threat, substituting German for foreign words and refining the language so as to make it fully expressive.

In line with its universalism, the Enlightenment favored established languages and cultures, namely, Latin, French, and English. A preference for an uncouth but authentic language of the people, however, fit well with the spirit of Romanticism, which was concerned not with generalities but with particulars. The German conservative Justus Moser challenged the Enlightenment claim to be concerned with humanity as a whole by saying that he had seen a German, a Frenchman, an Englishman, and a Turk—but never a man. The great intellectual Gottfried Herder also attacked the alleged universalism of the Enlightenment. He maintained that each nation should express itself in its own language and follow its own traditions, not absorbing outside cultural attributes even if they were better. Each nation should instead choose its own attributes, those which were appropriate to its spirit. However, as a child of the Enlightenment, Herder also claimed that all peoples were equal and that there was no absolute hierarchy of values. Taking his beliefs to the extreme, he maintained that the Hottentot criteria for beauty were as valid as those of Europeans. Kant, Hegel, and other eighteenth-, nineteenth-, and twentieth-century German thinkers were less scrupulous. For them there were clear hierarchies of race, most of which placed the Germans at the top.

Before developing this theme, I should like to glance at what can be called a "special relationship" between Germans and Greeks. Western Europeans found it hard to be too enthusiastic about the Greeks as long as the Byzantine Empire was a political power. It was only in the fifteenth century, when it was on the ropes—Constantinople finally fell in 1453—that Italians began to discover and glorify classical Greece. Soon thereafter, German scholars began to note that their language shared some features with Greek (four noun cases, infinitives ending with -n, etc.) that it did not share with Latin. Martin Luther played a critical role in this development, too, when he used the Greek Testament and the Septuagint to undercut the authority of Jerome's Vulgate. The perceived special relationship worked in two ways: First, it gave Germans a more direct connection to "pure" Christianity, and to antiquity as a whole, than that channeled through Rome. Second, it made the ancient Greeks honorary Teutons, which allowed them to be seen as manly heroes despite their apparent military weakness against the Roman Empire.

Concern with Greece dwindled in Germany—though not in all other Protestant communities—with the near collapse of German culture during the Thirty Years War. It revived with Romanticism and German nationalism in the mid-eighteenth century, when it provided another way in which to challenge the Franco-Latin cultural hegemony. This hegemony, damned as Catholic until 1789, then became linked to something that seemed even more evil, the French Revolution. It was in reaction to this that reformers, notably, Wilhelm von Humbolt, turned to the image of ancient Greece—improbably portrayed as harmonious—as the model by which Germany could reform its doomed autocracy without going through the radical horrors of the French Revolution. Thus, in the nineteenth century, the study of antiquity and of the Greeks in particular became the center of the Prussian humanistic education system. The meritocratic aspects of that system and its emphasis on Greece were attacked by reactionaries and German national extremists, but liberal nationalists quickly realized that, as they framed it, Hellenism provided a legitimizing universalism to their German ideology.

To return to the eighteenth century, the new Romantic historiography being promoted in Germany tried to escape from earlier history-writing, which was unfairly portrayed as mere lists of rulers and battles, by constructing the biographies of races. Now there was concern with the landscape in which peoples were formed, their laws, institutions, languages, and literatures. The new Romantic historians in Germany and elsewhere tended to turn away from the study of both antiquity and modernity and toward that of the Middle Ages, so despised by the Enlightenment. Thus they, too, were unable to avoid war and conquest; indeed, conquest became the mark of a "master race."

Despite an embarrassing number of cases, such as the Moors in Spain or the Turks in the Balkans, in which "inferior" races had conquered "superior" ones, the new historians were concerned with what they saw as the beneficial results of superior races' conquests of inferior ones. It was easy to tell the two apart, as superior races obviously came from more demanding and colder climates, hence from the north. This meant that the paler the skin, the better the people. The "natural nature" of such conquests was further helped by a force that I can only call "cartographic gravity." During the Renaissance it had been arbitrarily but significantly decided that the North Pole should be at the top of the map. Thus it was seen as easier to conquer downward than upward, although in Europe beneficial results could also come from horizontal conquests by races of the colder east of Central Asia. The conquests along these lines that particularly interested the new historians, however, were those by the Germanic tribes of the western Roman Empire: the Visigoths in Spain, the Lombards in Italy, the Franks in France, and the Saxons in England. These tribes were believed to have provided the dynamism that impelled Europe to conquer the world. Whatever was good about Western Europe was attributed to this Germanic element, while weaknesses were largely the legacy of the decadent subjects of the Roman Empire. However, images of gender played a role here, with the Celto-Roman natives seen as having provided a woman's touch that civilized the resultant culture. In many ways, this was viewed as the best possible basis for a new civilization. Nevertheless, the Romantic insistence on purity and authenticity led to some ambivalence over the extent to which the conquerors should mix with the conquered. There was a strong tendency to see the best Germans as those who had stayed at home in their own lands and not mixed with lesser races.

It should be emphasized here that such beneficial conquests were restricted to Europe; if a conquered people were categorically or continentally inferior, mixing with them was seen as miscegenation.

This view was based on the paradoxical belief of most racists that the darker/inferior feminine races always defeated the conquerors in the end by sapping the vital fluids of the lighter/superior masculine ones. The most "tragic" example was that of India, where the purest Indo-Europeans, the original Aryans, had succumbed to the dark Dravidians despite heroic efforts to keep their blood pure through the caste system. The only satisfactory way for Europeans to conquer the world—as was their right—was either to exterminate the inferior races, as in North America and Australia, or to keep a rigid barrier between the races, as in Africa and Asia. The Iberians, whose Germanic elements were attenuated, were thought to have been woefully remiss about racial segregation in South America.

With respect to the potentially beneficial conquests of Southern Europeans by Northern Europeans, the image of the Gallo-Romans' conquest by the Germanic Franks became politically crucial on the eve of the French Revolution. The nobles, unable to justify their outrageous privileges in terms of the universal values of the Enlightenment, turned to the newly conceptualized Middle Ages and appealed to a fictionalized descent from the Franks. Thus their superiority and special privileges were seen as deriving from their race and the right of conquest. They now saw themselves as ultimately Germanic. In the 1770s and 1780s, members of the aristocracy flocked to subscribe to a French translation of Shakespeare, who was seen as the epitome of a dynamic "natural genius," having broken all the classical dramatic rules of Aristotle and Seneca that were followed so carefully by the French playwrights Racine and Corneille.[9] The king, too, was swept up in this Frankish current, and whereas Louis XIV had been promoted as the classical Apollo or Hercules, and Louis XV had followed the rituals of a Chinese emperor, Louis XVI increasingly saw himself as a medieval king. However, where his models had generally (and sensibly) sided with the bourgeoisie to counterbalance the nobility, in the new world of race Louis XVI made the fatal error of placing himself at the head of his peers in opposition to the Third Estate.

The aristocrats' racial ideology backfired terribly, especially when they fled to Germany and England at the first whiff of trouble. The revolutionaries, assuming the guise of Roman republicans, were able to characterize themselves as French patriots driving the Germans back to their howling forests. I am not claiming that this was *the* cause of the revolution, behind which there were much more substantial social, economic, and institutional forces; nevertheless, it was a factor—an important one in its contemporary interpretation. The "racial" conflict between Teuton and Gallo-Roman loomed even larger in the German nationalist struggle against Napoleon after 1812.

The racial interpretation of the revolution established a link between "race" and "class." However, unlike the absolutism of the ancient distinction between free Hellenes and slavish barbarians, the new historians saw some good in the underclass—but only if it was European. Reactionaries believed that contact and conflict between European races/classes, especially those in which a superior masculine people triumphed over an inferior feminine one, could have a positive effect on the resulting culture. Thus the most renowned German Romantic historian of the first decades of the nineteenth century, Barthold Niebuhr, identified the dynamic of Roman history as the struggle between patricians and plebeians, and he maintained—on the basis of no evidence whatsoever—that those classes had originally been races. While he saw Roman slaves as irredeemably barbarian in accordance with ancient tradition, he believed the "free classes" to have been good because he supposed them to have come into Italy from beyond the Alps. (The patricians were the better class because they came from further north.) Niebuhr clearly related this schema to contemporary events, and his premature death was at least partly caused by distress over the July Revolution of 1830, which he and many of his contemporaries saw as a resurgence of the Gallo-Roman bourgeoisie against the Frankish-German aristocrats.

Once unpacked, the Romantic view of such struggle as the dynamic of history became the basis for the two great ideologies of the nineteenth century. Detaching race from class, Malthus, Darwin, and Spencer saw social and biological struggles for survival of the fittest as the engine of progress, and, although they fudged on the issue, there is little doubt that the late nineteenth-/early twentieth-century Chinese intellectual Yen Fu was right to interpret their image of the fundamental competition as one between races and nations.[10] Detaching class from race in the historical struggle was of course the basis of Marx's historical materialism, which, as Mudimbe points out, made class the dominant—though short-lived—concept of the Russian Revolution. (The question of whether Marx foresaw non-Europeans as capable of becoming positive proletarians remains moot.)

To return, finally, to the establishment of the Aryan model of Greece in the 1840s, we can see that, whatever internalist reasons there were for its postulation, the idea of the masculine, dynamic master race of Hellenes sweeping down and conquering the feminine, passive pre-Hellenes (who were safely European) fit perfectly with the nineteenth-century Romantic historians' image of progressive history as it ought to be. The Ancient model did not.

Notes

1 Martin Bernal, *Black Athena: The Afroasiatic Roots of Classical Civilization*: Vol. 1, *The Fabrication of Ancient Greece*, and Vol. 2, *The Archaeological and Documentary Evidence* (London and New Brunswick, 1987, 1991).

2 Aristotle, *The Politics*, 1327B; see *The Politics of Aristotle*, trans. Ernest Barker (Oxford and New York, 1958), 296.

3 A.-C.-H. Clérel de Tocqueville, *L'Ancien régime et la révolution* (Paris, 1988), bk. 3, chap. 2, p. 245.

4 Aristotle, *Politics*, 1255a, in *Politics of Aristotle*, 16.

5 See Frank Snowden, *Blacks in Antiquity* (Cambridge, MA, and London, 1970); and *Before Color Prejudice: The Ancient View of Blacks* (Cambridge, MA, and London, 1983).

6 St. Clair Drake, *Black Folk Here and There*, Vol. 1 (Los Angeles, 1987).

7 See Benedict Anderson, *Imagined Communities: Reflections on the Origin and Spread of Nationalism* (London, 1983).

8 See Allen J. Frantzen, *Desire for Origins: New Language, Old English, and Teaching the Tradition* (New Brunswick, NJ, 1990), 15–22, 203–7.

9 See C. Le Tourneau, *Shakespeare*, 19 vols. (Paris, 1776–83); list of subscribers appended to Vol. 1. I am indebted to Professor Kenneth Larson for drawing my attention to the list.

10 See Benjamin Schwartz, *In Search of Wealth and Power: Yen Fu and the West* (Cambridge, MA, 1964), 74–80.

Dominique Colas

Civil Society: From Utopia to Management, from Marxism to Anti-Marxism

During the 1993 electoral campaigns in Poland, Bronislaw Geremek, a famous medieval historian and former advisor to Lech Wałęsa, the leader of Solidarność and now president of Poland, underlined the role to be played by "civil society" in the dramatic changes affecting his country. "Civil society," not the government or administration, should play the most important role in the construction of a liberal society. Along the same lines, the struggles of churches, civic associations, trade unions, human rights activists, and illegal political parties during the Communist Party's domination of Poland have been jointly described as the struggle of civil society against the totalitarian state.

It must be kept in mind, however, that "civil society" is a concept with a long history, a comprehensive term which has received a cluster of different meanings. For example, in the nineteenth century, when the Roman Catholic Church spoke of civil society, it meant the state, as opposed to the church; but when Marx used this term

The *South Atlantic Quarterly* 94:4, Fall 1995.
Copyright © 1995 by Duke University Press.
CCC 0038-2876/95/$1.50.

Table 1. Semantic Variations on "Civil Society"

Author	Term	Synonym	English
Aristotle	koinonia politiké	polis	civil society; state; political community
Augustine	societas terrestra	civitas respublica	earthly city; state
Aquinas	communicatio; politike commu- nitas	societas	political associa- tion
Giles of Rome (Aegidius Romae)	societas civilis	civitas	civil society
Luther; Melanchthon	societas civilis	civitas respublica	civil society
Hobbes	civil society	commonwealth	
Spinoza	societas civilis	imperium	civil society; state
Rousseau	société civile	Etat	civil society
Ferguson	civil society		
Hegel	bürgerliche Gesellschaft		civil society
Marx	bürgerliche Gesellschaft		civil society
Durkheim	société civile	peuple; nation	civil society

Table 2. Civil Society as Part of Various Conceptual Systems

"Civil Society" versus:	Value of civil society	Author
family and "people" (*ethnos*)	+	Aristotle
family and City of God	−	Augustine
family and state of nature	+	Hobbes
family and state of nature	−	Rousseau
family and state	±	Hegel
family and state	+	Marx

it more or less meant the economic basis of society, as opposed to the state (see Tables 1 and 2).

"Civil society" is a legacy of Greek political thought, mainly that of Aristotle, who used the term *koinonia politiké*—in Latin, *societas civilis*; in English, "political association" or "civil society"—as a synonym for city or state. Aristotle also used the term interchangeably with the Greek word *polis*, from which we derive "politics," "political," "politician," and so forth. Aristotle differentiated between civil society and all other kinds of association (*ethne*)—household, family, army, or guild.[1] While each of these associations has a specific function and a particular goal—raising children, producing consumable goods, fighting enemies, organizing the worship of a deity—civil society has a broader function and thus encompasses and includes all of these other local, specific associations. As such, civil society aims to serve the interests not of any one specific group, but of the society as a whole. Because civil society works in the common interest, because it seeks the common good, Aristotle considered it the most sovereign of all goods. As the association of associations, the community of communities, the polis exists by nature, even if not all men live in this kind of association. According to Aristotle, therefore, man, an animal who is capable of speech, is by his very nature an animal who is intended to live in a polis: he is a political animal.

What also must be underlined is that civil society represents a specific type of power structure: it is defined by citizenship, and citizenship is a link between equals. In the polis or city, according to Aristotle, every citizen has the right to be a ruler. Civil society is thus very different from the power structure we find in a household (*oikos*): a Greek household included slaves, permanent dependents on a master who had uncontrolled and sole authority over them. A political association, however, as an association of "equal and like" members, or citizens, is defined by the principle of *isonomie* (*iso*: equal; *nomos*: law).[2]

Equal rights of citizens in civil society, in the body politic, are characteristic of civilized peoples, and the people whom the Greeks called barbarians did not, according to Aristotle, have the psychological qualities, the virtues, which made men able to live in cities. Not even all Greeks had the capacity for a political association. Those who did not have it lived in "ethne," which can be translated as "a people" or "a nation." This term is, of course, the root of such English words as "ethnic," "ethnicity," and "ethnology." As a kind of society, ethne can probably be likened to what cultural anthropologists call segmentary society, in which kinship is the main social tie.

═════

While Aristotle considered civil society the most valuable kind of association and believed that only Greeks, as opposed to barbarians, could live together as citizens, it's another kind of dualism that we find eight centuries later in Augustine's theory of civil society. In his theological, eschatological vision, the opposition is between the City of God and the earthly city, or City of Evil, with which civil society seems at first glance to be identified. Augustinian dualism opposes the City of God to the City of Evil, Heaven to Earth, Jerusalem to Babylon. Citizens of the City of God are like pilgrims journeying on Earth toward Heaven; they are in exile, and, after the Last Judgment, they will live for eternity in the love of God, while citizens of the City of Evil will endure eternal punishment.

It sounds like a binary opposition between Caesar's city and God's city, but the Augustinian opposition is a mystical one and the distinction between the two cities is not that simple. First, we must not forget that on earth the two kinds of citizens, those of the City of God, blessed with God's grace, and those of the City of Evil, are mixed up together. Second, according to Augustine, we can find on earth a prototype or anticipation of the City of God, for not all political regimes are bad. While the Roman emperor Nero was cruel and clearly driven by an evil will to power (*libido dominandi*), Augustus was a sort of rough anticipation of Jesus Christ, in Augustine's view. The criterion for distinguishing good political regimes from bad ones, according to Augustine, was peace. In the City of God, eternal peace reigns; thus the civil society that seeks to live in peace imitates life in the City of God and is therefore better, more worthy, than a civil society (state or empire) whose aim is to dominate others through war. Even though "libido dominandi" might be, according to Augustine, a major trait of the Roman character—with the murder of Romulus, which Augustine interpreted as a kind of repetition of the murder of Abel, a foundational example—it was a drive that could be curbed. A perfect human society would never be possible, but an acceptable one could be realized and could function on earth. Thus, in spite of the strong polarization between the two cities, a kind of junction or associative nexus of the two was not precluded by Augustine. As we shall see, this idea was clearly relevant to the political attitude of Martin Luther, who had read and annotated Augustine's *City of God*.

From the very beginning of his rebellion against the Roman Catholic Church, Luther compared it to Babylon: Catholic Rome, like the Whore of Babylon in the Apocalypse, had to be destroyed. Luther denied any correspondence between pope and king, between the heavenly and earthly kingdoms; the Church, he said, must not be ruled like a state, and the pope had no business meddling in earthly matters. Luther clearly believed that the City of God and civil society were separate and meant to be so.

On one side, Luther fought against the Roman Catholic Church, while on the other he was forced to confront a radical political protest by "iconoclasts" and "fanatics." These were the terms with which Luther identified the rebels and extremists who wanted to destroy not only images—paintings and sculptures—in churches, but also political authority in civil society. They rejected any kind of representation, political as well as religious. More particularly, "fanatics" were also those who wanted to establish—*hic et nunc*, here and now—the kingdom of God on earth; recognizing no king but God and no law but the Gospel, they refused to recognize any earthly political authority and wanted to abolish private property as well. For Luther this was equivalent to abolishing the essential distance or gap between heaven and earth: Had not Christ proclaimed, "My kingdom is not of this world"? Luther believed that because of Original Sin man was under the power of evil and that without political authority all of humanity would be destroyed by war. So he defended what he saw as the legitimate violence of the German princes against insurgent peasants as well as the right of a good Christian to be both a landlord, a merchant, or a priest and a soldier, a warrior, or a statesman. One could, he said, legitimately pursue an earthly calling (*Beruf*), working for one's personal benefit and for the common good of civil society.[3] In this sense, Luther's political thought clearly anticipated Max Weber's sociology, in which the state is defined as the institution that has a monopoly on legitimate violence. Marx's political thought, however, was largely a rejection or contradiction of Luther's choices and attitudes.

Another opposition—between man living in civil society and man living in a state of nature (i.e., without political authority, even without law)—would become more and more important after the Protestant Reformation. I wish to make only two points here in regard to this complex debate. First, according to Hobbes, in the state of nature every man is threatened by all other men, or, in his famous phrase, "man is a wolf to man."[4] He has to contract with other men to live together under the control of a political authority, which in turn provides security for individuals in their quest for a better life. Hobbes called this kind of association a "commonwealth"—a body politic designed to promote common well-being—and he sometimes used "civil society" as a synonym for commonwealth (e.g., in *Leviathan*). Second, the idea that man can act rationally in society to increase his own welfare and wealth while at the same time serving the common good would become a fundamental tenet of the new science, founded in England in the eighteenth century, called political economy. Whereas in Aristotle's theory, economy was merely the art of household management, for Adam Smith, Adam Ferguson, David Ricardo, and others, economy became the science of civil society, in that the aim of civil society was thought to be the development of individual and general wealth. The progress of civilization no longer seemed essentially linked to either religious faith or civic duty, not to political virtue but simply to economic activity. This ideology prevailed among eighteenth-century thinkers—with the exception of Rousseau, who argued that man was better and happier in nature than in civil society.

Rousseau's judgment was one that Hegel, at the beginning of the nineteenth century, entirely disapproved of. Hegel called the totality of modern global society "the state." In his system, civil society was only one of three complex elements that together comprised the state: the family, civil society, and a third element, which he also called the state—the political government or its bureaucracy and administration.

Whereas the family was a natural institution (i.e., one with a biological basis) that had existed prior to civil society, as had the state (the Roman Empire is an example), civil society, according to Hegel, was a creation of the modern world; he associated its emergence with industrial development. Civil society could be said to have emerged as a social sphere once individuals were able to satisfy their needs through labor. Hegel's description of the economic aspects of civil society is actually very close to the analysis proposed by the English political economy theorists; for him, civil society made the production of goods and the accumulation of wealth possible by means of a systematic division of labor. Hegel believed that in modern society the individual will is not in conflict with the interests of society as a whole. Nevertheless, between individuals there is no spontaneous harmony because the process of economic competition forces them to be in conflict and to fight with each other. So civil society is threatened by the kind of warfare between all individuals—everybody against everybody else—that Hobbes thought would occur only in the state of nature.

Because individuals could act selfishly or only out of self-interest, a society without laws or regulations, without political authority in short, would be destroyed by its own internal conflicts and contradictions. In fact, Hegel saw civil society as a kind of blending or fusion of the economic and the political, and he analyzed it into three, intimately related parts: (1) the system through which needs are satisfied, (2) the administration of justice, and (3) the police and the professional associations or corporations. What Hegel meant by "police" was not a police force per se, but all those bodies concerned with public order and, more particularly, with the lawful regulation of the free market—through the supervision of industry practices, for example (consider the U.S. Food and Drug Administration). Without the enforcement of rules and regulations, a free market economy would be impossible. As for what Hegel meant by "corporations," obviously he was not referring to big business but to the modern equivalent of professional guilds. Civil and criminal courts, like the police and the corporations, operate as regulatory bodies within civil society, whereas it is outside civil society that Hegel situated the state. As the executive and legislative power, it writes the laws and decides how to deal with global social problems. We might say that the state organizes the management of civil society. To borrow a term from philosophy, the state is civil society's *condition of possibility*. In other words, just as we cannot imagine the state without civil society, neither can we imagine global society without the state, that is, without specific political institutions, outside and inside civil society.[4]

Turning now to the Hegelian citizen, we note that the term used by Hegel as the German equivalent of "koinonia politiké," or "civil society," is *bürgerliche Gesellschaft*. "Bürger" is a polysemic term, and Hegel made good use of this polysemy. A bürger was, first, an inhabitant of a city, that is, someone who enjoyed civic rights, a citizen. But a bürger was also someone who enjoyed an elevated social status—a master of a corporation, for example—and, according to Hegel, the typical member of civil society was just such a "bourgeois," in the French sense of that word.[5] However, at the same time that civil society was engendering a bourgeoisie as one of its poles, it was creating what Hegel called a "rabble" as its other pole—with a gap between the two that could only increase. One way to regulate civil society, according to Hegel, was to encourage what he considered surplus members of the rabble to go off and found colonies elsewhere. It is clear, then, that not all members of civil society were bourgeois, but that for Hegel it was on this social stratum that civil society was built—and, for all intents and purposes, defined.

Hegel's state is not a democratic one: political sovereignty resides not in the people or the nation, but in the king. Nevertheless, Hegel's citizen has a great many rights, including freedom of conscience. Hegel's modern society thus represents a kind of synthesis of subjective freedom with a social organization that amounts to a totality. The state guarantees the rights of individual citizens, but under one particular set of circumstances individual citizens must give something to the state in return. Sometimes, conflicts between nation–states can be settled only by war because no law holds between nations except the law of nature; according to Hegel, relationships between nations are the same as relationships between individuals in the state of nature. On those occasions, the bürger–cum–bourgeois in civil society must serve his nation as a soldier. It's a kind of exchange: the state makes peace possible, that is, creates the conditions of possibility for commerce, business, and the common welfare, but, in return, it sometimes requires its citizens to make war and, if necessary, to sacrifice their lives on its behalf.

≡≡≡

Marx's view was utterly different from Hegel's. He believed that modern civil society—modern bourgeois society—is not designed for human welfare and peace, but for economic exploitation, and that the class struggle which consequently divides modern society is a form of civil war. Marx claimed that he wanted to radically alter Hegel's philosophy, to make Hegelian idealism walk on the ground, to bring it down to earth. While Marx explicitly agreed with eighteenth-century economists that civil society was equivalent to the economic sphere of society, he disagreed with Hegel's view of the state as the basis of society as a whole. Civil society was that basis for Marx, and history was the process of civil society's evolution. It was only during certain historical stages that civil society could blend with the political. While in Hegelian political theory the fusion of the political and the economic was what effectively endowed civil society with reality, Marx saw politics and the state as, under certain conditions, parasites of civil society.

If history equals the process of differentiating the state from civil society, what exactly does such differentiation mean? It means a separation between the two, which creates a specific economic sphere. From Marx's point of view, concepts or abstract ideas could be used to understand every period of history, even if social reality corresponded to those concepts only when capitalism triumphed. The concept of civil society could therefore be applied heuristically to the distant past. According to Marx, the state and civil society originated as two spheres which were fused during history's first stage. (He was referring here to the epoch of German tribes described by the Roman historian Tacitus.) After this era, the state and civil society no longer coincided, but underwent a progressive split, division, scission, differentiation—the word used by Marx is *spaltung*. During this first phase, called "primitive communism," the state, or the political sphere, and civil society, or the economic sphere, formed a single, unique sphere. There was no personal ownership; the state was a collective landlord, owner of the land and of all wealth. Individuals had no property rights; rather, they were allowed to cultivate community land. Personal ownership of property came later, first as ownership of movable property (furniture, arms, or animals, for example), then of nonmovable goods, namely, real estate. The state and civil society thus became different—but not yet totally distinct; instead, they represented two, partially overlapping spheres.

Capitalism, of course, produced the main shift in civil society's history. Industry and private property not only drastically reduced the economic role played by the state, but, once capitalism triumphed, the state's economic role vanished entirely. More accurately, the capitalist state could be said to fulfill two functions, operating on the one hand like an organization (Marx used the German term for "labor union") and working for the common interests of the bourgeois class and, on the other hand, like a power apparatus, using the police and the military to protect the bourgeoisie against the working class. Bureaucracy and violence, then, are the two functions of this highly political state.

Here we have a paradox, for the very moment the state becomes completely autonomous, ceasing to fulfill an economic role, it becomes a tool for the bourgeoisie, an instrument for class domination by the capitalists. This dramatic change from the first stage of history—the stage of primitive community, or the tribe—to modern society can be summed up in a formula: in the primitive community, the state owned everything; in capitalist society, capitalists own the state. As a matter of fact, capitalists in modern society can literally buy the state, that is, by purchasing treasury bonds on the stock market.[6]

According to Marx, the state and its laws had no real history, but were part of the reign of ideas, the world of phantasy and illusion. The fact that the state could play a role in society at a precapitalist historical stage did not enhance its value for mankind. Marx viewed the French Revolution, for example, as mainly a political one and therefore a revolution only in appearance, of appearances. While it recharacterized man as a citizen, defined by his political rights—and for Marx the citizen was merely a Hegelian abstraction—it had nothing to do with man as a member of civil society, man as a worker or producer; the French Revolution, and political revolutions in general, had nothing to do with real men.

The state in Marx's system was destined to disappear eventually, after the real, proletarian revolution, which would give birth to the dictatorship of the proletariat. In Marx's view, of course, the dictatorship of the proletariat would emerge as a reaction or response to bourgeois dictatorship. Although in modern society the state became the property of capitalists, as I have said, this was not to be the last stage of political development. Marx, of course, considered the class struggle in France to be a paradigm, and he thought of the French state as a model for general historical development. Napoleon Bonaparte's coup d'état in December 1851 put an end to the Second Republic, the product of the 1848 revolution, and resulted in a new kind of state. Bonaparte (Napoleon III, "Napoleon le petit") needed political support, and he favored and initiated the development of a bureaucracy. Marx considered these bureaucrats and petty officers to comprise a "caste," not a class, because they had no function in civil society other than providing political support for the Napoleonic state. Since this bureaucracy had no role in the economic sphere, Marx considered it a parasite or vampire, and he regarded the Paris Commune of 1871 as a revolution by civil society against this ghoul state.[7]

In Augustine's terms—and turning his values upside down—we could say that Marx saw the Commune as the secular city's protest against the celestial city, the revolt of earth against heaven. In fact, we are now in a position to contrast, however generally and briefly, Marx's political theory with those of Augustine, Luther, and Hegel— to all of whom Marx made reference in his writings. Unlike Hegel, Marx considered civil society, not the state, to be both the basis upon which history had developed and the ultimate aim of that development. Unlike Luther and in agreement with the so-called fanatics of the sixteenth century, Marx believed that political authority had to be destroyed. We could even say he was an iconoclast in that he viewed the state as a fake reality, the representative state as a trick, a falsification, an illusion—and he saw humanity as needing to be liberated from all such alienation, most notably from political alienation. Finally, we could say that, like Augustine, Marx distinguished between heaven and earth, but for him heaven—that is, the perfect society, or utopia—was the city of mankind, the human society that would be realized by the proletarian revolution.

═══

Marx's critique of the political as a factor in human alienation would take on another meaning in Lenin's doctrine and action. The Bolshevik leader proposed a paradigm for a new kind of social organization on the basis of his belief that Russia was a capitalist society *without* a political civilization. The autocratic czarist state in Russia made the development of civilization impossible, so civil society had never developed there. Lenin's theory can be described as the theory of the missing social class: in Russia, there was no civilized class, no bourgeoisie in the Hegelian sense; there was, however, a despotic state, which had to be destroyed so that a single political party could impose its will as the sole will of the whole society. The role played by the bourgeois class and by the bourgeois revolution in Western Europe (especially, of course, the French Revolution) would have to be played in the Russian Empire by the Bolshevik Party. After the revolution of October 1917, the main mission of this unique political party became the destruction of all the debris of the former society, particularly the parasitic peasantry, the kulaks, whom Lenin compared to insects, lice, and whom he planned to eradicate.[8] Mass terror, targeting selected groups of people, would be one of the key aims and methods of such a totalitarian regime.

Marx had described the history of the accumulation of capital in England as the process of "clearing estates."[9] From Lenin's point of view, the Party likewise had to sweep away all the debris of the old society: in the first Communist constitution, drafted in 1918, political rights were reserved for workers; politically and socially, the society had to be purged of those whom Lenin saw as useless or harmful. What Lenin was prescribing, and what he began to put into effect, was of course a process of purification—in this case, class cleansing. The place for those he classified as undesirables was in concentration camps or, for political opponents, in lunatic asylums. Such camps and asylums were already operating by 1918.

Totalitarian society can be described as one in which the single political party that rules the state makes autonomous civil society impossible. The party seeks to play the role of the infrastructure, the very role that Marx attributed to civil society. In the political sphere, citizens have no civil rights: the fundamental freedoms—of association, speech, the press, conscience—have all been abolished, and the economic sphere is controlled by centralized planning.

The end of Communism can thus be understood as the condition of possibility for the birth, or rebirth, of civil society. But at least two obstacles remain. First, since the Communist ideology created no foundation for civic political life, the tendency toward nationalism has become all the stronger; it is simply easier for individuals to think of themselves as members of an ethnic group than as members of a political association. Nationalist ideology can help a dictatorial power mobilize people, and nationalist struggle can seem like an attractive alternative to the very difficult work of accomplishing economic change. Second, satisfying urgent needs through a free market economy is made more difficult because a free market presupposes a state ruled by law. Without professional lawyers and a set of commercial laws, a rational organization of the economy is hard to achieve.

In this sense, we can say that the Leninist legacy in the former Communist countries is a deep and negative one: the Marxist struggle against the Hegelian concept of civil society has been successful.

Notes

1 "Observation tells us that every state is an association, and that every association is formed with a view to some good purpose. I say 'good' because in all their actions all men do in fact aim at what they think good. Clearly then, as all associations aim at some good, that association which is the most sovereign among them all and embraces all others will aim highest, i.e., at the most sovereign of all goods. This is the association which is 'political' [*koinonia politiké*]"; see Aristotle, *The Politics*, 1252a1, trans. T. A. Sinclair, revised by Trevor Saunders (Harmondsworth, 1981), 54.

2 It may be noted of the place of women in Aristotle's civil society that although women clearly did not have political rights, those who were daughters of citizens did not have the same status as slaves. In Aristotle's view, a specific feature of barbarian peoples, as opposed to Greeks, was that *they* treated women as slaves.

   In Athens, a citizen was defined as the son of an Athenian father *and* an Athenian mother, and he had to perform two years of military service, between the ages of eighteen and twenty. The link between citizenship and compulsory military service is, of course, still very important in modern society; on this issue, see Aristotle, *The Athenian Constitution*, §42.

3 Melanchthon wrote a commentary on Aristotle's *Politics* in which he criticized fanatics, mainly the Anabaptists, using Leonardo Bruni's 1418 translation. In Bruni's translation, which was very different from the older one by Moerbecke (1260), *koinonia politiké* was rendered as *societas civilis*, a formula used, if rarely, by Cicero. It was only in a 1598 English translation (from the French) of the *Politics* that the term "civil society" first appeared. For more details about the history of this term and concept, see Dominique Colas, *Le Glaive et le fléau: Généalogie de la société civile et du fanatisme* (Paris, 1992), or *Civil Society and Fanaticism, Conjoined Histories,* trans. Amy Jacobs (Stanford, in press).

4 "Civil society is the stage of difference which intervenes between the family and the state, even if its full development occurs later than that of the state; for as difference, it presupposes the state, which it must have before it as a self-sufficient entity in order to subsist itself"; see G. W. F. Hegel, *Elements of the Philosophy of Right,* trans. H. B. Nisbet (Cambridge, 1991), 220, §182 Addition.

5 "The object . . . is in civil society, the *citizen* (in the sense of *bourgeois*)" (ibid., §190).

6 Marx presents his theory of the separation and differentiation between state and civil society in *The German Ideology*; see Robert C. Tucker, "The Relation of State and Law to Property," in *The Marx–Engels Reader* (New York, 1972), 150–51. This

issue is also at the core of his analysis of modern civil society in *On the Jewish Question*; see Tucker, "Relation of State and Law to Property," 24–51.

7 See Karl Marx, *The Civil War in France: The Paris Commune* (New York, 1993 [1871]), 68.

8 See V. I. Lenin, *How to Organize Competition*, in *Collected Works*, Vol. 26 (Moscow, 1963 [1917]).

9 See Karl Marx, *Capital*, trans. Ben Fowkes (London, 1976 [1867]), bk. 1, chap. 27, p. 877.

Wyatt MacGaffey

Kongo Identity, 1483–1993

The invention of the primitive in the nineteenth century organized the peoples of the
world into essentially different primordial
communities, the inferior type of which were
called tribes. If such primordial communities exist anywhere, we would expect to find
them in Africa. For the BaKongo of what is
now Lower Zaire we are fortunate to have an
extensive documentary record covering over
500 years; according to Jan Vansina, the number of contemporary pages written on Kongo
from 1500 to 1800 amounts to over half a million, more than on any other African area of
comparable size.[1]

The BaKongo, whoever they are, inhabit
most of an area lying three to seven degrees
south of the equator and extending about
400 km between the Atlantic coast of Central
Africa and Kinshasa. There may be as many
as six million BaKongo distributed among the
Republic of Congo (formerly French Congo),
Zaire (formerly Belgian Congo), and Angola.
(Note that *Kongo*, the area inhabited by the

The *South Atlantic Quarterly* 94:4, Fall 1995.
Copyright © 1995 by Duke University Press.
CCC 0038-2876/95/$1.50.

BaKongo, is distinct from the much larger area of the former colonial territories called *Congo*.)

I referred above to "the BaKongo, whoever they are," because their identity is my topic. Their history can be divided into four periods: the Old Kingdom, Kongo of the Atlantic trade, colonial Kongo, and Kongo today.

In 1483, Portuguese sailors arrived at the mouth of the Zaire River and made contact with the governor of the Nsoyo province of the Kingdom of Kongo, whose capital, Mbanza Kongo, lay inland in what is now northern Angola. At this time the kingdom dominated a roughly rectangular area bounded by the Atlantic coast from Luanda north to the Zaire River and inland to Kinshasa. Once the Kongo nobility had converted to Christianity and adopted Portuguese titles (for reasons that won't be discussed here), missionaries and other Europeans could travel throughout the interior of Kongo. Their reports tell us that in the fifteenth century the kingdom controlled eight major provinces overseen by governors who were appointed by the king and sent tribute to the capital. The principal governors probably belonged to one or another of the clans installed at Mbanza Kongo, among whom the rules relating to marriage and succession to office gave them a share in the Crown itself. The provinces had probably once been independent polities that were incorporated in the kingdom under circumstances upon which we can only speculate.

One reason for the kingdom's establishment may have been its position at the intersection of two important trade currents, one between the coast and the interior, south of the Zaire River, and the other the route by which copper was brought from the north to the Angolan savanna. Although this commercial theory appears to be supported by the fact that the king controlled the source of a widely used form of currency—a certain seashell found only at a point off the Angolan coast—it does not explain either the extent or the boundaries of the kingdom, nor why there were eight major provinces with boundaries of their own. These provincial borders were perhaps defined by ecological factors, such as the distribution of natural resources, but it would be a mistake to overemphasize the role of frontiers; precolonial African polities were defined by centers of power rather than by fixed boundaries.

In the sixteenth century the king's control, always precarious, was in various ways both strengthened and weakened by his alliance with the Portuguese and the new commercial relations entailed by that alliance. This is not the place to discuss these developments; suffice it to say that at this point Kongo was a political rather than a cultural entity. The neighboring coastal kingdoms of Ndembo to the south, Ngoyo, Kakongo, and Loango to the northwest, and Tio to the northeast were related by language, social organization, and culture. Indeed, it can be argued that all the societies in which western Bantu languages are spoken, from Cameroon to Angola and from Gabon to eastern Zaire, were local variations of a single cultural system adapted to different environments and historical circumstances.

"Kongo" referred to a polity whose boundaries varied with the political fortunes of various noblemen, but whose center remained the capital, Mbanza Kongo. The word "kongo" itself signifies a socially organized space. The meaning of "MuKongo," or *mwisi Kongo*, was relative to the existence of the kingdom, referring to someone living at court, as opposed to *muvata*, or *mwisi vata*, a villager. The notion of a distinct people called "Kongo" was by the sixteenth century, then, already an artifact of European expectations.

In the mid-seventeenth century, rivalries within the ruling group, as well as the fact that Kongo kings were no longer able to monopolize European trade, contributed to the downfall of the kingdom, with the king's forces defeated by the Portuguese at the Battle of Mbwila in 1665. Thereafter, a new political and economic system arose to carry out the function of mediating between the interior and the coast in the rapidly developing Atlantic slave trade. In relation to this trade, the geography of the lower Zaire generated a new social configuration. The course of the Zaire River (*Nzadi*, in KiKongo) between Malebo Pool (Kinshasa) and the estuary beginning at Matadi is interrupted by a number of cataracts that restrict navigation to short stretches. Slaves, ivory, and other goods brought from the interior in canoes by highly organized *riverain* transportation groups had to be warehoused at Malebo before being transferred to the custody of Kongo traders. These traders used a new network of routes that partly bypassed Mbanza Kongo to reach the coast directly. Inland transportation was provided by the labor of porters, including slaves. At each of the ports, which were by then frequented not only by Portuguese but also by Dutch, English, and French ships, new polities arose to broker the import–export exchange.

This new configuration shifted the area that could be called Kongo northward. Much has been made of the alleged northern migration of Kongo groups and their displacing of others. In my view, although much local movement undoubtedly occurred, the Kongolization of the north was primarily a matter of adaptation by northern groups, who never markedly differed in language or culture from those to the south, to the new commercial system. Within this system, independent communities varied in scale and power according to how well placed they were for trade. Those situated at the coast and at crossings or intersections in the interior were wealthier than others; wealth gave rise in turn to relative centralizations of power commensurate with the social stratification of chiefs, the freeborn, and slaves. Elsewhere, villages whose subsistence depended primarily or entirely on their own agricultural production remained poor and relatively egalitarian. The only identifiable unity among them was a common institutional system, adapted to their function in the trade, but that did not sharply distinguish them from other areas and communities. Mbanza Kongo became one village among others, though still relatively important because of its position in the trade network; it retained its traditional mystique as the source of the magical powers by which local chiefs and headmen authenticated their claims to office.

From the seventeenth to the nineteenth century, the BaKongo thought of themselves as adherents to this or that matrilineal clan, which might itself be linked to other clans in the neighborhood by ties of patronage and ritual dependency. According to local legends, ambitious men and their followers would move to new territories, building new villages and acquiring insignia of office from patrons (i.e., the chiefs of established groups) in exchange for tributary fees. This political activity was expressed and understood in ritual terms as the acquisition of occult powers associated with witchcraft and the ability to combat it. Descent groups affiliated in this way, or claiming to have been so at one time, took the names of their patrons, with suitable modifications and additions; these names themselves often referred to the magically powerful insignia that distinguished one patron from another. Neighboring clans lacking such insignia or affiliated with a different patron were known by different names, in an ever-shifting kaleidoscope of political alignments. An example of the sort of configuration that focused on a particular ritual tradition is the Nsundi chiefship complex, which probably originated in the Nsundi province, the northernmost province of the Kongo kingdom. The nineteenth-century center, or perhaps centers, of Nsundi chiefship lay in the district north of the river, now called Manianga.[2] Some scholars have assumed that this Nsundi entity was a tribe, but the indigenous theory of what these units were supposed to be like, complex in itself, cannot be fitted into such European categories as the state, tribe, or ethnic group.

This system, with internal modifications over time and space, remained in effect until 1885, when the European powers divided up this part of Africa into what became the colonies of Moyen Congo (French), Angola (Portuguese), and Belgian Congo.

≡≡≡

By 1860 or so, anthropology, developing as the science that specialized in the knowledge of peoples then coming under European control, had begun to use the concept of tribe. Highly ambiguous then as now, this concept has been largely abandoned in anthropology, although it continues to be used elsewhere.[3] Part of the nineteenth-century sense of "tribe" derived from a scheme of social evolution in which primitive societies were thought to advance from the leaderless "band" organization characteristic of hunters and gatherers to a "tribal" stage initiated by the acquisition of metal-working skills and eventually to "civilization" and the nation–state; in other words, primitive peoples were expected to evolve into Europeans, or at least into conformity with the model of themselves that Europeans entertained until quite recently. The historical development of Kongo from kingdom to village, however, ran counter to these social-evolutionary expectations.

In the nineteenth century, what later became the "four fields" of anthropology in the United States—cultural anthropology, archaeology, physical anthropology, and linguistics—were merged, so evidence from any one of them could be used to pinpoint a given tribe's place on the evolutionary scale since all four functioned as complementary indices of the essential nature of the group. For example, if members of the group had round rather than elongated heads, they could be expected to exhibit matrilineal rather than patrilineal descent, agricultural activity rather than pastoralism, and monosyllabic rather than compound words in their language. (I am not making this up.) In Belgian Congo and other colonies, members of a given tribe were expected to share not only the same set of institutions at the appropriate level of primitiveness, but also common physical and psychological traits. The same expectations applied to "sub-tribes." Accordingly, at the 1897 International Exhibition in Brussels, visitors to the pavilion of the Congo Free State (the predecessor of Belgian Congo) were told that a Kongo "sub-tribe" called the Basundi were "the true savage types of Lower Congo; their reddish hair falls in long locks, neither combed nor plaited." Another group, the Babwende, was said to be taller and recognizable by a chest tattoo representing a crocodile. Those called "the BaKongo," meaning those who lived south of the Zaire, were distinguished by the absence of upper incisors; "they have mild habits, feeble and wretched dispositions." All over colonial Africa, tribes were characterized by their European colonizers as uniformly warlike, lazy, docile, good workers, or the like, and assigned to appropriate places in the colonial economy.

In the context of colonial occupation, "tribe" effectively meant a social unit that lent itself to convenient administration, or (from the point of view of missionaries) to convenient evangelization. Intended to be a province of a modern state, namely, a colony, the tribe was thus obliged to demonstrate some of the characteristics of the state, though not, of course, its "modernity." As a not-yet-fully-evolved state, it supposedly had boundaries marking it off from other tribes, as well as a central administration that made it theoretically possible for the newly arrived district commissioner to say, "Take me to your chief." In Belgian Congo, territorial administrators were given specific instructions to identify chiefs, no matter how minor, or to invent them if necessary.[4]

Although the evolutionary scheme of nineteenth-century anthropology might appear to have been dynamic by implying a slow but continuous development over time, in practice it was really a spatially organized and fundamentally static model. Civilization was at home in Europe, while extreme primitivism was to be found in places remote from Europe, such as Patagonia, Australia, and southern Africa. The notion of essential characteristics denied a role to dynamic factors like individual ambition, talent, or motivation to change and the ability of groups to adapt to new political and economic conditions.

One recent exponent of the "tribal" concept, who bases his extremist views on a considerable antecedent literature, is Raoul Lehuard, the leading expert on Kongo art. At the beginning of his two-volume 1989 study, he speaks of the collective term "Kongo" as a source of confusion and pours scorn on those who classify a given piece of sculpture as such when, in his view, it should be classified as one of no less than fourteen types, one of which he subdivides into thirty-two subtypes.[5] This taxonomic excess proceeds from the static essentialism of nineteenth-century anthropology and ignores the fact that successful Kongo sculptors established ateliers in which their individual styles were copied by apprentices.[6] Lehuard also attempts to relate the physical types represented in Kongo sculptures to those of the "ethnic groups" who produced them. Evaluating physical types in the nineteenth-century manner, he identifies craniofacial measurements as the significant features and quotes from a 1959 memoir by a French physician, "Dr. Chabeuf," who provided nasal indices and classifications of chin form, eye form, and the like, for groups called "Vili," "Yombe," "Bembe," "Lari," "Sundi," and "Kunyi," together with figures for the average stature of these groups and observations on which ones have thinner lips. Physical anthropology of this sort was already old-fashioned in 1959 and was recognized as absurd long before 1989.

As for the art styles that Lehuard has more usefully identified, these have nothing to do with ethnic classification. In his own mapping of them, their distributions, which supposedly correspond to sub-tribes defined by physical type, overlap considerably; the styles he calls "Bwende" and "Manyanga" occur throughout the administrative district called Manianga, and both of them overlap with two other styles in part of that area.

An exhaustive 1973 survey of "ethnic" labels by Olga Boone, who compiled everything written on the subject, revealed the unsatisfactory results of generations of ethnographers' and district officers' efforts to classify the BaKongo. Although Boone herself frequently complained of the absence of good data and noted that most of the names were either recent or regional, or both, she nevertheless went on to draw maps of ethnic distributions and boundaries. Among other things, her own evidence on these purported sub-tribes shows that "Mayombe" is the name of a region, not an ethnic group (the word originally meant "savages in the interior"); while "Bayombe," the name of those who live in Mayombe, is not what the Bayombe call themselves, using instead the name of their district or clan.[7] "Bwende" is likewise the name of a region, not an ethnic group, and it may be a nickname for the BaLari.[8] The people around Luozi call themselves "Kongo," but are called "Manianga" by others; the latter, originally the name of a famous market and later that of a region to which this market gave access, is not an ethnic label.[9] "Ndibu," which came into use at the turn of the century, refers to a speech mannerism allegedly characteristic of the inhabitants of a region. "Nsundi" ("Sundi," "BaSundi," etc.) cannot be said to designate a territory because it is often considered a clan name.[10]

———

The first indication of BaKongo thinking of themselves as "BaKongo" dates from 1910. That year, a leading evangelist of the Swedish mission, Simon Kavuna, wrote an article in the mission journal urging his countrymen to respect the KiKongo language and not to let it degenerate into the crude version used by the government in a much larger area than that of Kongo proper.[11] The context of his plea was the recent institution of the first relatively orderly native administration in Belgian Congo and the consequently urgent need, already voiced by his fellow teachers, to press collectively for benefits and privileges. Fifty years later, the theme of respect for the language motivated a solidarity movement among the Kongo elite that developed into the country's first political party.[12] Meanwhile, in 1920, a Kongo business-man named André Yengo had formed a group called "the Congomen," who urged the government to live up to its own ostensible standards in its treatment of the natives; this group, denounced in the settler press as a terrorist organization, was suppressed.

During the twentieth century several subgroups have emerged among the BaKongo, shaped by such modern factors as the zones of influence created by mission organizations and new transporta-tion routes that gave a sense of common identity to people who rode the same trucks. The principal groups effective in politics were and still are, from west to east, Yombe, Manianga, Ndibu, and Ntandu.[13] These groups are unequivocally regional. The origins of their names vary; "Ntandu," for example, was apparently the name that desig-nated those who lived up-river (*ku ntandu*) at the turn of the century. In the 1960s, the BaYombe rarely called themselves by that name, variously electing to use the name of their administrative territory or that of their clan or clan fraction.[14] Today, a European who goes around asking people what sub-tribe they belong to may hear any one of a number of names because the BaKongo are not well versed in nineteenth-century anthropology.

Kongo politics in the 1950s and 1960s featured rivalries among the principal groups, who competed for government benefits and other advantages. Within each group, schisms appeared whenever an indi-vidual leader and whatever following he could attract believed that they were not getting their due, or that agitation could improve their lot. In the former Belgian and French colonies, however, the BaKongo have always had a strong sense of both their unity and their superi-ority to other "tribes." These others were also colonial inventions, with labile identities that could change in response to political pres-sures.

A well-known case in point is that of the Bangala. Just before Independence, the Belgians permitted local government elections in Kinshasa, the Belgian Congo capital, where the BaKongo were in the majority. The rest of Kinshasa's population came from various parts of the vast country; in Kinshasa, lacking a common language, they adopted Lingala, a lingua franca developed by the government to facilitate administration. Consequently, they became known as Bangala and, as an adventitious "tribe," constituted the opposition party in these elections, the real issue of which was control of political patronage. Similar developments occurred among the BaKongo themselves as they competed for office in Kongo towns such as Boma.

BaKongo will discourse at length on the moral and intellectual failings of "the Bangala." In 1980, when I lived in Kisangani, a city in northeastern Zaire, I found that the Bangala (i.e., speakers of the vehicular language Lingala) were as strongly detested there as they were by the BaKongo in Lower Zaire. But it was an unpleasant surprise for me, ethnographer of the BaKongo, to find that these "Bangala" included the BaKongo, who were obliged in that part of the country to speak Lingala in order to make themselves understood!

Independence for the French, Belgian, and eventually Angolan territories has had its own effects on Kongo identity. At first there was talk among intellectuals about a possible revival of the old Kingdom of Kongo, but this romance faded in the hustle of national politics. Spread out over the three countries, BaKongo now have only personal ties to one another, at best. (I have heard educated people say of a given individual who, in fact, came from Mbanza Kongo, the fabled former capital, "Oh, he's not a MuKongo, he's an Angolan.")

In Zaire, as in other colonial and postcolonial states, ethnic identity is established by an entry on one's "identity card," on the strength of which one may be identified as a MuKongo without ever having lived in Kongo or spoken the KiKongo language. The government of President Mobutu fosters rivalry among the "tribes," but is careful to refer to BaKongo as belonging to this or that subdivision in order to deny their unity, which would pose a potential threat to the regime. In recent years, Kongo intellectuals have published texts in KiKongo so as to counter Lingala imperialism, and, with an eye to the apparently impending collapse of the Republic of Zaire, they have revived talk about a possible Kongo state. They have also founded a university, whose officers were carefully chosen to represent the various divisions, with three separate campuses in Lower Zaire. These moves have once again manifested the ambiguities of external and internal political relations, of unity and schism.

At another level, two observations are pertinent to the more general themes of this special issue of *SAQ*. First, there are clear signs of a developing national consciousness in Zaire (as in Nigeria and other African countries, I believe), one that is a product of a unified national experience within the boundaries of the Zairean state despite, or even partly because of, a general popular disgust with the present government. Such signs include the increasingly widespread familiarity with Zairean popular music all over Africa, and even in New York and Paris, since 1965. Zairean national dress, an invention of the president's that has now fallen into disrepute, nevertheless identified citizens as such at international gatherings and even led other Africans to remark on a distinctive Zairean style or attitude. With distinctive political histories having served to individuate a formerly inchoate mass of "Africans," an increasingly extensive and populous Zairean diaspora has generated Zairean communities from London to Johannesburg whose common experience is of national origin and exile.

Second, there are no clear signs of either race or class consciousness, except among the few who have been extensively exposed to European ideas on these subjects. In their own cultural environment, the BaKongo traditionally thought of themselves as belonging to this or that clan and affiliated patrilaterally to this or that other clan, depending on how marriages were arranged. In the "modern" world, that is, the world of European institutions introduced by colonial conquest, they adopted the identities of "tribe" and "sub-tribe," manipulating these opportunistically as political instruments. There is no essential Kongo entity. Although the group or groups it is convenient to call "BaKongo" are identified by dialects which linguists assign to a single category, it was only in the twentieth century that a unified (and simplified) "KiKongo" readily intelligible to all became established as a by-product of literacy and printing. In the cities, however, the young no longer speak it.

In Kongo, an area where one would expect to find tribes if such things existed, we find instead a constant flux of identities. It is always possible, in Africa as elsewhere, to establish ties of kinship or cultural affinity when political expediency requires them—what international diplomatic communiqués traditionally refer to as "the special relationship between our two countries." Such ties are equally easy to break in the name of fundamental cultural differences.

The best framework within which to understand the definitions and redefinitions of identity that have occurred in Kongo over the centuries is that of political anthropology, with its concept of segmentary relations. In a segmentary system, groups who think of themselves as different will unite against another group of like order when their common interests are threatened. Pervasive politicization of social relations, marked by incessant fission and fusion of this sort, occurs wherever an absence or weakness of hierarchical authority opens the way to competition for public resources.

That is what has happened in the retribalization of Europe since 1980. Politics always resorts to metaphors of kinship, community, and common ancestry to mobilize and define its constituencies. In Europe today, propagandists appealing to the United Nations or the European Community for political vindication have revived nineteenth-century assumptions about ethnicity as a primordial, essential, and virtually prehistoric identity. Their appeals, often on behalf of groups that have formed quite recently as products of state policies, such as those of the Balkan states, for example, have propaganda value because, intellectually speaking, the nineteenth century is not yet over;[15] the twentieth century lives on the ideas of the nineteenth.

Politically motivated European folk notions have little value as concepts with which to interpret non-European events, except insofar as BaKongo, for example, may have adopted them in their own political context. It may be a peculiarity of modern Western thought to expect everyone to belong to some original and primitive group. In this respect, "ethnic group" and "tribe" are very similar to "race," although the latter term has currently fallen out of favor; it may be worth remembering that in the last century the Slavs, for example, were referred to as a "race," supposedly identified by their round heads. Like "race," the terms "tribe," "nation," and "ethnic group" lack objectively verifiable truth conditions, as my review of their application to Kongo history has shown. Although both "tribes" and "ethnic groups" are imagined communities,[16] the difference between them may be that while an ethnic group imagines itself, a tribe has been imagined by others.

Notes

1 Jan Vansina, "The Kongo Kingdom and Its Neighbors," in *General History of Africa* (London and Berkeley, 1992), 5: 546.

2 See J. M. Janzen, *Lemba* (New York, 1982), 63, fig. 3.

3 See A. Southall, "The Illusion of Tribe," *Journal of African and Asian Studies* 5 (1970): 28–50.

4 See Wyatt MacGaffey, *Custom and Government in the Lower Congo* (Los Angeles, 1970), 259–76.

5 Raoul Lehuard, *Art BaKongo: Les Centres du style*, 2 vols. (Arnouville, 1989), 40.

6 An exhibition by François Neyt of Luba art from central Zaire at the Dapper Foundation, Paris, in 1993 classified the objects exclusively in terms of ateliers.

7 See Olga Boone, *Carte ethnique de la République du Zaire: Quart Sud-Ouest* (Tervuren, 1973), 90–103.

8 Ibid., 104–8.

9 Ibid., 109–13.

10 Ibid., 129.

11 See Wyatt MacGaffey, "Ethnography and the Closing of the Frontier in Lower Congo, 1885–1921," *Africa* 56 (1986): 269.

12 See Laurent Monnier, *Ethnie et intégration régionale au Congo: Le Kongo Central, 1962–1965* (Paris, 1971).

13 Ibid., 370.

14 See Albert Doutreloux, *L'Ombre des fétiches* (Louvain, 1967), 30.

15 See, for example, L. M. Danforth, "Competing Claims to Macedonian Identity," *Anthropology Today* 9 (1933): 3–10.

16 Benedict Anderson, *Imagined Communities: Reflections on the Origin and Spread of Nationalism*, 2d ed. (London, 1991 [1983]).

Jocelyn Létourneau

The Current Great Narrative
of Québecois Identity

Historiography, defined as the body of works on which the "great narrative" of a community of communication is partly based, plays an important role in the process of identity construction by establishing and framing the historicity of that community. With regard to the history of Quebec, a dialectical link can be discerned between the historiographical representation of the Quebecer and the actual process of identity transformation that this collective subject is experiencing.[1]

The great narrative of the Quebecers is being rewritten from a new perspective in which the emphasis is placed on four criteria that, in a way, typify the collective subject in time: utilitarianism, liberalism, cosmopolitanism, and urbanity. Indeed, the historical work currently being produced is clearly endeavoring to show that the Quebecer, throughout the course of history, has been a completely rational being, marked by contact with the Other (whether Amerindian, English, or American, for example),

The *South Atlantic Quarterly* 94:4, Fall 1995.
Copyright © 1995 by Duke University Press.
CCC 0038-2876/95/$1.50.

open to all kinds of influences, and shaped by an environment that was quite urban and far more secular than has usually been supposed. This historical representation of the Quebecer is obviously quite different from the received one, which stressed the rural, homogeneous, traditional, and distinctive character of the French Canadian in North America.

Neither the deconstruction of a great narrative nor its subsequent reactualization as a new variant originates in a strictly intellectual process marked by linear advances in knowledge (i.e., on the principle that the more is known about a field of study, the better it can be described), but rather from what might be called a societal impulse, which, in the Quebecer's case, has expressed itself as a profound change in the collective subject's self-identification. In other words, a collective transformation of identity has opened up a new set of questions, among historians in particular, and, consequently, a new way of actualizing and reanimating the past; this has led to the "discovery" of various aspects (previously forgotten or neglected) of Québecois identity and has made it possible to develop a new version of the great narrative, with this new version and the Quebecer's changing identity reinforcing one another.

What are the consequences of using the four criteria mentioned above to reinterpret the major episodes of Quebec's history and to reshape the historical course of this community of communication? The new version of the great narrative evinces the following four effects: (1) historians are no longer thinking of the Quebecer's historical evolution in terms of being "out of step"; (2) a new chronology, together with new temporal and other reference points for situating the Quebecer within the main stages of history, is being established; (3) the representational significance formerly accorded to the "pre-Revolutionaries" has given way to the dominance of a single reference point or period, that of the "moderns";[2] and (4) a new historical status has been bestowed on the Quebecer, who is now typified as a subject developing at the same rate as its Other(s) (thereby universalizing the Quebecer's historical itinerary), although following certain distinctive paths. The question that historians used to ask— "How and why was Quebec's development not like that?"—is now being posed without the negative ("How and why was Quebec's development like that?"), affirming the displacement of the vanquished, demoralized, and humiliated subject (the Old French Canadian) by the mature, ambitious, and enterprising one (the New Quebecer).

─────────

If we accept the idea that identity is an *account* of oneself and others in a relationship of reciprocity and mutual recognition, then the crucial issue of the human experience is not, as Shakespeare formulated it in *Hamlet*, "to be or not to be, that is the question," but rather *to be or not to be a well-told, well-communicated history—that is the question*. What then becomes obvious is the fundamental role played by historiography in the foundation of a collective identity. I define "identity" as the given narrative in which a community of communication recognizes itself. Borrowing from Jürgen Habermas, we can define a "community of communication" as a group of people who participate, by way of communicational activity, in an interaction which coordinates their projects in accordance with their shared perception of the world; a group of people who also share a life–world, that is, a type of horizon that defines their particular stock of cultural facts, interpretations, and explanatory models.

Although identity is embodied in attributes that, becoming more firmly entrenched over time, eventually seem natural to us, it nevertheless begins with a narrative in which a community of communication establishes its group thematics, evokes its origins, reestablishes the preeminence of its memorialized state, and recites its incantations. In this respect, the narrative which the Québecois, through the discourse of their intelligentsia, remembered about themselves— that is, the way in which they defined themselves in relation to their Other(s)—has varied over time. During a good part of the nineteenth century and up to around 1940, this narrative represented French Canadians as an isolated and sectarian group, forsaken and enclosed, crucially affected by British subjugation since 1759; a group that nevertheless survived, becoming concentrated around its elite, mainly comprised of clerics; a group that held to its traditions and learned how to protect itself from harmful outside influences so as to preserve its specificity—a special status granted by the divine power and expressed as a community mandate to memorialize its Golden

Age—continually reviving its sacred past and its recollected renown. Gradually, during the 1940s, sufficient numbers of intellectuals became trained to constitute a critical mass that could "think beyond the thinkable." Therefore, by the 1950s, this problematic of a nation that had been defeated politically, yet had triumphed nonetheless in terms of its morale, its group loyalty, and its traditions, was increasingly being regarded as an anachronic society.

Without getting into the details, suffice it to say that this problematic enjoyed a grace period in the 1950s, for it would be subsequently criticized in its original formulation. This problematic entailed reversing the account of the collective past of French Canadians and introducing the idea of a negative or pessimistic group identification. According to this new version, the history of the French Canadians was a painful one, and their determination to preserve their traditions was one of the leading causes of the group's unfortunate and inferior condition. Indeed, in spite of having made some progress toward becoming an urban, industrial society, the Province of Quebec still lagged behind other states and provinces, notably, Ontario and the United States. This lag was particularly striking with respect to its political institutions, its collective representations and imaginaries. In other words, if French Canadian society was not really traditional at the level of its infrastructure—contrary to the way it had been depicted by a certain faction of its intelligentsia—then its infrastructure (its *being*) was clearly out of sync with its superstructure (its *consciousness*). On the whole, French Canadian society was not entirely, or even sufficiently, modern—and thus was flawed. The political inference drawn from this evaluation of Quebec's history was self-evident: it was a question of nothing less than getting to the root of this flaw, that is, picking up the pace of progress and reorienting the historicity of the community toward its future, away from its past. Henceforth, the community would seek its salvation in the shaping of its future, which would consequently become the source of its happiness; at the same time, the community would break with its past, which had only been a source of unhappiness and a failure to thrive.

One has to understand the importance of these notions of Quebec as being out of step, being behind, inferior, frozen in time, all of which pointed to a single generative fault, that of inadequacy. These words cannot be considered simple qualifiers used in characterizing a societal state. They effectively define the conditions of being a community and characterize a collective subject in relation to its Other(s): the French Canadian subject was flawed as a result of having been influenced by rulers with limited horizons (i.e., clerics and conservatives) and was in the process of missing out on its current historical moment, namely, modernity. It was imperative to dissociate the community from this reactionary elite and to register it in a new temporality, one that would allow the community to eventually reach this idealized evolutionary stage of other contemporary societies—the stage of liberalism, democracy, and modern progress. More to the point, modernization was not just the order of the day, but a vital necessity for the regeneration of the entire community and for the complete development of a collective subject hitherto caught in the stranglehold of the past.[3]

We now understand why the 1960s produced so much social-scientific research on where Quebec stood in relation to other societies, particularly that of neighboring Ontario, which was considered highly developed. Certain books and articles published in the late 1950s and early 1960s soon became classics of modernizing Québecois thought. Through these pioneering studies, it was hoped, the reasons for the gap could be identified and the distance that separated the French Canadian subject from its Other(s)—especially the relatively privileged English Canadian subject—measured. Discovering the conditions under which a society could take off—the means by which the group could better itself, or even rise a bit above itself— such were the targeted aims and objectives of this research.

And so it went until the mid-1970s. At that point, the Quebec social-scientific milieu—and particularly the universities, which had rapidly expanded with a large influx of young francophone scholars—began to feel the impact of a group of intellectuals for whom the Quiet Revolution had been decisive in shaping their political and historical imaginations. As a result, the great collective history of the Québecois gradually began to be revisited and revised, notably, as a normalization of the historical course of that collective subject, who had by now come to resemble its Other(s) and to belong to the

mainstream of history. This reexamination of the past entailed seeing it differently, posing new questions that arose spontaneously or
were inspired by the problematics then in vogue in foreign intellectual milieux, most notably those of France, where many newly hired
faculty had been trained. In a very long article which reviewed much
of the scholarly work on Quebec history published in the 1970s, Fernand Ouellet showed how this intellectual group had attempted to
clear the way for, and link various research efforts to, a new agenda,
identifying new sites for exploration that still mark the landscape of
historical research in Quebec today, such as rural economic history,
urban history, demographic shifts, intercultural connections, social
stratifications, and gender relations, among others.[4] It was through
this research program that the general interpretation and vision of
the Quebecer in time has dramatically changed. The condition of this
subject has been normalized,[5] with the Quebecer's existential status
and historical course having been brought into alignment with those
of others.

To illustrate this point, let's take a look at the current literature on
the history of Quebec, as reflected in the 1991 *Guide d'histoire du Québec du Régime français à nos jours*, a volume edited by Jacques Rouillard in which some well-known local historians endeavor to provide
a panorama of current scholarship on Quebec's history by highlighting its principal tendencies.[6] Tackling works that cover the French
regime, John Dickinson and Jacques Mathieu note their tendency to
emphasize (a) the rational minds of the peasants (*habitants*); (b)
the economic, demographic, and cultural linkages between town and
countryside; (c) the mutual influences among ethnic groups, including Amerindians, that became part of the social fabric; and (d) the
social mobility that has marked the whole collectivity and brought
about a new representation of New France, one that has helped to
dislodge the traditional representation of the French regime period.
Hence the persistent image of a homogeneous and static, egalitarian and immobile, enclosed and entrenched society has yielded to
a new representation strongly anchored in the idea of movement,
out of which general matrix such notions as dynamism, hierarchy,
strategy, mobility, differentiation, and stratification may be derived.

The actual research on New France, then, has contributed to the construction of a general representation of the French subject which coincides exactly with four features now thought to typify the contemporary Québecois subject (being economics-minded, open to alien influences, in step with the times, and capable of engineering change). This suggests the extent to which historians can reactivate the past on the basis of what they call "a new questioning," that questioning being informed by the existential categories on which a group draws in attempting to revise its past while establishing its historicity for the long term.

The relationship between the configurations of contemporary French Quebec identity and its historical reincarnation is equally evident in the tendencies that mark the historiography of the English regime (1760–1867). An excerpt from an article by Jean-Pierre Wallot and Pierre Tousignant, leading historians in their field, again reveals the dialectic between the present and the past:

> L'ensemble des études [portant sur le Régime anglais] tend à montrer . . . que les Canadiens français (tout comme d'ailleurs les colons britanniques) se situaient dans un contexte atlantique en pleine mouvance, qu'ils participèrent aux idéologies et aux transformations de tous ordres qui se produisirent entre la Révolution américaine (1774–1783) et la Révolution française, à compter de 1789, et la Confédération (1867), en passant par diverses formes de gouvernement, une autre guerre avec les Etats-Unis (1812–1815), des insurrections (1837–1838) et le gouvernement responsable (1848). Sur le plan politique, ces études soulignent le rôle important des Canadiens français dans l'obtention et l'utilisation habile d'un régime parlementaire restreint. . . . Sur le plan économique et social, loin d'être fondamentalement irrationnelles et conservatrices, les classes moyennes canadiennes-françaises auraient plutôt cherché à lancer des initiatives à leur avantage et à s'accaparer du pouvoir; les masses paysannes et urbaines auraient réagi avec une rationalité limitée, certes, mais avec une bonne dose d'adaptation aux mutations qui se dessinaient déjà au tournant du XIXe siècle (restructuration et mo-

dernisation de l'économie sous l'impact du marché) et qui se déploieraient dans certains cas jusqu'à la Confédération malgré divers obstacles.

Recent studies [dealing with the British regime] tend to demonstrate . . . that the French Canadian settlers (like their British counterparts) situated themselves in an Atlantic context that was rapidly moving on, that they were open to ideologies and part of all sorts of transformations that happened between the American Revolution (1774–1783) and the French Revolution (1789), and the Confederation (1867), along with diverse forms of government, another war with the United States (1812–1815), the insurrections of 1837–38 and the responsible government (1848). Those studies also suggest that, on the political side, the French Canadians played an important role in controlling and cleverly exploiting the constraints on the parliamentary regime. . . . On the economic and social front, far from being irrational or traditional, the French Canadian middle classes tried rather to launch initiatives to their advantage and also to monopolize power; the peasants and urban French Canadians, although reacting with a more limited rationality, adapted themselves positively to the mutations that already marked Lower Canada at the beginning of the nineteenth century (restructuring and modernization of the economy in response to market forces) and that would last, despite certain obstacles, up until the Confederation.[7]

Here we find some interesting terms used to describe the behavior and attitudes of French Canadians: "moving on," "open to," "part of," "rational," "clever," and adapting to change "positively." All of these qualities help to demonstrate the normality of this subject in relation to its Other(s), particularly in relation to its secular alter ego, the English subject—a counterimage to the one promoted by English Canadian historiography, which portrayed the British as liberators of a population that was behind the times. But this representation also contradicted the previous image of French Canadians as a close-knit community upholding traditional values. With such notions as similitude, convergence, and parity now prevailing, the boundary between *ourselves,* or the collective Self, and *our Others* (*nos Autres*) would soon shift to different grounds, as would the bases of Quebec identity.

The idea of normalizing and universalizing the historical course of the collective subject—and thus of endowing that subject with a new historical consciousness—is particularly evident in the works dealing with the period from 1867 to the present. According to the new account, Québecois society was marked by internal divisiveness and class struggles (which did not always take the form of an ethno-linguistic conflict between the English and the French, even though the national question has always been linked to the social question). Again, contrary to what had often been alleged, Quebec society was now said to be open to other cultures and to be characterized by intensive migration and positive absorption of foreign influences. The idea of Quebec as out of step or a late developer, which had dominated so many of the works published during the 1950s and 1960s, was abandoned by these new historians. Indeed, French Canadian society was depicted as already urban and even showing signs of proto-industrialization in the countryside as early as the beginning of the nineteenth century. Overall, the territory and the society of Quebec were part of the global changes that were sweeping North America then, so Quebec was experiencing the same trends that were happening elsewhere. One other important feature that was played up by the new historiography concerned the demythification of clerical hegemony over Quebec life and, accordingly, the new emphasis placed on the role of the State and civil society. Indeed, the Quebecer was not so much a messianic subject as a civic subject, manifesting a political culture and showing a strong interest in democratic/parliamentarian institutions. Moreover, the State apparatus had been central to Quebec's history since at least the beginning of the Confederation, and its development, considering the limited financial resources available during this time, was comparable to that of neighboring states. Needless to say, the French Quebecer was, like the ideal of the Westerner, a techno-scientific subject who had founded institutions (and much earlier than has been thought) and had participated in the quest for knowledge—mainly by means of ingenuity, admittedly—but also by following the systematic procedures of the scientific method.

It should be clear by now that contemporary historiography is linked to, and has even reinforced, the transformation which the Québecois have been undergoing for thirty years or so at the level of their identity and their collective representation. Initially described as different from their Other(s) but actually superior to them, the Québecois, thanks to the emphasis brought to bear by the new *Aufklärer*, became aware of their shortcomings and tried to overcome them, to normalize their condition. Liberated from the strains of its guardianship role vis-à-vis tradition and made more self-confident by the success of the Quiet Revolution, this collective subject rediscovered its soul and reestablished its place in history while revisiting and revising its past, emphasizing its similarity to others and universalizing its historical course. Provided with this new, more positive identity that historians are even now constructing, the Québecois can anticipate a promising future and can also, once and for all, give up the siege mentality that has kept them in the ranks of the "small."

Let's move on now to the second question that I posed at the beginning of this article: How has the new representation of the collective subject led to a reinterpretation of the major periods of Québecois history and to a reevaluation of the historical trajectory followed by this collectivity? We have already seen how the current historiography of Quebec has endeavored to show that, from its beginnings as a colony and frontier society to its contemporary realization as an open society with a decisively French character, Quebec evolved more or less comparably to other societies. If, in the preceding great narrative, the Other (especially the English Other) was continually depicted as an adversary, an alien, and an antithesis, the new version of this great narrative lays the foundation for a reconciliation with this Other, who is now perceived as an enriching factor, a positive input into the collective development.

In other words, in the process of normalizing the Québecois and refurbishing their self-image, these historians have defined the conditions that favor a greater openness on the part of the Québecois toward their Other(s). Moreover, this new self-image reflects the important positive role played by exotic influences in the shaping of

Quebec culture. Accordingly, the Québecois subject is no longer perceived as historically idiosyncratic, but rather as the expression of a synthesis which renders it comparable, if not equal, to its Other(s), from whom it no longer needs to separate itself; now that the relationship is one of alignment, the Québecois subject can finally justify its long-standing claim to political autonomy.

So much the better, then, that the image of the out-of-step Québecois is now in the process of disappearing. The way is therefore open to restoring a temporality which starts with the universal rather than falling back on the singular or the local. Although the effort to link the history of Quebec with mainstream Western history dates back to the late 1970s, it is only recently that it has been incorporated in the argument of a history textbook.[8] The authors of that textbook later published an article in which they criticized their predecessors and called for a new temporality, a different periodization, with which to historicize Quebec and its development as a society. On the basis of modes of production and exchange, these scholars would restructure Quebec history as a series of six unequal periods, each of which was briefer than the last and represented a discrete stage of economic development:

(1) Before 1650: native exchange systems;
(2) 1650s–1810s: the preindustrial period;
(3) 1810s–1880s: the transition to industrial capitalism;
(4) 1880s–1930s: industrial capitalism;
(5) 1930s–1960s: modernization;
(6) 1960s to the present: contemporary Quebec.[9]

This periodization, in which the Marxist time line and its evolutionism are implicit, reconciles the historical trajectory of Quebec society with the broad parameters of Western history by locating Quebec on the same time line as other Western states. By means of this process of harmonization, the collective subject is not only fortified via historical normalization, but is further reinforced as part of mainstream history—as a group in the forefront, on an equal footing with those whom it had always (until very recently) viewed as models to imitate. Henceforth, the Québecois could consider themselves cured of their inferiority complex and raised to the ranks of the Other, since their history, contrary to what they had been led to believe, was in its own way a success story.

If this periodization universalizes the Québecois and authorizes them to liberate themselves from their confinement at the margins of the historical center, it also makes possible a total shift of the moderns (versus the pre-Revolutionaries) to the center of Quebec history. Because the historical narrative inevitably constitutes a dialogue between Memory and Oblivion, it opens up the possibility of a new relationship between recollection and amnesia, with significant consequences for the collective genesis and development of the group. Hence to reconstruct Quebec and the Québecois society as modern is to deny the idea that their development has been slower than— or out of step with—that of other states and societies. It is also to open up the possibility of seeing that society as competitive from the beginning. Again, to seek signs as far back in Quebec history as possible of the presence of a modern, pluralistic subject, liberal and urban, economical and rational, is to reject the past that suited the traditionalists, who maintained that Quebec was a longtime peasant society. Acknowledging this past so as to show that Quebec farmers sought business opportunities and were economics-minded is to deny that the Québecois had ever been a traditional, relatively immobile society exclusively concerned with the preservation of their heritage. As a result, the historicity and the historical consciousness of the community have been constructed on a new basis, one that lays the ground for the moderns' ascendancy over the group's historical configuration.

What is left unresolved by this reinterpretation of Quebec history, this universalizing of Québecois society, is the issue of distinctiveness. One major effect of the new periodization has been to challenge the status of the conventional stages of Quebec's history (i.e., Conquest, rebellions, Confederation, etc.), and one major consequence of that challenge has been to place in question the actual significance of the founding episode of New Quebec, an episode with which the historicity of the elite is identified, namely, the Quiet Revolution.

Now, contrary to what one might believe, both of these questions— Quebec's distinctiveness and the significance of its Quiet Revolution—have been resolved by the authors of the new version of Quebec's great narrative. On the one hand, the normalization of the collective past through the rediscovery of a much more optimistic and brilliant history has supported the claim to a glorious destiny of a group of people who have long been disdained as "woodcutters," "waterbearers," and "pea soup eaters." Moreover, instead of questioning the past negatively ("How and why was Quebec's development not like that of others?"), historians have attempted to understand and interrogate it on the basis of the particular conditions under which this society developed ("How and why was Quebec's development as it was?") in order to stress the specific and original character of the Québecois past. As a result of that approach, the defeated and demoralized subject was transformed into an accomplished and ambitious one.

As we know, identity is largely realized through a dialectical relationship with one or more Others who are often construed as enemies and, if need be, as the cause of one's misfortunes. In the case of the French Quebecer, this Other was the English (who replaced the "Indian" in this role). However, in the new version of the great narrative, the antithetical role of this figure has been modified and is treated as some sort of objective factor. The English subject remains part of the picture but is now characterized as one who had certain advantages over the French subject, notably, a privileged position in information and communication networks. In other words, the English subject is no longer a malevolent figure, having been reconstituted in much more neutral terms as a mode of production and exchange. Accordingly, the French subject is no longer a victim of inherent inertia or its associated inadequacy, having been reconceived in relation to a series of situations over which it had practically no control. The French subject is thus relieved of responsibility for its condition. Furthermore, in spite of the restrictions under which the French subject developed, that subject has shown, throughout history, an ability to find innovative solutions to the problems with which it has been confronted and to profit from the opportunities that have arisen. Overall, the French subject has had to be acknowledged as every bit as competent as others were in dealing with the difficulties of life. More specifically, by relativizing the dichotomy oppressed/oppressor, on which the old version of the great narrative was based, the authors of the new version made the Québecois an audacious and ambitious people, consistent with the new collective hero—the entrepreneur—in Quebec's own pantheon.

Although, as I said earlier, historiography has been in the process of revising the conventional periodization of Quebec's past, this has not included downgrading the significance of the Quiet Revolution. Representing a period of about six years during the 1960s when a new political class, inspired by the principles of state interventionism and technocratic planning, defined the conditions of its relative and absolute mobility in the social and political spheres, the Quiet Revolution led to a set of measures which effectively reversed not only the general functioning, but also the imaginary, of the collectivity. Most people would now admit that this date of 1960 is only a convenient means of pinpointing a global change that was brought about over a period of several years. That being said, the impression of the Quiet Revolution as a turning point for the collectivity, in the sense that the Québecois wouldn't have overcome their anachronic trajectory and attained the stage of modernity without the vision and leadership of the technocracy, has simply been reinforced by the new narrative.

In fact, the Quiet Revolution was, for the technocracy, a turning point in the realization of its own identity as a ruling class.[10] But there is another reason why the Quiet Revolution could not be easily eradicated from the collective imaginary of the Québecois. In English Canadian historiography, the Conquest of 1759 used to be interpreted as a virtual liberation of the French, given the benefits they acquired and the advances they made, at least from the perspective of Continental values and institutions. In the great English Canadian narrative, the Conquest represented a blessing for the conquered, and the British a force of liberators who allowed and enabled the conquered to inscribe their historicity alongside that of the conquerors. The destiny of the Québecois was from the beginning, then, dependent on the goodwill of the British (or of the English Canadian, which amounted to the same thing), that is, of the Other. Can we conceive of a destiny as tragic as the dispossession that renders one a spectator of one's own history? The Quiet Revolution, as the starting point of an identity reversal for the Québecois, allowed them to free themselves from this alienating perspective and to reinstall themselves as the true heroes of their own liberation. In other words, the Quiet Revolution gave them back the role of actors in and commanders of their own historicity. The Quiet Revolution reversed the terrible defeat of the Conquest and authorized the Québecois to view themselves as historical victors. As a result, the exorcism of the collective subject's negative identity is finished and its defeat has been compensated.

Notes

1 For further elaborations of this argument (as well as additional bibliographic references), see Jocelyn Létourneau, "La production historienne courante portant sur le Québec et ses rapports avec la construction des figures identitaires d'une communauté communicationnelle," *Recherches sociographiques* 36 (1995): 9–45.

2 These notions of "pre-Revolutionaries" and "moderns" are relative to Quebec's Quiet Revolution, which is considered a watershed in its history and has played a crucial role in the advent of a new temporality by which everything is defined as either pre– or post–Quiet Revolution. Associated with those two periods are two, mutually exclusive subjects, although the actual narrative promoted by historians tends to modify this vision. See Jocelyn Létourneau, "La saga du Québec moderne en images," *Genèses* 4 (1991): 44–71.

3 For further elaboration of this idea, see Jocelyn Létourneau, "The Unthinkable History of Quebec," *Oral History Review* 17 (1989): 89–115.

4 Fernand Ouellet, "La modernisation de l'historiographie et l'émergence de l'histoire sociale," *Recherches sociographiques* 26 (1985): 11–84.

5 As rightly pointed out by Ronald Rudin in a very subtle article, "Revisionism and the Search for a Normal Society: A Critique of Recent Quebec Historical Writing," *Canadian Historical Review* 73 (1992): 30–61.

6 *Guide d'histoire du Québec du Régime français à nos jours: Bibliographie commentée*, ed. Jacques Rouillard (Montreal, 1991).

7 Ibid., 62; my translation.

8 John Dickinson and Brian Young, *A Short History of Quebec: A Socio-Economic Perspective* (Toronto, 1988).

9 John Dickinson and Brian Young, "Periodization in Quebec History: A Reevaluation," *Quebec Studies* 12 (1991): 1–10.

10 See Jocelyn Létourneau, "Le 'Québec moderne': Un chapitre dans le grand récit collectif des Québécois," *Revue française de science politique* 43 (1992): 765–85.

Daphna Golan

Between Universalism and Particularism: The "Border" in Israeli Discourse

I live in No-Man's-Land, on a hill between what used to be the borders of Israel and Jordan. The village is a small community of Arabs and Jews who wanted to create an egalitarian society where all Israelis could live together. My children learn both Arabic and Hebrew; they celebrate Christmas and Chanukah and Id el Fitter. My six-year-old daughter talks about the 415 Palestinians who were deported to Lebanon in December 1992. She wants to grow up to be a pilot so that she "can fly and bring back the deportees."

To be a pilot is the typical Israeli boy's fantasy. Pilots are our heroes. They go across the borders and bomb people they do not see. They do not have to look in somebody's eyes before they kill them. In any case, they do not kill people; they bomb "strategic military targets"—and they usually come home safely.

But my daughter wants to be a pilot—not to make war, but to do justice. And I am very proud of her for that. Her fantasy reminds me, however, that there is no possibility of

The *South Atlantic Quarterly* 94:4, Fall 1995.
Copyright © 1995 by Duke University Press.
CCC 0038-2876/95/$1.50.

raising children in Israel and keeping them insulated in No-Man's-Land. The creation of an island of Jews and Arabs living together does not necessarily mean obliteration of the boundaries between the two communities—in fact, my children are exposed daily to the drawing of lines. And instead of the universalistic education I envisaged, they get a double dose of nationalistic messages.

This paper conveys my personal confusion. On the one hand, my work in the human rights movement is based on universal norms of justice and an ideology which stresses that each person, regardless of nationality, deserves basic dignity and rights, superseding nationalism; I have a simple, John Lennon understanding of "imagining" that the world would have been a much better place without national struggles. But then, I am not sure that there is such a thing as No-Man's-Land in a country where the basic conflict revolves around control over land, and I have come to the conclusion that the only viable political solution is to draw a clear border between an Israeli and a Palestinian state.

This paper has two themes: One pertains to the Israeli peace camp and the apparent contradictions in its ideology—between universal notions of justice and the political venture of drawing the borders of the country. This paradoxical position is shared in various degrees by all of the Israeli Left—and, as I will show, those who propound the doctrine of peace tend to be Israeli first and only then "peace camp." In order to understand these prima facie irreconcilable positions (to which I will return), we must take up my second, closely related theme, namely, the nature of the borders and their effect on Israeli society. By "the nature of the borders" I mean the relations between the crude geography and the perceptions of people regarding the physical existence of the territory and the mysticism surrounding it.

The relationship of Israeli society to its borders evolved over four periods. The first period, extending until 1949, covered the drawing of the borders between Israel and its neighbors—the so-called green line. During the second period, from 1949 to 1967, the Israelis lived within this border and perceived themselves as a frontier society. In the third period, following the 1967 war, when Israel captured the West Bank, the Sinai Peninsula, and the Golan Heights, a series of

Israeli governments attempted to erase the green line. The fourth period, which began in 1987 with the Palestinian uprising (*intifada*), simultaneously emphasized and erased the border. In many ways the recent agreement signed between the PLO and Israel is a step forward in a long process in which both Israelis (or most of them) and Palestinians (or at least some of them) have learned that they must deal with each other's perception of the border.

In describing these four periods and their effects on the process of marking and erasing this border, I refer mostly to Israeli Jewry. The experience of the Arabs living in Israel, who comprise about 18 percent of the Israeli population, has been quite different and calls for treatment in its own right. The borders of Israel not only tore Israeli Arabs from their families in what became the Occupied Territories and in neighboring Arab countries, but also made them a minority in what became defined as a Jewish state.[1]

Period 1: The Formation of the Border. Throughout the ages, Israel has represented the Holy Land for most Jews. For many, it constituted their homeland and in their imagination the land of Israel had no borders. But the Jewish community in Israel, or what was called Palestine until 1947, was very small, not even owning much land. The Jewish national movement, better known as the Zionist movement, acted in three ways to acquire land in Palestine. First, through diplomatic negotiations, the Jews gained the recognition of the international community. Eventually, the Peel Commission suggested a partition of the area between the two nations that claimed it.[2] The Jews also bought land. Since 1901, donations from Jews around the world have helped the Jewish National Fund purchase parcels of land. Through the spare change they put in little donation boxes, Jews could contribute to the realization of the Zionist dream, participating in the "redemption of the soil."[3] Finally, though, the borders of Israel were defined by the lines drawn up at the time of the cease-fire that ended the 1948 war (Israel's War of Independence). The armistice frontiers after the war extended the area under Israel's control by some 2,000 square miles beyond the 6,000 square miles allotted to the Jewish state in the partition plan.

Throughout the late nineteenth and twentieth centuries, the message of the Zionist movement was that Israel had been waiting for 2,000 years for the Jewish people to come and save it, or, as the slogan went, "A land without a people for a people without a land." Contrary to the Zionist myth, however, the land was not empty, and the war that established Israel's independence rendered some 700,000 to 800,000 Arabs refugees. Many were deported, while many others fled the fighting and were never allowed to return to their homes.[4]

During the 1948 war, David Ben Gurion, describing the flight of Arabs from Haifa, wrote in his diary:

> During the night of the bombardment there were 30,000–35,000 Arabs in the town, and they started running away—to the port, to the German neighborhood [which was under British rule], boarding boats and buses. . . . Now there are less than 10,000, maybe 6,000. . . . A ghost town. Except in one place we saw two old people sitting in a half-empty store, and in another alley we met an Arab woman walking with her child.[5]

A month later, after dozens of villages had been emptied, Ben Gurion established a committee to "clean up these villages, cultivate them and settle them."[6] In reality, according to B. Morris, this meant the "standard Haganah [precursor of the Israel army] and IDF [Israel Defense Army] practice" of rounding up and expelling "the remaining villagers (usually old people, widows and cripples) from each site already evacuated by most of its inhabitants mainly because the occupying force wanted to avoid having to leave behind a garrison." Morris argues that there was no national political decision to expel the Arabs, but "it was understood by all concerned that, militarily, in the struggle to survive, the fewer Arabs remaining behind and along the front lines, the better and, politically, the fewer Arabs remaining in the Jewish state, the better."[7] When Israel was declared the state of the Jewish people, its population consisted of some 650,000 Jews and 165,000 Arabs. Most of the 385 villages formerly occupied by Palestinians were destroyed, and Jewish kibbutzim or villages were created on their sites.[8]

But there were also those who thought that the borders drawn in 1949 were not the true borders of Israel. They believed that one day it would become the Greater Israel of biblical days—Israel as it was promised to Abraham by God, Israel stretching from the Euphrates to the Nile. They made a distinction between the *state* of Israel, which has internationally recognized boundaries, and the *land* of Israel, which is four or five times greater in size, with its borders drawn by God. This mystical notion of the land and yearning for a "Greater Israel" has always had a somewhat vague presence in Israeli politics, but it became more dominant after the occupation of the West Bank in 1967 and was even strengthened after the 1977 change of government, when the right-wing Likud Party took over from the Labor Party. *Gush Emunim*, a faction within the Zionist movement rooted in a long history of intertwined religious and secular fundamentalist Zionist ideology, made "redemption of the greater land of Israel" its goal. Rabbi Z. Y. Kook, who gave Jewish/Zionist fundamentalism its spiritual base, argued that the state of Israel was envisioned by the Prophets and thus embodied the very fulfillment of the messianic ideal—but not without those parts of the land of Israel "which were torn from the live body" with the territorial partition of 1948, especially Hevron (Hebron), Jericho, and Shechem (Nablus).[9] He maintained that Judaism consists of three elements—the people, the land, and the Torah—and that "when one inch of the land of Israel is taken away, it is as if a word is erased out of the holy book."[10] Although the concept of *Eretz Israel* (Land of Israel) was never central to the Israeli collective identity, it had an important influence on shaping it. The collective identity of the Israelis can be seen in terms of a state/land continuum: although the social boundaries in the state of Israel are officially defined by citizenship, among other things, and the Jewish nation–state can accommodate non-Jews with equal rights, the Eretz Israel concept, which includes kinship as the criterion of membership in the collectivity, is very powerful. It is this concept that defines non-Jews as "strangers within our midst" (*goyim*) and endows them with a different status.

≡

Period 2: Living with the Border. The literature on life on the frontier in America or South Africa emphasizes the fact that a group becomes more united as the dangers it faces become more evident: the group stresses its own unique characteristics—its common language, history, and culture—in order to clearly draw the boundaries of exclusion and inclusion. Israeli society evinces most of the characteristics of a frontier society, that is, one which has always perceived itself as a threatened minority fighting for its survival. Its wars with neighboring Arab countries that do not recognize Israel's right to exist have, until recently, erupted every few years and are new episodes in the long history of Jewish persecution all over the world. Those who do not participate in guarding the borders of society are excluded from its center. And the dominant culture is that of men who know how to fight wars.[11] Israel, cramped within such narrow borders, feels that it is all border, that it is in a permanent stage of siege, that "the whole nation is an army."[12] Thus it has become a society with very little tolerance for the difference of the other, for those who do not participate in defending the borders.

The new Israeli wanted to create a society that would be diametrically opposed to what he had left behind in Europe: no more wandering Jews who were not allowed to own property, but a people who worked their own land; no longer a minority without power, but a nation with a powerful army. In the face of an urgent need to create an image of the "New Israeli," everything that was *galuti* (of the Diaspora) was ridiculed.

This admiration of power, combined with the perceived importance of the land, caused a great deal of tension when the survivors of World War II and the Holocaust began arriving in Israel. These individuals, who had come back from hell and were a far cry from the self-sufficient New Israelis, were not always well-received. They tended to remind the New Israelis of exactly what they did *not* want to be.[13] The negative perception of these survivors was reinforced by Zionist leaders such as Ben Gurion, who, at a November 1945 JAE meeting, asked "Are they a hindrance, an obstacle to Zionism, or a benefit?"[14] And Eliyahu Dobkin, co-head of the Jewish Agency's immigration department, described a group of Jewish refugees from Poland in May 1942 as "broken in spirit, despairing, lacking in hope." Reporting to the Mapai Central Committee, Dobkin declared, "According to past criteria, we would never have agreed to approve [them] for Aliya" (immigration to Israel).[15] Alterman, a leading poet of the labor movement, summarized the ambivalent attitude of the New Israeli toward those who had survived the war and the Holocaust: "They were different . . . in language, logic, image, way of walking, line of action . . . reaction of fear and laughter. . . . At night . . . we carry them . . . on our backs [from ship to shore, in illegal immigration], we feel the cracking of their weak bodies and their hands closing on our throats."[16]

Others who were not accepted as part of the hegemonic center were the Jews who emigrated from Arab countries in the early 1950s. These new immigrants were perceived as too much like the Arabs: they spoke Arabic; they listened to Arab music; they ate Arab food— so they were sent to live on the borders, as close to Arabs as possible. There were, of course, practical reasons for this policy: the number of immigrants arriving within a relatively short time span was huge compared to the established Israeli community, and Israel wanted settlement of the border areas for its protection. Between 1948 and 1951, the Jewish population doubled. In other words, by 1951 one out of two Israeli Jews was a newcomer.[17] Oriental Jews were expected to integrate with the dominant Western (Ashkenazi) culture and were made to feel that their culture was inferior. In response to their need to conform to the hegemonic culture, they began to identify Arabs in the stereotypical terms bestowed upon an enemy.[18]

And then there were the women. Because women did not play an equal role in guarding the borders, they were marginalized. Their role was to be the "hero's wife,"[19] to take care of the men, to worry about them and to help them. The outbreaks of border wars every few years—and the consequent need to ward off threats to the physical existence of the country—in which almost all Israeli men (age permitting) participated, were highly conducive to strengthening patriarchal family life. Women were supposed to look after their families when the men were protecting the country.[20]

The predicament of Israeli Arabs, however, is even worse. Those who did not flee and were not deported have faced constant discrimination as an unwanted minority in Israel. They have been seen not only as a security threat, mainly because of their affiliation with Arabs on the other side of the border, but also as a "demographic" liability—a potential danger to the definition of Israel as a Jewish state.

Although those Arabs who remained in Israel in 1948 became Israeli citizens with equal political and civil rights, there were at least three mechanisms which kept their discrimination in force. First, in accordance with the British Defense (Emergency) Regulations (which were incorporated into Israeli law with the establishment of the state), all Arab-populated areas were placed under the control of the military, which closed the areas and allowed only holders of special permits to enter and leave, a state of affairs that continued until 1963. The military commanders in those areas were authorized to detain these citizens without trial or to deport them "for reasons of security,"[21] although this authorization, too, was canceled in 1963. Second, those Arabs who had fled from Israel during the War of Independence were not allowed to return. Their lands were resettled by new Jewish immigrants, and their property was confiscated.[22] Third, the 1950 Law of Return and the 1952 Nationality Law underscored the perception of Israel as a distinctively Jewish state. The Law of Return legalized the immigration of "every Jew" into the country, while the Nationality Law automatically bestowed citizenship on anyone entering the country under the Law of Return. Arab residents, as well as other non-Jews, could acquire citizenship through residence, birth, or naturalization.[23] These mechanisms were part of a "too many Arabs in Israel" ideology.[24] As the advisor on Arab affairs to Prime Minister Joshua Palmon put it:

> I opposed the integration of Arabs into Israeli society. I preferred separate development. True, this prevented Arabs from integrating into the Israeli democracy. . . . The separation made it possible to maintain a democratic regime within the Jewish population alone.[25]

Period 3: Attempts to Erase the Border. The third period commenced at the end of the 1967 war, in which Israel had acquired the Sinai Peninsula, the Golan Heights, the West Bank, and Gaza—the areas that came to be called the Occupied Territories. Over the next twenty years, Israel tried to rub out the borders, as it were, to treat these areas as part of Greater Israel, while at the same time refusing to fully admit them into Israel proper.

Israel, in referring to these areas, has never used the term "Occupied Territories"; instead, it has called them the "Administered Territories," which, of course, implies a very different attitude. The former term indicates a temporary state of military occupation, a status that will someday change. Israel, however, has been unwilling to accept that eventuality. Yet Israel was also unwilling, or unable, to annex the Occupied Territories not only because of opposition from the international community, but also because annexation would entail granting civil and political rights to the Palestinians living there. With annexation, the Palestinians would comprise one-third of the Israeli citizenry and, by sheer numbers alone, would soon pose a threat to the Jewish majority.[26]

On state-owned radio and television (until recently there were no privately owned television stations), the Occupied Territories of the West Bank are called by their biblical names, "Judea and Samaria," to remind listeners and viewers that these lands were part of the Jewish kingdom in biblical times. Only a few months after the end of the 1967 war, the Israeli government decided to erase the green line from all official maps, which would henceforth show the new cease-fire lines instead. Since then, the Occupied Territories have been depicted on all maps as officially part of Israel. In everything from textbooks to guidebooks, the green line—the border between Israel and the Occupied Territories—has disappeared. But much more was erased than the symbolic borders on maps. Soon after the war ended, Israel began to physically efface the actual boundaries, building roads on and across the border, confiscating some 50 percent of Arab lands in the West Bank, and beginning to settle Jews in the Occupied Territories.[27]

The plan to build Jewish settlements in these territories was aimed at—in the words of the right-wing Likud government—"creating facts on the ground," thereby making it impossible, or at least extremely difficult, to redraw the green line. The ultimate goal was to increase the Jewish population in the West Bank to 2.6 million, or some 40 percent, by the year 2010.[28] The government provided these settlers with low-cost housing, income tax reductions, a good education system, and virtually free land for cultivation. While all of these economic benefits were widely publicized, no mention was made of the fact that the housing projects were in the Occupied Territories. In any case, approximately 85 percent of the settlers live close to Tel Aviv and Jerusalem, and many of them moved to the territories for the sake of these economic benefits rather than for ideological reasons.

East Jerusalem, the Arab section of the city, was the first area annexed by Israel, immediately after the end of the 1967 war. The reunification of Jerusalem was enacted by the Knesset and is now celebrated annually as Jerusalem Day. The government made the building of Jewish neighborhoods in the eastern half of the city a policy initiative, and about a third of the Arab-owned land in East Jerusalem has since been confiscated. Today, approximately 35 percent of Jerusalem's Jewish population lives across the green line.[29]

Despite these efforts to erase the border, boundaries between the two societies—Israeli Jews and Palestinians—remained. In fact, the more intense the attempt to blur the green line, the more distinctly divided the two population groups became. The Jews in the Occupied Territories are Israeli citizens who enjoy full civil and political rights in Israel, although they live outside its borders; the Palestinians in these territories, on the other hand, live under military rule and have no political rights at all. The manifestations of their different status are numerous: Jewish settlers can buy cut-price land confiscated from the Palestinians; they use about nine times as much water (a scarce commodity in the region) as their Palestinian neighbors; and their settlements include a top-quality, Israeli-built road system, while in the areas inhabited by Palestinians there is not even a single traffic light.

One poignant example of this policy of discrimination was the distribution of gas masks during the Gulf War. In January 1991, when Saddam Hussein threatened Israel with chemical weapons, the government provided all citizens with gas masks—except the Palestinians in the Occupied Territories, on the grounds that they were not in the danger zone. Yet Jewish settlers living among the Palestinians in that very same zone did receive gas masks. The Israeli High Court ruled that this was a clear case of discrimination and ordered the army to provide gas masks to the Palestinian population.[30] Nevertheless, by the end of the Gulf War, the army had distributed only 70,000 gas masks among the 1.8 million Palestinians in the Occupied Territories.

In short, for many years after the 1967 war Israel's ambivalent attitude toward its borders prevailed. While there were always those, individually and as part of various social movements, who opposed the occupation, most Israelis accepted the overall benefits of cheap Palestinian labor and a captive market for Israeli goods and services; eventually, many forgot that there had ever been a border between Israel and the West Bank.

Period 4: Redrawing the Green Line. This attitude began to change in the mid-1980s after Israel's war with Lebanon, when many Israelis started questioning the wisdom of such military ventures as this one, which was euphemistically called "Operation Peace for Galilee." The change that led to the reinstitution of the green line, however, began in December 1987 with the launching of the intifada. The Palestinian popular uprising was aimed at ending the Israeli occupation by means of civil disobedience and work strikes as well as violent actions against Israel. Jerusalem became redivided between East and West, between its Arab and its Jewish populations, not by walls or signposts—but by fear. Israeli Jews who had become used to shopping and walking around in the Arab neighborhoods soon felt too uncomfortable, even too frightened, to do so any longer. Virtually no Jews felt at ease in Gaza or Nablus. The stone-throwing incidents, school boycotts, strikes, and demonstrations that took place in the Occupied Territories served to remark the borders, and many Israelis began to realize that their army was stationed in a land where perhaps it did not belong.

Here I finally come to the paradoxical position from which I started: the position of the Israeli peace movement, which would redraw the border between a Palestinian and an Israeli state on the basis of universal norms of justice. Again, I will address only the Israeli side of the border, although its marking was initiated and continued mainly by the Palestinians with the intifada.

Since the mid-1980s, a few different Israeli peace groups have called for the redrawing of the green line. They differ from each other in their focus and ideology, and in their understanding of how much they can distance themselves from the consensus of Israeli society. What they share, however, is the problematic tension that marks their work—the tension between universalistic notions of human rights and justice, on the one hand, and their political efforts to draw political boundaries between an Israeli and a Palestinian state, on the other. These individuals, who in Israel are considered part of the Left, but who would probably be considered liberals anywhere else, feel uneasy about Israeli society's tendency toward chauvinism, with its characteristic nationalism and militarism. Yet this critical position is always compromised by their loyalty to a certain reading of Zionism.

The largest and best-known Israeli peace group is the Peace Now organization, which was launched in 1978 by a group of combat officers who challenged the right-wing government headed by Menachem Begin for dragging its feet over the peace talks with Egypt. To this day, Peace Now has tried to legitimize its dovish message by focusing the limelight upon those of its members who hold high rank in the military reserves.[31] Peace Now represents the intellectual elite of Israel and is composed of a relatively small group of well-educated and affluent Ashkenazi Jews who are closely connected to the Labor Party, which heads the current government. The organization's slogan, adopted in September 1993 in support of the recent peace initiative, is "Peace is my security," which reflects Peace Now's opposition to the occupation as harmful to Israeli democracy and underlines the moral values of Israeli youth. This "enlightened self-interest" assumes that the present status quo is untenable, but that annexation of the territories, entailing civil rights for the Palestinians residing there, would create a "demographic problem," as Jews would then become the minority in a Jewish state.[32]

The Peace Now position has been criticized by a smaller group, *Yesh Gvul*, as a policy of "shoot and weep," or serve first, ask questions later. Yesh Gvul claims that it is not enough to protest immoral actions post factum, but rather that one should actively refuse to countenance them as they are occuring (i.e., oppression of the Palestinians in the Occupied Territories). Yesh Gvul was formed during the Lebanon War in 1982 by a group of soldiers who requested exemptions from military duty in Lebanon. In a petition to the prime minister, these reservists explained that they were willing to serve their country, but they did not want to fight a redundant war against a civilian population.

"Yesh Gvul" has three meanings in Hebrew: (1) "there is a bor-der"; (2) "there is a limit"; and (3) "enough is enough." The play on these meanings in the group's name is deliberate—the movement supports those who refuse to cross the borders, including those who have had enough of (border) wars. Yesh Gvul has not attempted to define alternative political or ideological borders, but leaves it up to each member to define his limits of obedience.[33]

There were soldiers who went to Lebanon but refused to fight civilian populations; there were others who did not go at all, while some went after voicing their protest. Later, Yesh Gvul members shifted their focus to the Occupied Territories and asked to be relieved of military duty there. In a letter to the prime minister published in May 1986, they wrote: "We swore to defend the peace and security of the State of Israel, and we are loyal to this oath. We therefore ask you to allow us not to take part in the process of oppression and occupation in the territories." Signed by thousands of reservists, each of whom gave his rank, this letter set off a wave of refusals to serve in areas outside the green line. Although it is hard to estimate how many refused for ideological reasons and how many simply thought that "enough [was] enough," the fact is that since then thousands of soldiers have refused to serve in the Occupied Territories. Some (180) went to jail, most of them during the first two years of the intifada, before the authorities decided to refrain from jailing refuseniks so as to play down the issue.

Yesh Gvul is unique not only among Israeli peace groups, but also relative to other antiwar movements elsewhere in the world. Its mem-bers are not pacifists, nor do they object to serving in the military per se. On the contrary, they stress the fact that they are ready and willing to do so and that some of them are even officers and soldiers in elite units, but they argue that there should be a limit to the obedi-ence required of them. In a country where the rights of conscientious objectors are not recognized and where military service has always carried a considerable moral imperative, Yesh Gvul's position is rela-tively radical. Not surprisingly, it was this issue of selective refusal that cleaved the Israeli peace movement into two quite distinct fac-tions. Peace Now saw loyalty to Israeli democracy and law as a sine qua non, while Yesh Gvul emphasized the uncompromisability of personal moral codes, even to the point of breaking the law and facing the threat of imprisonment. Attempts to delegitimize Yesh Gvul by characterizing it as merely a marginal group of traitors were made not only by the establishment, but also by members of other Israeli peace groups who continued to live a double life, doing their military reserve duty in Gaza and then agitating for an end to the occupation.

The issue of loyalty, and the conflict between universal ethics and loyalty to the State of Israel, is also evident in the tension felt within the Israeli human rights organization *B'Tselem*, which was established in 1989. B'Tselem, the Israeli Information Center for Human Rights in the Occupied Territories, was formed much along the lines of Amnesty International or Human Rights Watch. Its name represents some of the dilemmas that it faces. "B'Tselem" means "in the image of God" and is taken from Genesis: "In the image of God He created him. Man and woman He created them." As its name suggests, the organization stresses the universal notion of human rights, notably, that all human beings are born equal in terms of dignity and rights, yet the name is a Hebrew one, drawing on specifically Jewish associations. In keeping with this dual identity, the organization strives at once to uphold the international principle of human rights and to direct most of its work to an Israeli audience. A crucial ongoing controversy within the organization pertains to the language in which B'Tselem should publish its reports: Hebrew and English or Hebrew only. The Hebrew-only people maintain that B'Tselem should view Israelis as its primary audience, aiming to change Israeli public opinion and to influence Israeli policy makers, and that, as Israelis, its members should not publicly (i.e., internationally) criticize their country.[34] On the other hand, there are those who claim that the human rights movement is conceptualized on the basis of universality, including the idea that all people are responsible for safeguarding the rights of others, regardless of nationality, religion, race, or sex. This tension between the opposing factions—or between conflicting loyalties to the State of Israel and the human rights community—remains unresolved, with every member of B'Tselem positioned somewhere along this continuum from the patriotic to the universalistic.

My last example of an Israeli peace group is also the one whose position is farthest from Israeli consensus and closest to the border. The Alternative Information Center is almost at the fringe of Israeli society, and it publishes only in English. In November 1989, a three-judge panel imposed a prison sentence of twenty months plus a ten-month suspended sentence on Michael Warschawski (Mikado), as well as a $5,000 fine on the Alternative Information Center, which he directs. Both were convicted of typesetting a booklet that the judges attributed to the Popular Front for the Liberation of Palestine (PFLP). The booklet described interrogation techniques and torture allegedly perpetrated by the Israeli security services and offered advice on ways to withstand such interrogations. While the court found that Warschawski had not known of the booklet's PFLP origins, he was nevertheless convicted of "shutting his eyes" to its source.[35] Twenty months for shutting one's eyes is a very heavy sentence, especially when compared to penalties imposed for similar offenses even by Palestinians. Warschawski told a group of Israeli peace activists that "the verdict" was directed at them "as a warning sign: Beware of the Border! We warn you, the border is a dangerous area, keep away from it!" As a matter of fact, Warschawski is one of the very few political activists in Israel who does position himself at the border—at the margins of Israeli society—on the border that divides the permitted and the prohibited, the Israelis and the Palestinians. Describing his political work in promoting Palestinian rights, Warschawski said:

> My work could not have been done from the center—from the heart of Israeli society and its consensus. This could have been done only from the border and on the border. Only there was it possible to meet, talk, and act jointly. Therefore, I have always refused to sit in the warm bosom of the consensus, and already in 1968 I chose my place on the border, on this side of the border, as part of my society, but as close as possible to the other part.[36]

———

Every national movement is fraught with tensions that arise between particularism and universalism. The Zionist ideology is no different in this regard. Like all movements, it stresses the unique, the particular, in Israel's struggle to be like all other nations. Israeli society has lived under constant threat from its neighbors since Israel achieved independence; this society also lives with the memory of the Holocaust and of a long history of anti-Semitism and persecution. The more insecure Israel was about its geographical boundaries, the more rigid it became toward its social boundaries, failing to develop much understanding or compassion for the other, for those who were—or chose to be—different. The Israeli peace camp has been affected both by the strong pressure to conform and by the memories of Jewish persecution; and, when all is said and done, it shares the nationalistic sentiments of most other Israelis.

Here, I have tried to show some of the tensions and paradoxes inherent to Israeli ideologies of peace in the post-Zionist era. What I have omitted may be at least as interesting as what I have chosen to discuss, at the expense of some of the same questions that I have criticized the peace camp for not posing: Is Zionism the answer to world anti-Semitism? Was the creation of a Jewish state justified, even at the expense of Arab lands? Is it possible to form a state that is at once Jewish and democratic? And what are the bases of legitimation for the State of Israel?

I began by referring to the importance of geographical location to life in Israel. The position of the Israeli Left toward housing development in Israel summarizes some of the tensions and paradoxes in the various post-Zionist ideologies. An essential componenet of Israeli left-wing ideology is the refusal to live in the Occupied Territories. Although housing there is cheap by virtue of government subsidies, Israeli leftists do not want to live in developments on land that was confiscated after the 1967 war. Yet some peace movement leaders reside in houses that once belonged to Arabs who fled during the 1948 war. In fact, owning an old Arab house in Jerusalem has become a status symbol. What is the essential difference between the houses occupied since 1948 and the lands occupied since 1967? The limit of memory? The edge of convenience? The border of empathy with the other? Is the difference due to the impact of an era which "discovered" human rights? Or does living in these houses say that there is a certain moral price Israelis are ready to pay (and that they are willing to force Palestinians to pay) for the establishment of a Jewish state, but that there is no price at which Israelis are willing to buy the expansion of the state after the 1967 war? Or does it come down to a very practical position based not on objective or moral reasons for the existence of a Jewish state, but on the desire simply to end the wars?

In September 1993, when Israel recognized the PLO, it openly faced the need to withdraw from at least part of the territories it had occupied since 1967. The first controversy that arose after the signing of the agreement was over how to define the Jericho area that would be subject to Palestinian jurisdiction: Should the region be defined according to biblical terms, British maps, or Jericho municipality plans? This debate, in fact, touches upon a much deeper issue, notably, the state's bases of legitimacy. Ostensibly a dispute over borders, this entails the recognition of the possibility of creating a new Palestinian state neighboring the State of Israel—which is what I hope there will be in the end: one border between two independent states, with flags and hymns and leaders—everything I do not like, but still would like to see become reality.

Notes

1 See N. Rouhana, "Collective Identity and Regional Arrangement—The Palestinians in Israel" (unpublished paper); A. Abed Elrazik, R. Amin, and U. Davis, "Problems of Palestinians in Israel," *Journal of Palestine Studies* 7 (1978): 31–54; M. al-Haj, "The Arab Internal Refugees in Israel: The Emergence of a Minority within the Minority," *Immigrants and Minorities* 7 (1988): 19–65; and I. Lustick, *Arabs in a Jewish State: Israel's Control of a National Minority* (Austin, 1980).

2 On the partition plan, see M. Gilbert, *The Arab–Israeli Conflict* (London, 1974).

3 Between 1905, when they made their first land purchases, and 1948 (when Israel gained independence), the Jewish National Fund acquired 936,000 *dunams* of land; see U. Davis and W. Lehn, "And the Fund Still Lives," *Journal of Palestine Studies* 7 (1978): 3–30.

4 The exact number of refugees is in dispute, with estimates ranging from 600,000 to 900,000; I rely on B. Morris, *The Birth of the Palestinian Refugee Problem, 1947–1949* (Cambridge, 1988; Oxford, 1990).

5 David Ben Gurion, *War Diary* (in Hebrew), 1 May 1948 (Tel Aviv, 1984), 1: 378, 381; my translation.

6 Ibid., 2: 487 (5 June 1948).

7 B. Morris, "The Origins of the Palestinian Refugee Problem," in *New Perspectives*

on Israeli History: The Early Years of the State, ed. L. J. Silberstein (New York, 1991), 47.

8 Morris, *Birth of the Palestinian Refugee Problem*, appendix. Some small villages which were destroyed are not indicated on Israeli maps.

9 These areas were later occupied by Israel in the 1967 war and are now part of the West Bank.

10 G. Aran, "Jewish Zionist Fundamentalism: The Bloc of the Faithful in Israel (Gush Emunim)," in *Fundamentalism Observed*, ed. M. E. Marty and R. S. Appleby (Chicago, 1991), 268.

11 This is one of the reasons for the discrimination against women in Israel; see L. Hazelton, *Israeli Women: The Reality Behind the Myths* (New York, 1977).

12 D. Grossman, *Sleeping on a Wire: Conversations with Palestinians in Israel* (New York, 1993), 316.

13 See A. Elon, *The Israelis: Founders and Sons* (New York, 1971); T. Segev, *The Seventh Million: The Israelis and the Holocaust* (New York, 1992); and *1949: The First Israelis* (New York, 1986).

14 Quoted by D. Porat, "Attitudes of the Young State of Israel towards the Holocaust and Its Survivors: A Debate over Identity and Values," in Silberstein, ed., *New Perspectives on Israeli History*, 172.

15 Ibid., 162.

16 Ibid., 167; quoting Alterman's *Ir Hayona*.

17 See the *Statistical Yearbook of Israel: 1992*, No. 43, which estimates that there were 716,700 Jews in Israel by the end of 1948, but 1,404,400 by the end of 1951.

18 The last decade has seen the rise of Israeli peace movements among Jews with origins in Arab countries who stress their cultural links with the Arabs, the best known of which is East for Peace. These movements, however, have failed to attract a large following of "Arab Jews" in Israel.

19 In Hebrew, the words for man/male—*gever*—and hero—*gibor*—have the same root.

20 Discrimination against women in Israel is rooted in two cardinal aspects of daily life: one is the national security aspect to which I refer here, while the other is the fact that Israel's marriage laws are dictated by the Jewish religious establishment.

21 Regulations 111 and 112 of the Defense (Emergency) Regulations of 1948 can still be applied today, both in Israel proper and in the Occupied Territories; see D. Golan, *Detained without Trial—Administrative Detention in the Occupied Territories* (Jerusalem, 1992).

22 See D. Peretz, "Early State Policy toward the Arab Population, 1948–1955," in Silberstein, ed., *New Perspectives on Israeli History*, 85.

23 Ibid., 96–97.

24 For such remarks by Israeli leaders, see Segev, *1949*, chap. 2, n. 13.

25 Ibid., 67.

26 This ambiguous situation is directly related to the legal status of the Occupied Ter-

ritories in terms of international law: Israel does not recognize the applicability of the Fourth Geneva Convention's human rights provisions to these territories. For the official Israeli view, see M. Shamgar, "The Observance of International Law in the Administered Territories," *Israel Handbook on Human Rights* (Jerusalem, 1971); and *Military Government in the Territories Administered by Israel, 1967–1980: The Legal Aspects,* ed. M. Shamgar (Jerusalem, 1982). By not recognizing these lands as "occupied," Israel is avoiding the legal consequences of not recognizing the basic human rights of civilians whose lands are occupied. On the role of the Israeli High Court in upholding human rights violations, see D. Golan, "La Deportation," *Le Monde Diplomatique* (March 1993).

27 See M. Benvenisti, *The West Bank Handbook* (in Hebrew) (Jerusalem, 1987); M. Schwartz, "Sharon's Star Wars: Israel's Seven Star Settlement Plan," *Challenge* 3 (1991).

28 See International Center for Peace in the Middle East, *The Settlements in the West Bank and Gaza* (in Hebrew) (Tel Aviv, 1993).

29 A few months after the Six-Day War, rebuilding began in the Jewish quarter of the Old City of Jerusalem; in addition, housing was built in a few new Jewish neighborhoods located in an area between West Jerusalem and Mt. Scopus, which until the war had been an Israeli enclave in Jordanian territory. In the second stage of this initiative, beginning in 1970, four large, suburban satellite developments were created; and, in the third stage, a major housing project was built on the northeast edge of the city. See M. Romann and A. Weingrod, *Living Together Separately: Arabs and Jews in Contemporary Jerusalem* (Princeton, 1991), which includes data from Jerusalem municipality records and from the Jerusalem Institute for Israeli Studies, *Statistical Yearbook of Jerusalem, 1991.* See also M. Benvenisti, "Jerusalem: A Study of a Polarized Community" (The West Bank Data Base Project), 33.

30 See D. Golan and Y. Ginbar, *Human Rights in the Occupied Territories during the Gulf War* (Jerusalem, 1992).

31 See P. Kidron, "A Limit to Obedience," *New Outlook* (May 1988).

32 See D. Hurwitz, *Walking the Red Line: Israelis in Search of Justice for Palestine* (Philadelphia, 1992).

33 Literally, *his*, not his or hers, because the female component in Yesh Gvul membership is negligible.

34 I have been the research director of the organization since its foundation in 1989 and have participated in these debates.

35 *News from Within*, 29 November 1989 (published by the Alternative Information Center, Jerusalem).

36 Michael Warschawski, speech at the solidarity meeting in his honor, *News from Within*, 29 November 1989. This powerful speech made me think for the first time about the importance of the border issue to the Israeli peace movement.

Miriam Cooke

Reimagining Lebanon

> We must resist the *formation* of national, ethnic, and other myths, as they are being formed.
> —Eric Hobsbawm

The end of the twentieth century has produced two paradoxical global phenomena that suggest the need for a new approach to defining the nation. First, macroeconomic forces are aligning groups that see no other reason for unification. In the overall drive for realignment, differences are highlighted, even created, and then used to forge new alliances that often conflict with the interests of the larger socioeconomic group. The establishment of multinationals and supranational coalitions has coincided with the proliferation of multiple political identities, each demanding autonomy and recognition. Second, the transport revolution has scattered people in search of a haven or of economic advancement all over a shrinking world. Mass migration has thus coincided with affirmations of political attachment to particular parts of the world, even if from afar. Global unification

The *South Atlantic Quarterly* 94:4, Fall 1995.
Copyright © 1995 by Duke University Press.
CCC 0038-2876/95/$1.50.

versus local differences, world citizenship versus parochialism—how are we to address these apparent contradictions?

I shall attempt to do so here by proposing degree–zero definitions of "nation" and "nationalism" that will allow us to span the spectrum between individual and collective identities. For many, the nation is that geopolitical entity from which nationality is derived. However, whereas the use of nationality as an identity marker is not in itself subject to debate, the nation which gives rise to particular nationalities is. Eve Sedgwick has defined the nation as a "set of discursive and institutional arrangements that mediate between the physical fact that each person inhabits, at a given time, a particular geographic space, and the far more abstract, sometimes even apparently unrelated organization of what has emerged since the late seventeenth century as her/his national identity, as signalized by, for instance, citizenship."[1] I shall develop that more abstract concept of national identity in terms of a specific understanding of the nation, using "nation" to denote a psychic space in which individuals feel rooted and to which they feel they belong. This space can be, but is not necessarily, coterminous with a political entity, a piece of land, or a human collectivity organized around a culture, a religion, or a language. "Nationalism," accordingly, is action motivated by that feeling of connectedness. In general, its goal is to foster a conceptual community which shares an understanding of what constitutes a given nation. Thus construed, nationalism may be primordial. It may indeed be traced to the earliest records of human history that describe men fighting together as members of a chosen people to assert or defend their right to and control over a piece of land promised to them because they spoke the language of their god. However, what is different about today, the expanded today of the post-Enlightenment, is that nations are imagined, and nationalisms played out, within the context of nation–state ideology.[2] In other words, each nation, once imagined, is almost obliged to agitate for the political autonomy of a state or, at the very least, for what Francis Fukuyama has called *thymos*: recognition of personal dignity. This context must shape our considerations of the nation and of nationalism.

Lebanon makes a good subject for a case study because it has long been a site of contestation over the meanings attached to "nation" and "nationalism." Although some claim that its civil war renders Lebanon an anomaly, I am not persuaded of that. In light of the developments since 1989 in the former Soviet Union, in Eastern Europe, and especially in Bosnia, it seems rather that Lebanon encapsulates a global, postcolonial situation. As the poet Rashid al-Daif puts it, "The whole world is Beirut / Lebanon."[3] Providing a special lens on the rest of the world, Lebanon reflects trends that are also manifest, but less visibly, elsewhere.

More than most countries, Lebanon has experienced a drain on its human resources for the last 100 years. Ever since the 1860s, with the first Druze–Maronite clashes in the mountains, many Lebanese have opted to make physical homes for themselves—while attempting to maintain their cultural homes—elsewhere. Current estimates put the number of Lebanese living outside the country at five to six times the number remaining on the soil of Lebanon. While the poet Henri Zghaib has succinctly articulated the expatriate understanding of the Lebanese nation as not only its *soil*, but, most importantly, its *soul*,[4] for those living on Lebanese soil, especially after the ravages of a seventeen-year war, the sense of nation has been less mystical. As demonstrated by the writings I analyze below, the soul of Lebanon has been tightly bound to its soil. In fact, it was for hegemony over this stretch of land that many men fought to the death. Lebanese nationalism was invoked under the different banners of competing ideologies which were generally organized into autonomous groups, tribal militias, each of whom claimed to represent the best interests of a Lebanon that in fact often served only their individual interests. The labels attached to these groups could be political (e.g., Marxist or Nasserite), religious (e.g., Maronite or Shiite), or feudal (e.g., Zghorti or Jumblati), yet however particular these identifications might be, they always had a nationalist connotation. Only members of the Kataib (an extreme right-wing Maronite militia) or of Saiqa (a left-wing Palestinian group) or of the Ahrar (another Maronite militia) or of Amal (a moderate left-wing Shiite militia) or of Hezbollah (a

pro-Iranian, Shiite fundamentalist organization) could really understand and therefore be qualified to respond to Lebanon's needs and to
represent its aspirations.

Women's literary constructions of the nation in 1980s Lebanon
emerged in response to a sense that not only had these nationalist/
ideological projects failed, but that they had been responsible for the
carnage of the civil war. Such constructions challenge the generally
accepted use of "nationalism" to denote advocacy of the principle
that a state should conform to the wishes and beliefs of the majority,
however that majority may be defined. This kind of nationalism can
be called "statist" because of its insistence on the overlap between an
imagined community, the nation, and a public entity, the state.

Political scientists, historians, and sociologists have variously
labeled the different forms of nationalism "popular," "official,"[5]
"romantic," "racist," "cultural," "authoritarian," "ethnic," or "religious." Yet these classifications are in general subsumed by the broad
category of what I am calling statist nationalism. In the nineteenth
century and up to the end of the Second World War, nationalist movements in Asia and Africa grew out of popular dissent and provided
the mobilizing rhetoric for peoples who recognized—and found unacceptable—the fact that their states were under foreign rule.[6] In the
second half of the twentieth century, statist nationalisms have prolif-
erated globally. Some, like the Palestinian and Kurdish nations, have
long struggled to win autonomy in and control over their own lands,
yet not every nation can have its own state. John Hall has written of
the 250 minorities worldwide who are now seeking states and, quoting Ernest Gellner, of the 8,000 "natural" languages that "could be
used to put forward nationalist claims."[7] In its extreme form, statist
nationalism can become radically xenophobic, with all foreigners—
whether in power or not—fair game. But who are these foreigners?
Foreignness is a matter for negotiation and even construction. The
fragmentation of centers in the postcolonial era has provided groups
who never thought of themselves collectively before with the possibility of autonomous ethnic purity. Highlighting (some might say
inventing) differences can divide what once seemed to be homogeneous communities. New myths of origin allow groups to remember or discover or create a uniqueness which "spontaneously" pro-

duces a shared identity and promises the fruits of a common destiny. These groups then segregate themselves and exclude those who do not fit, those who threaten their freshly constructed and thus fragile group ethos.

This process is inherently violent because it involves imposing ideology on geography. Statist nationalists place the state first and the nation second—but always as though the nation were at once primordial and immortal. Since, as Gellner notes, "nationalism emerges only in milieux in which the existence of the state is already very much taken for granted,"[8] statist nationalists are usually involved in a conflict with the state's existing power that may escalate into a war. Wars ensure nationalist sentiment of an outlet so that it can serve as bedrock for the foundation of the new nation–state. "The advent of the nation–state," according to Anthony Giddens, "stimulates divergent and oppositional nationalisms as much as it fosters the coincidence of nationalist sentiments and existing state boundaries."[9] Ross Poole sees war as "important for national identity, not so much because individuals have shown that they are prepared to kill for their nation . . . but because men—and sometimes women—have been prepared to suffer and die on behalf of their nation."[10] Vaclav Havel goes even further, calling nationalisms "the instigators of modern wars."[11] This is the danger of statist nationalism: it is inherently violent.

Statist nationalists claim to represent all the people comprising their imagined community. In general, however, these nationalists have been indigenous male elites who invoke, without listening to, others' voices—which is not to say that statist nationalism is either evil or inherently masculine. Globally, women are as much at the forefront of violent statist–nationalist movements as they are advocates of nonviolence. To cite only three examples of what Jean Bethke Elshtain calls the Ferocious Few, women of the Shining Path are fighting peasants in Peru, Serbian women are blocking aid convoys to Muslim civilians in Bosnia–Herzegovina, and Israeli feminists are establishing Zionist settlements on Palestinian land. Yet women have rarely, if ever, been the leaders of these movements. Highlighting the gender of nationalist groups and their leaders reveals what is at stake for each group in advocating a particular identity. Once such stakes have been made transparent, individuals are seen to be talking not so much about and for others, but about and for themselves—those who dominate the group that aspires to dominate.[12] Such decentering of a particular nationalist discourse assigns it a place *alongside* others.

If all competing nationalist ideologies of all centers within the confines of a single state are given equal consideration, then nationalism would seem to be not only a collective ideology, but first and foremost an individual state of mind, a way of expressing a sense of belonging to an entity that is thus created as something to which people may choose to belong. This complex of emotions is what I call humanist nationalism. Whereas statist nationalism is absolute and constructed within a binary framework of differentiation and recognition, positing the nation as "out there" from time immemorial and awaiting discovery by those who "naturally" belong to it, humanist nationalism construes the nation as dialectic, as both produced and productive.

Humanist nationalism is a program of action that may be pursued without reference to a state. It unites individuals and accommodates the subjectivities of several communities: those who are usually lumped together as anonymous "nationalists"; those who are not, strictly speaking, nationalists at all because they do not belong to a group that designates itself, first and foremost, as nationalist; and those who call themselves nationalists but whose individual needs have been marginalized, such as women's groups. Radhakrishnan believes that, faced

> with its own repression, the women's question seems forced either to seek its own separatist political autonomy or to envision other ways of constituting a relational-integrative politics without at the same time resorting to another kind of totalizing umbrella. . . . Nationalist totality . . . is an example of a "bad totality" and feminist historiography secedes from that structure *not to set up a different and oppositional form of totality, but to establish a different relationship to totality.*[13]

In outlining my definitions of nationalism, I am mindful of the neglect of individual motivations that Terry Eagleton deplores, saying that the metaphysics of nationalism speak of the entry into full self-realization of a unitary subject known as the people. . . . If subjects have needs, then we already know what one at least of these needs must be, namely, the need to know what one's needs are. The metaphysics of nationalism tend to obscure this point, by assuming a subject somehow intuitively present to itself.[14]

The 1980s poetry and fiction of Lebanese women allows us to connect the first stirrings of nationalist sentiment in the individual psyche—the identification of individual need—with its mobilization and organization as a collective movement when the nation imagined by the individual requires its invention by the collectivity.[15]

Lebanese women's writings redefine nationalism and extend it to its humanist dimensions. They reveal the individual's construction of links with a piece of land, the geopolitical dimensions of which are rarely defined, that then becomes instrumental in an individual's self-definition. This focus on individual agency in constructing political selfhood makes it possible to see nationalism as a meaningful and dynamic way of belonging and caring, rather than as a way of dominating what Gellner calls an "anonymous, impersonal society with mutually substitutable atomized individuals."[16] Redefining nationalism from the perspective of the individual subject position would seem to vindicate Fredric Jameson, whose claim that throughout the twentieth century third world writers have produced national allegories has been contested. For him, citizens of this so-called third world cannot write of themselves except as metonyms of their nations. Some have questioned Jameson's totalizing narrative and have suggested that it is dependent on the omission of all literature except that written by indigenous male elites.[17] However, if we accept the premise of humanist nationalism, then it may well be that twentieth-century, and particularly postcolonial, male and female writers of all classes and all nations—not only those of the third world—may be engaged in a nationalist enterprise. Their project begins in the individual imagination and may in some cases ally itself with others and become elaborated into some form of statist nationalism. They are inscribing a sense of belonging in the face of a global economy that is less and less hospitable to the individual and of a world that is increasingly fragmented just when it seems to be more unified; their goal is to accommodate, reintegrate, and empower its alienated citizens.

Since 1982, Lebanese women have produced several humanist–nationalist allegories: some critical, others constructive; some political, others mystical. In *Hajar al-dahak* (The Laughing Stone), Huda Barakat examines the ways in which nationalism drives men to reject their blood kin so as to create new families out of a military matrix. There is the merchant whose wife is convinced that the Virgin Mary will appear to her, for example. Ostensibly to give her some rest, but really to free himself to take over the leadership of a militia, he sends her to his family village. The fact that this militia is sponsored by a neighboring country and not by some local political or religious group allows him to claim "irrefutably that belonging was not to the religion but to the nation [*watan*]."[18] Barakat may ridicule this nationalist, but she does not trivialize the compelling attraction of statist nationalisms.

Khalil, the antihero, describes his brief membership in a nationalist group as empowering. He recalls the joy he had experienced in being part of "a group, even if only on its margins," with comrades dropping by whenever they needed anything and confiding their fears and their dreams to each other:

> In front of you they strip off their family to choose you. . . . When you leave the group you become a real orphan because you have lost your chosen family, to whom you gave birth because you had become a man. Your friend becomes your ultimate father and you forget the first one. You have relegated him to the edges of childhood memories so as to be able to create new loved ones.[19]

Khalil creates his surrogate fathers, who include, in addition to these companions, Dr. Waddah. This doctor had successfully operated on Khalil for an ulcer, and, when Khalil came out of his coma, he turned his savior into both father and mother. In the recovery room, he felt the touch of Dr. Waddah's hand, the warmth of which "gave me more than the umbilical cord that had connected me to my mother. . . . While I slept, he looked at me more than my mother had when I was a child. . . . Like my father, when I recovered he was happy with me." Later, leaning his head against Dr. Waddah's chest, Khalil finds himself nestling between two large breasts and realizes that this man is "more than my mother, and his eyes are more than her milk." [20]

These created parents are more real and loving than Khalil's natural ones. He is particularly repelled by his beautiful mother. Toward the end of the novel, when Khalil has come to terms with his homosexuality, he thinks about his mother, whose beauty makes him hate her "because beautiful mothers cannot be mothers for us. . . . When we grow up and become leaders [zuʿamaʾ] we hate [them] and completely destroy [their] beauty." [21] He compares his mother unfavorably with the women of Carthage, who cut off their hair and melted down their precious metals for the national fleet; his mother, shame of shames, "laughs a lot. Khalil began to hate his mother a little, and laughter a lot, and he came out at the top of his history class." [22] It is almost as if despising his mother and her foolishness garnered him academic rewards.

Through Khalil, Barakat demonstrates how the nationalist group displaces the individual member's family by means of a reconceptualization of birth—men's birth, at both the passive and the active level. To give birth to the new family, the boy must become a man, but how does he do so? In the passage describing the transformation of the boy into a man, Barakat uses a simple, causal conjunction: "*because* [he] had become a man."

Looking elsewhere for elucidation of masculine birth in a nationalist context, we find Klaus Theweleit's analysis of German Freikorps writings of the inter–World Wars era. Theweleit claims that all military formations provide a womb for the gestation and birth of the properly masculinized man, the only person qualified to be a citizen. The military corps renders the mother's body irrelevant and redundant. The mother cannot give real birth to real men, real citizens. This real birth must be out of the all-male fighting, killing corps, whether an official military unit or a civilian militia. [23] The mother must be eliminated. Barakat, however, takes this transferral of the birthing function further than Theweleit does. She proposes that the real birth, with its attendant militarized masculinity and right to citizenship, relegates not only the mother, but also the *father*, to the margins of memory. Khalil does not even long for a better father; he wants to imagine new bonds that are based not on kinship, but on ideology.[24] Masculinization gives birth to new beings, and the masculinity of these new men is proved by the fact that they kill. Barakat presents this lethal masculinity through Khalil's necrophiliac desire: whenever he reads the paper, he becomes excited by photographs of dead militiamen laid out, "their firm, naked bodies affirm[ing] without a shadow of a doubt that they are men and that the acute igniting of their masculinity was what had led them to kill."[25]

How are we to recognize real nationalism? It is to be found in those who exhibit nationalist feeling (*hiss watani*). How can we recognize such feeling? Tongue in cheek, Barakat announces that there are telltale signs, such as the censure of laughter. Only extreme seriousness and a willingness to consort with death are truly indicative of nationalist feeling. Hence Khalil spends most of the novel preoccupied with death—that of the men he has desired, that of their families and his, and his own death:

> Nationalist sentiment suffers when it is far from death. History is constructed by death alone, full of hatred and contempt for laughter. Khalil had known two history professors. He remembered them well. Neither had laughed. Both were infatuated with nationalist sentiment and with death.[26]

Laughter is a sure sign of nationalist inconstancy, if not betrayal. The list of those who laugh is telling: those involved with militias laugh a lot; they tell terrible jokes at parties and burst their sides laughing. Laughter rings loud when the bombing starts because this is the signal that a holiday has begun. Women laugh because they can then meet each other to chat. The shopkeeper and the baker laugh because everyone is panic-buying. The restaurateur also laughs because people care less about their safety and risk dining out. The gas-station owner laughs because suddenly he is powerful and may even become a political leader. The money-changers laugh because remittances start to pour in. Poets laugh because their moral authority is renewed by their elegies for the newly dead. Foreign correspondents laugh because they are sure of a good story. Everyone in real estate laughs because bombs are good for business. Worst of all, "even the mothers of the dead laugh because new delegations will join their sons and thus lessen the loneliness of the mothers." But the ones who laugh most are the armed forces: "blue-blooded laughter turns black from laughing . . . dies from laughing. You, Khalil, who coldly drink your tea, why do you not laugh?"[27] Khalil, it seems, is the only one in this carnival of laughter, of antinationalism, who maintains his dignity and composure, his nationalist sentiment.

Khalil can easily control his laughter, but he has no stomach for that aspect of nationalist sentiment which is obsessed with death. When he sees the fountain of blood at the Ministry of Tourism exhibition, he faints.[28] This is a fountain that he will later revisit in his dreams. Yusuf, the object of his passion, has been shot to death and appropriately buried, but here he is again being led to the fountain by the wife of the "President of the Organization." She attaches two wings to his back that are held in place by white silk bands threaded through his bullet wounds. After embracing him, she seats Yusuf on the fountain and blood starts to flow from the top of his head, but without discoloring his wings. Dream then blurs into reality as Khalil vomits blood because his ulcer has become irritated. Mortified that he cannot be a better nationalist, he thinks of the people of Tyre, who had immolated themselves for their nation, and weeps "for love of his nation and for sadness at its miserable fate." Khalil loves his nation and understands its prohibition on laughter, yet after meeting Yusuf he always laughs—and with "nationalist feeling" when Yusuf once returns alive from some mission.[29] Knowing that nationalism demands seriousness and the affirmation of death, Khalil nevertheless laughs when his beloved is not killed, explicitly calling what he does and what he feels "nationalist." Although both laughter and the affirmation of life are antinationalist, Khalil's love defiantly redefines them. Has his love for Yusuf turned the negative mandate of nationalist feeling into something positive? Or is his desire a threat to his nationalism?

Yusuf, like Khalil's earlier infatuation, Naji, is killed. Khalil even fantasizes, as Yusuf lies dying in the ambulance, that it is he who has pumped Yusuf's body full of lead. Khalil mourns deeply and painfully for a long time, cutting himself off from everyone until his bleeding ulcer forces him to go to the hospital. After recovering from surgery,

Khalil suddenly sees the world differently. Instead of pondering death, he begins to feel that he deserves to live and to live well, happily. He gives in to his old friend Nayif, who has been trying to convince him for weeks to start working for his militia's newspaper. Khalil goes to a party thrown by the militia and discovers that the editor is interested in him sexually. Although Khalil does not reciprocate the editor's interest, he becomes involved with him anyway, knowing that such an affair will change his life. It does. Now he can convince himself that morality and nationalist sentiment are meaningless in Beirut, that what really matters is to love oneself even if that love means hating others. By the end of the novel, Khalil has taken this philosophy so far as to have raped the woman who lives upstairs from him. He has succumbed to the temptations of the drugs and arms trade and to the lure of the group—the real family—that makes him one of the boys. He laughs with the others now at black humor.[30]

On the last page, the narrator interrupts, saying wistfully:

> How you have changed since I described you in the opening pages! You have begun to know more than I do. Alchemy. The laughing stone. Khalil has gone and become a male who laughs. And I remain, a woman who writes.[31]

Khalil is now the laughing stone, the polar opposite of his own conception of how a nationalist should feel and act. As a stone he feels nothing, but he laughs nonetheless. Khalil joins a nationalist unit, but in defiance of what he had believed to be the necessary conditions for nationalist sentiment.

When I read this novel, I was shocked by its ending. Relentlessly optimistic to the end, I had hoped to read of a man who could stay in Lebanon during the war and not become involved in the fighting, not give in to the immorality and violence. I immediately wrote to Barakat and asked her why. Why, having started to do so, could she not construct a model for humanist nationalism that would not be undone by its own project? Less than two weeks later, I received her reply. She was happy that her novel had made such a strong impression on me, but I had to understand that this war was different from any other war, including the Spanish civil war, which had had two clear sides. In other wars in which the enemy is clear, *hiss watani* can develop as a kind of defense of identity and belonging. But what I wanted to say was that, in the Lebanese civil war, all the fighters were corrupt and violence and hatred had reached the point of absolute evil, so that all claims of defending a cause—whatever it might be—became a lie and a crime.

In such a situation, Barakat's letter continued, individuals have the

choice between being the executioner, which Khalil rejected at the beginning, or the despised victim. In the latter case, the outcome is *madness*, drugs or escape. I wanted to write an accusation, a complaint. I wanted to understand how an entire people turns into criminal fighters. What human resources do we draw on when legal protection is withdrawn and the body consumes itself from within? I wanted to convey the deepest impact of the civil war on human society and how it changes and rots when the only enemy is ourselves.[32]

Barakat's next novel, *Ahl al-hawa* (People of Passion), which was written in 1993, a year after the war ended, explores one of the outcomes of victimization: madness. The narrator is a man who had been kidnapped and tortured. His sister, Asma, commits him to a psychiatric hospital run by nuns, whom he upsets with his singing and his crazy perspective on the world outside. At times of danger, the patients flock to him, however, "believing that I was their father. They would crawl under me as though I were a great hen."[33] This description is reminiscent of Khalil's reaction to Dr. Waddah; in other words, the main character here is both mother and father to the patients.

The narrator talks about "them," about their thinking that he must have been driven mad by his torture and his failure to end the war. However, he thinks that his real problem is his obsession with images of the woman he had captured during a bombardment and whom he imagines he has killed. He rehearses again and again the sensuousness of her body and tries to convince himself that he was indifferent to her, did not really care that she had tried to leave him. But perhaps the real reason for his madness is that he has lost the ability to function morally in his society. The reference to laughter may provide a key. He and his friends become uncontrollably amused—antinationalist?—whenever they hear the word "society." The doctor tries to calm them down by suggesting other words: *ahl* (people of the family), *nas* (people), or *al-kharij* (the outside). But the "preferred words are *umma* [state], *qawm* [nation or tribe], or *shaʿb* [populace]." The patients do not like these alternatives and assure the doctor that there is really no need to find another word because they like the word "society" very much. Finally, "we agreed to a neutral phrase like the ones used by the doctor and we began to say 'the people outside.'" This "society" that gave rise to so much mirth and hilarity was tearing itself apart with anger and violence. It was a society that expected men to prove themselves by killing. The narrator could not relate to such a society and its gendered expectations, so he became fascinated with androgyny, "jealous of animals and plants reproducing themselves because they have male and female organs. This sex is freed from torment." Since he has been unable to satisfy his society's demands in connection with masculinity, the narrator finds that he has become one of those "who do not fight in these wars. We have no sex to bring to our women. . . . Because we are no longer any good to fight or fuck they are taking care of us and not even asking our families for money."[34] He cannot—perhaps will not—do all the lethal things that a real man is supposed to do, and so he has become useless to his nation, sterile and thus unable to survive. He is fit only for an insane asylum.

———

What place do women occupy in such a system? Few are the stories of women joining nationalist movements, despite the fact that recent research has revealed the presence of women in several militias—in some cases, in combat roles.[35] Joining a military unit or a militia, however, is not the only way to be a nationalist. Lebanese women's writings during the civil war indicate that their conceptions of nationalism were no less strong than those of the men, but that they expressed themselves differently. In tandem with their global politicization and invention of women-specific strategies of resistance and opposition, women, particularly the school of writers whom I have called the Beirut Decentrists,[36] propounded a nationalism that was rooted in an individual, nurturing relationship with Lebanon. It was through a dynamic, reciprocal relationship that they belonged to the Lebanese nation, sometimes defined as the extended village or even family, because they had adopted a quasi-maternal responsibility for the people and, above all, for the land denoted by the name Lebanon.

However, women's nationalism also excluded. Like the militiamen, they discriminated between those who were qualified to assume Lebanese citizenship and those who were not. These qualifications did not pertain to membership in political, religious, feudal, or what Etel Adnan calls "tribal" groups.[37] For the women writers, citizenship in the Lebanese nation was earned through individual evidence of loyalty to the land, an entity that was at once concrete and amorphous because it never delimited or even defined. As long as people, usually men, left the country and allowed it to self-destruct, the war would continue. The Lebanese had to stay, loyal to the land, if they were to stay Lebanese. The Beirut Decentrists have called for a collective sense of responsibility that does not point the finger of blame and then smugly shrug, for, as Ghada Samman said in *Kawabis Bayrut* (Beirut Nightmares), "There are no innocents in an unjust society."[38] This sense of responsibility was not backward- but forward-looking, as it demanded that each person participate in the effort to end the violence. How could this loyalty to the land be recognized? It manifested itself in the impossible decision to stay in Lebanon, and to write of doing so as transformative; those who left forfeited their citizenship. Through fiction-writing, women came to understand their decision to stay. Their discourse then became part of the new social and civic contract between the Lebanese and their nation, as defined by these texts.

From the beginning of the war, Emily Nasrallah was creating maternal prototypes of the ideal Lebanese citizen. Nasrallah's citizen was not necessarily or essentially a woman, but one who was capable of what Sara Ruddick has called "preservative maternal thinking."[39] Even the devastation and despair wrought by the Israeli invasion did not undermine the contract. Lebanese women's writings after 1982 have reaffirmed the need to stay and to redefine nationalism as a positive force. Some imagine writing itself as that space in which the nation can be constructed. When Barakat contrasts Khalil, the man who laughs, with herself, the woman who writes, for example, she seems to be privileging discourse as the site for constructing the nation. ("Khalil has gone and become a male who laughs. And I remain, a woman who writes.") Nasrallah makes the connection between writing and the nation unequivocal: "The word has become a refuge and a lifeboat—the poem or story a substitute nation."[40]

Nasrallah wrote prolifically in the wake of the Israeli invasion, publishing two collections of short stories, in 1984 and in 1985. The later collection, entitled *Al-tahuna al-daʿiʾa* (The Lost Mill), deals with the difficulty of communicating nationalist sentiment, or what Barakat's Khalil calls *hiss watani*. In one story, "All of Them Are His Mother," she offers empathetic grieving as a form of nationalist sentiment, an ineffable feeling packaged paradoxically, yet inevitably, in words. Her narrator, the only audience member in an auditorium, assumes that the masked, screaming players on stage are acting for her alone. Yet they "seem oblivious" to her presence. When she tries to leave, she finds that she cannot: the theater has no exits; she must stay, compelled to observe, passively and uncomprehendingly. Then one of the players raises his mask. How long has she been there? "Since the curtain went up." Briefly, the boundary between stage and audience, between fiction and fact, is sketched in. So, she is in a real theater. "What did you see?" the player asks. "What I see now." "What did you understand?" She is relieved at the question: maybe the anonymous masked players were just screaming and there was nothing more to understand. However, her relief is short-lived: since she had understood nothing, why had she stayed? There were no exits. He pulls down his mask, plunging her back into confusion and frustration. Her illusion of communicating and understanding—that the screams were screams—shatters.

Next, a woman separates herself from the mass of actors. How, the narrator wonders, does she know that this is a woman? "From the voice. Yes. It was a wounding voice, erupting out of the depths of creation and fluttering off into space, spreading fear and pain. 'She's weeping for her son.' A voice from nowhere reaches me."[41] The woman's voice is distinctive. Even though it utters no words, it imparts meaning by creating spontaneous empathy.

Then the father (inexplicably recognized as such) joins the mother, and they scream together. At this point, when the parents' voices melt into a single scream, the narrator feels the foggy barriers that surround her understanding dissipate. She begins to weep, to share the feelings of those people with whom she could not otherwise communicate. She has tapped into the core of the others' intensity. Although Nasrallah is not explicit in her description of this shared emotion, it is suggestive (especially in the context of contemporary women's writings on the civil war) of grief for the nation. This grief is not the proscriptive seriousness of nationalist sentiment demanded by Barakat's Khalil and his comrades in *Hajar al-dahak*. To grieve during this war is to *feel with*, to belong, and only then somehow to communicate nationalist sentiment. However, at the very moment of identification with that grief, the same disembodied voice tells Nasrallah's narrator that, unlike the rest of the actors, she is not "his mother." The narrator insists:

> "But I am his mother." The voice replies: "Your tears are outside the theater. Remember, you're the audience." "But I'm the participating audience." I was delighted with my courage. The voice was silent, or maybe it had left me to watch the scenes. Then I saw the mother's shape separate for the second, third, and fourth time. Then that recurrent mother began to form a wide circle, and the others became a dot to that circle. All of them are his mother.[42]

The symbiosis of dot and circle, of mother and (m)others, is assured through the maintenance of the scream. The story ends when one of the mothers approaches the narrator with arms outstretched like "ropes of unearthly light," beckoning her up onto the stage. The narrator is about to react when the mother turns into a huge tree, and the voice explains that she has "taken root in the soil."[43] The materiality of the soil is vivid. It is as a mother that she unites with the soil. When the voice becomes silent, the narrator realizes that the theater has become a forest. All of the mothers are now trees whose roots reach down to the "living principle." This ending, the transformation of a mother into a tree, echoes other works about women's growing strength during the Lebanese civil war. All who wish to consider themselves Lebanese must stay in the country and become an organic part of its regenerative soil. But who can plant such roots? People who feel jointly and intensely for something that is at once their child and, paradoxically, their parent, the source of their communal identity.

Nazik Yarid has been more tentative than Nasrallah in prescribing nationalist action. In 1986, she published a novel, *Al-sada al-makhnuq* (The Stifled Echo), which examines the consequences of emigration. In contrast to earlier works that portrayed men who leave and women who stay, Yarid's protagonist in this novel, Najib, is a man who stays, while his wife, Amal, emigrates to Paris, "for the sake of the children." As in most fiction about Lebanese war emigrants, the one left behind does not censure the one who left. With time, however, and particularly after a sojourn in France, where the Lebanese live easily and distantly from the war, Najib becomes embittered. No longer feeling guilty about the tentative affair he has begun with Nuha, he justifies having cut himself off from the wife who left him. All but one of the characters in this novel have been corrupted by the apparent necessity of leaving Lebanon; the exception—and the only character to elicit sympathy—is Najla. She has done the right thing, having stuck by her husband when he decided to go to Paris. Yet she can never banish her country from her mind. When friends rebuke her for not taking advantage of the joys of Paris, she responds:

> My nerves may be tired. But I feel as though people here are looking at me with some contempt because I enjoy safety and contentment while my country burns and my compatriots are dying. I feel ashamed. . . . I envy those who are in Beirut. How can you enjoy living here, Amal, when you could be at home?[44]

Not only does Najla remain firmly loyal to Lebanon, but she fosters in her children the same kind of loving loyalty. Unlike Benedict Anderson's "long-distance nationalists," who buy their peace of mind and their citizenship with money, Najla remains connected to her nation through love and loyalty. By teaching love of nation to others, in this case to her children, Najla seems to be involuntarily becoming a long-distance, yet humanistic, nationalist.

An anthem to the Lebanese nation, Nur Salman's 220-page poem, *Ila rajul lam yaʾti* (To a Man Who Did Not Come), immediately signals its tone and message with its title.[45] This is a love poem filled with blame and pain. Salman's dedication indicates her audience: "To my mother, Zahiyya, and to my sisters, Najla and Widad and Saqala." On behalf of the women in her family, she is writing to the men who did not come to Lebanon, without being explicit about who or when. Yet in the context of women's literature on the Lebanese civil war, it is likely that she is referring to the expatriates, many of them men, who watched the war from a safe distance. The accusation directed at absent Lebanese recalls criticisms by Aijaz Ahmad and Benedict Anderson of emigrants who claim exile status. Both insist on the importance of clarifying the terms of what Anderson calls "long-distance politics without accountability" among "emigrés who have no serious intention of going back to a home which, as time passes, more and more serves as a phantom bedrock for an embattled metropolitan ethnic identity."[46] In an era of mass migration when 100 million people are wandering the globe, it does make a difference if this wandering is forced or chosen. The economic migrant will have a different sense of attachment to the country to which s/he may return than the exile who knows that his/her chances of returning are slight. The statist nationalist in London, New York, or Paris who sends regular remittances to relatives fighting the enemy back in the home country does not necessarily intend to return to the land for which he is paying others to die and to kill. His publicized contributions serve rather to assure him of a securer space wherever he is now. His choosing to settle in a land that is far from the nation that continues to shape his identity pushes against international frontiers so that they are made to serve as national boundaries.

Throughout *Ila rajul lam yaʾti*, the poet summons and then immediately repels Ya Baidi, "My Distant One." The use of *baʿidi*, from the root *bʿd*, recalls the elegaic formula *la tabʿad*, meaning "do not be distant," but also "do not perish."[47] While the poet's lover may not in this case be dead, he would have done better to die than to have remained distant from the war. The poet grieves for him, but never so much as to compel her to escape to him. Again and again, she calls to him, even begging him to "be a man for my nation!" Yet, almost in the same breath, she warns him not to come.[48] She fears for him "the narrowness of the pavements":

> I fear for you our wailing, our lamentations
> Our screaming in small valleys.
> I fear for you our confusion. Our wretched delusion.[49]

As the poem progresses, her warnings, always sad and never angry, escalate. He, like the others who left, is not safe in this land of martyrs, prophets, and poets who have lived through the terrors and have learned to break down the barriers between death and life, and between life in death and life in life. There is in them a life that death cannot touch, these martyrs who are

> the creators of the single echo
> They are the ones who remain . . .
> All that remains of the body of the nation are its martyrs.[50]

These martyrs, human vestiges of the nation, are the prophets whose lives were cut short so that "we might live," yet these are martyrs who do not die. They are the bedrock of the new nation. How can others become like them? By staying, especially if they are sons of the new nation: "A thousand woes to a nation whose *sons* are not where they should be!" It is the absence of the men that is so painful, and the poet mourns "my house without a boy, my nation without its sons. They are the babies of orphan births."[51] They must stay, but they also must write because the poets

> plant the nation in the earth
> Master creators. They fertilize our history with fire
> . . . The earth holds its head high because of them and is called
>   nation.[52]

The poets will return "my nation to its land," for these people who have stayed, these martyrs/prophets/poets,

> are united by the fact that
> Their dream is one with their waking. Death with life.
> Thirst with its quenching. Love with love.[53]

These martyr/prophet/poet survivors are dangerous for those who have not shared their experiences. The poet is threatening her lover, while claiming to be protecting him, as a mother, against the harm that will surely befall him. She is warning him, somewhat ominously, against herself: "I fear for you the voracity of my fading / I fear for you the voracity of my loneliness." Finally, Cassandra-like, she intones the prohibition:

> Beware of coming!
> Do not come to our grief [nation], Ya Baidi . . .
> I longed for you. Do not come tonight![54]

The only relief lies in this final, pro-tem prohibition—"tonight!" Is she offering hope for an ultimate forgiveness? There is a possibility that he can find a niche in this dangerous place if, once he has returned, he can learn to love the land.

The poet's feelings for Ya Baidi are fraught with paradox. She loves him and wants him to return, yet she needs him to remain distant. His absence creates a longing, and this longing defines her: "I loved your distance because I was the path to it." His absence makes her productive.[55] She fears his return, lest

> My body end in a blocked pulse. . . . We are doomed to
>   miscarry we
> Who are caught between our own wombs, the wombs of time
>   and place
> A dead fatherhood and a crippled motherhood.[56]

She is trying to survive in a death–world that has destroyed the possibility of parenting. The dream of Ya Baidi enables her to hold on to her own individual power of reproduction, to be in fact both mother and father. She dreads his return lest his presence render her body sterile. She has managed to retain her fertility because of her dream of him, the dream that made her a mother:

> How this distance brings me close to your absence
> I cling to you and sleep in a dream
> The dream has made me into the mother of a child . . .
> This is our child, Ya Baidi

... O the poverty of a love that does not beget life
Before me is my child ... my boy ... my son
He is the most important. Indeed, he is the axis planted in the
    deepest depths of existence
He is the one that joins the "I" of the masculine with the "I" of
    the feminine.[57]

This child that is the product of her dream of her love is at once feminine and masculine; above all, s/he is *her* child. As in *Hajar al-dahak*, the new social formation cannot survive unless it excludes the father, for the father may become destructive: "I am afraid of the days that will change me against my will into a frightened, bereaved Sheherezade. / And turn you into a tyrannical, careless, and possessive Sharayar." [58]

The absent presence of Ya Baidi remains the muse of her poem and of her love, which is creating the nation. Her love for him feeds, and is in turn fed by, her love for her nation, with each of these loves made possible by the greatest love of all, that of the nation for its people:

Your love brought me love of nation
My love for you would be worth nothing if my nation did not
    love me
My love for you would be worth nothing without a nation for
    me to love
... Our love is not enough for my nation
It loved me more, more, more
I dissolve into the earth.[59]

What is the nation? For Salman as for Nasrallah, the nation is the grief of the people who have stayed and survived, and whose staying has allowed them to put down roots in the soil, the land of the nation. This grief of the survivors is an empathy that links and creates a community out of those who have experienced it. Women have the greatest share of grief, of the nation: "I am a woman whose only right is to grieve." The earlier association of grief with nation allows us to read the woman whose only right is to grieve as the humanist nationalist writ large. This nationalist, this grieving woman, is powerfully creative because grief, when it occurs in the body of a woman, is "fertile with the mercy of childbirth."[60] Indeed, the grief/ nation—like the anguished dream of the beloved—makes a woman's body fertile. Salman anchors her hope in this notion of intellectual fertility: as long as the land/woman is fertile, the nation will survive because blood will not beget blood.

Who is this fertile woman? She is both mother and writer: the mother who nurtures and the woman writer who sows fear. The poet's father, "the man who was jealous of the thin pen," had warned her mother when she was small that her pen would "turn into nails in the coffin of her happiness." How is the reader to understand this mother/ writer who represents both an ethic of care and a symbol of terror? Through the transformation of the meaning of the nation, which becomes the product, as well as the source, of the citizen's love. The mother/writer is the source of the new nation; she is the one who has "no choice but to love because [she] constantly give(s) birth."[61] Her work, and by extension herself, is at once productive and the product of the nation. Each needs the other to exist and to survive.

A recurrent image in this poem is that of the womb. This quintessentially female organ becomes in Salman's hands the symbol of renewal. As such, it is no longer attached to a particular body or gender, but rather becomes generalized. How does it work? Twice Salman repeats that, like Saraswati, the Hindu goddess with the many hands, the woman writer has many wombs:

> A woman's body has more than one womb
> My hands are a womb
> My heart is a womb
> My eyes are a womb
> My lips are a womb.[62]

In a move that I read as strategically essentialist, Salman extols woman's body as powerful in its pride, seclusion, pain, creativity, and freedom. She then goes on to declare:

> Woman's body has no sin. It has no sin.
> It was squeezed into the mold of sin so that it should become
>   the body of sin

It is free, proud, the knots of civilizations have shackled it with
brass rings.
In civilizations it is their conscience, their feeling, and the
qibla of their birth.[63]

This woman's body recreates "a nation that has left her," defying the
blades of male logic to release "the glorious labor pains which weave
the body to the soul for constant childbirth."[64] Again, the poet insists that women writers give birth not just to people, but to nations,
which constantly regenerate themselves through the mother/poet's
many wombs. She, the poet, prophet, and thus martyr, must write
the abandoned nation back into existence by giving birth to sons who
will replace the sons who are where they should not be.

Is Nur Salman excluding men from citizenship in a nation for
whose production everyone should be responsible? What is she saying
with her emphasis on the woman's body and on the sons of the nation
whom women must produce? Does the womblessness of men's bodies
disqualify them from producing new sons and creating the nation?
Does she deny that men are capable of producing alternative communities? Surely not, but the answers to these questions are to be found
in her focus on the woman's reproducing body. For just as Salman
seems to be connecting the production of a nation to the reproductive
capacity of women's bodies, she undermines the gender specificity of
the connection. She displaces the womb from its natural place so as
to allow it to proliferate throughout the body and function in systems
that are not gender-specific. This dislocation and multiplication of a
woman's reproductive organs extends an invitation to men to join in
this process of self- and nation-regeneration.

The writings of Huda Barakat, Emily Nasrallah, Nazik Yarid, and
Nur Salman engage the nation in such a way as to produce what
Radhakrishnan has called "a critical and deconstructive knowledge
about nationalism. . . . It is on the basis of such knowledge that postcolonial subjects can produce a genuinely subaltern history about
themselves and not merely replicate . . . the liberal-elitist narrative
of the West."[65] The nation that these women have written into exis-

tence is not an ideological construct, despite its discursive nature; it is, rather, an individual sense of belonging, and then of responsibility, which radiates out from multiple centers. It is first of all personal, and it *may* become collective. This nation is the context within which each individual constructs a center for her/himself, the new citizen. Citizenship is neither a birthright nor a reward for military service; it is an affective identity that becomes a building block in the construction of the nation, the center of a humanist nationalist. The process is circular and keeps renewing itself in terms of itself. For those who are humanist nationalists, there is no single polity but multiple, fragmentary projects that are continually disassembling, but also reassembling and regenerating, because they foster, above all, survival.

Notes

I would like to thank Elisabet Mudimbe-Boyi, Stephen Dodd, Hitomi Endo, Satti Khanna, Victor Mair, Jing Wang, and particularly Sherif Hetata and Bruce Lawrence for their comments on an earlier draft of this essay.

1 Eve Sedgwick, "Nationalisms and Sexualities in the Age of Wilde," in *Nationalisms and Sexualities*, ed. Andrew Parker, Mary Russo, Doris Sommer, and Patricia Yaeger (New York, 1992), 239.

2 Francis Fukuyama argues convincingly that the Industrial Revolution (and to a certain extent, the French Revolution) influenced the growth of a specific form of nationalism. He sees the increasing sophistication of arms technology as creating "powerful incentives for national unity; [nations] must be able to mobilize resources on a national level. . . . They must break down various forms of regional, religious, and kinship ties which potentially obstruct national unity." He posits national consciousness as the product of new socioeconomic relations:

> Rulers and ruled had to speak the same language because both were intertwined in a national economy; peasants moving from the countryside had to be made literate in that language. . . . Older social divisions of class, kinship, tribe, and sect withered under the pressure of requirements for continual labor mobility, leaving people with only a common language and common linguistic culture as their major form of social relatedness. Nationalism was therefore very much the product of industrialization and the democratic, egalitarian ideologies that accompanied it.

See *The End of History and the Last Man* (New York, 1992), 73, 269.

3 Quoted by Mona Takieddine-Amyouni, "Style as Politics in the Poems and Novels

of Rashid al-Daif" (paper delivered at the annual meeting of the Middle East Studies Association, November 1993).

4 Quoted in comments made during the Lebanese literature panel discussion at the Middle East Studies Association annual meeting, November 1993. See also Mai Ghossoub, "Etre Femme Libanaise après la Guerre" (paper delivered at the Institut du Monde Arabe, Paris, 1993), who states: "Je crois que c'est cela être Libanaise: une appartenance multiple, cette possibilité de vivre notre individualité, tout en sachant l'agencer avec les exigences de nos grandes familles, et cela quelque soit notre lieu de résidence."

5 Benedict Anderson writes of "official nationalism" as an "anticipatory strategy adopted by dominant groups which are threatened with marginalization or exclusion from an emerging nationally imagined community," and of its policy levers as "compulsory state-controlled primary education, state-organized propaganda, official rewriting of history, militarism . . . and endless affirmations of the identity of dynasty and nation." According to Anderson, "Such official nationalisms were conservative, not to say reactionary, *policies*, adapted from the model of the largely spontaneous popular nationalisms that preceded them"; see his *Imagined Communities: Reflections on the Origin and Spread of Nationalism*, 2d ed. (New York and London, 1991 [1983]), 101, 110.

6 Evelyne Accad has pointed out, however, that even at this earliest, "positive" stage, nationalism was not all good. She shows how women were used as indicators of cultural superiority during colonial rule, when segregating, secluding, or veiling one's women proved that one was honorable. Moreover, the exploitation of women in nationalist ideology continued beyond this first, "good" stage, with women then asked to fight for their country, which they had previously been made to represent and for which they were expected to reproduce; see her "Transnational Aspects of War and Violence: Peace as an Alternative" (paper delivered at the War and Gender conference, Bellagio, August 1993).

7 John A. Hall, "Nationalisms: Classified and Explained," *Daedalus* 122 (1993): 22.

8 Ernest Gellner, *Nations and Nationalism*, 2d ed. (Oxford, 1988 [1983]), 4.

9 Anthony Giddens, *The Nation–State and Violence* (Berkeley, 1987), 220.

10 Ross Poole, "Structures of Identity: Gender and Nationalism," in *War/Masculinity*, ed. Paul Patton and Ross Poole (Sidney, 1985), 77–78.

11 Vaclav Havel, "How Europe Could Fail," *New York Review of Books*, 18 November 1993, 3.

12 See Jean Bethke Elshtain, *Women and War* (New York, 1987). Cf. Fukuyama, *End of History*, 266; his explanation, which attributes a need for "recognition of group dignity" to these leaders, seems vague, evasive, and unwarrantedly benign.

13 R. Radhakrishnan, "Nationalism, Gender and Narrative," in Parker et al., eds., *Nationalisms and Sexualities*, 78, 81; his emphases.

14 Terry Eagleton, "Nationalism: Irony and Commitment," in *Nationalism, Colonialism and Literature*, ed. Terry Eagleton, Fredric Jameson, and Edward Said (Minneapolis, 1990), 28–29.

15 For a discussion of the differences between imagining and inventing nations, see Hall, "Nationalisms," 4.

16 Gellner, *Nations and Nationalism*, 57. Such a nationalism, he says, is "held together above all by a shared culture, in place of a previous complex structure of local groups, sustained by folk cultures reproduced locally and idiosyncratically by the micro-groups themselves."

17 See Aijaz Ahmad, *In Theory: Classes, Nations, Literatures* (London and New York, 1992), 243; he rejects the automatic reduction of third world literature to "the unitary insignia of nationalism," followed by its designation as "the determinate and epochal ideology for cultural production in non-Western societies." See also Miriam Cooke, "Literary Criticism: The State of the Art in Arabic," *Al-Arabiyya* 20 (1987): 277–96.

18 Huda Barakat, *Hajar al-dahak* (Beirut, 1990), 103.

19 Ibid., 122–23.

20 Ibid., 204–5.

21 Ibid., 243.

22 Ibid., 133.

23 See Klaus Theweleit, *Male Fantasies* (Minneapolis, 1989).

24 The Freikorps writers "*desire* a father—a man less weak than their own fathers were in reality. . . . While real fathers are silenced by the soldier males, their texts express unmistakable desires for better ones" (ibid., 369).

25 Barakat, *Hajar al-dahak*, 170.

26 Ibid., 131.

27 Ibid., 145–50.

28 Ibid., 130.

29 Ibid., 132, 135.

30 Ibid., 129.

31 Ibid., 250.

32 Huda Barakat, letter of 28 October 1992, Paris; my emphasis.

33 Huda Barakat, *Ahl al-hawa* (Beirut, 1993), 19.

34 Ibid., 95, 88, 154, 165.

35 See Lamia Rustum Shehadeh, "Sexual Conflict in Lebanon" (paper delivered at the Conflict Resolution in the Middle East conference, Larnaka, Cyprus, July 1993).

36 Miriam Cooke, *War's Other Voices: Women Writers on the Lebanese Civil War* (Cambridge and New York, 1988).

37 Etel Adnan, *Sitt Marie Rose* (Paris, 1978).

38 Ghada Samman, *Kawabis Bayrut* (Beirut, 1989), 315.

39 Sara Ruddick, *Maternal Thinking* (Boston, 1989).

40 Emily Nasrallah, *A House of Her Own* (Charlottetown, 1992), 12.

41 Emily Nasrallah, *Al-tahuna al-daʿiʾa* (Beirut, 1985), 197–98.

42 Ibid., 199–200.

43 Ibid., 204.

44 Nazik Yarid, *Al-sada al-Makhnuq* (Beirut, 1986), 160–61.

45   Nur Salman, *Ila rajul lam yaᵓti* (Beirut, 1986).

46   Benedict Anderson, "Long-Distance Nationalism: World Capitalism and the Rise of Identity Politics" (paper delivered at the University of Michigan, September 1992), 20.

47   Suzanne Pinckney Stetkevych, *The Mute Immortals Speak: Pre-Islamic Poetry and the Poetics of Ritual* (Ithaca, 1992), 169.

48   Salman, *Ila rajul lam yaᵓti*, 17, 7, 133, 139.

49   Ibid., 124, 190.

50   Ibid., 100, 104.

51   Ibid., 89, 129, 161, 166.

52   Ibid., 103.

53   Ibid., 167.

54   Ibid., 169, 172, 189–90.

55   Ibid., 205. This is in marked contrast to Rashid al-Daif, who in an interview claimed that when he wrote "From your absence comes the evening," he was expressing "the anguish of losing my beloved. This anguish is similar to that caused by war." In another poem, he expressed the fear of losing one's nation as follows:

> WATANI (my nation)
> You've lost your W
> You've lost your A
> You've lost your T
> You've lost your N.

All that is left is the "I," which in Arabic denotes the first-person singular, possessive pronoun. All that is left is the possessing, not the belonging, individual; see Takieddine-Amyouni, "Style as Politics," 2.

56   Salman, *Ila rajul lam yaᵓti*, 221.

57   Ibid., 94.

58   Ibid., 79.

59   Ibid., 15.

60   Ibid., 134, 120, 205.

61   Ibid., 41, 38, 43.

62   Ibid., 153, 159.

63   Ibid., 156–57.

64   Ibid., 11, 159.

65   Radhakrishnan, "Nationalism, Gender and Narrative," 86.

Thomas Lahusen

The Ethnicization of Nations:
Russia, the Soviet Union, and the People

Hiding in nostalgia for a recent past, speaking from spaces and cultures that no longer exist, Tadeusz Konwicki's or Andrzej Wajda's exegesis on Poland's borders, and other themes of "exile" formulated in Valentin Mudimbe and Bogumil Jewsiewicki's general argument all have specific counterparts in Russia's literary "imagined communities" of the last three decades. During the 1960s and 1970s, the nostalgic portrait of the Russian village on the brink of extinction in Siberia or in the Russian North was received as progressive, sometimes even as dissident, relative to the official Soviet cultural "monolith." Post-Stalinist Soviet "village prose" is often said to have been inaugurated by Alexander Solzhenitsyn's story "Matryona's House," published in 1963, a year after "One Day in the Life of Ivan Denisovich." These are the first lines of the story:

> In the summer of 1953 I was returning from the hot, dusty wastelands, making my way aimlessly back to Russia. No one had sent

The *South Atlantic Quarterly* 94:4, Fall 1995.
Copyright © 1995 by Duke University Press.
CCC 0038-2876/95/$1.50.

for me and no one was waiting for me, because my return had been delayed by a little matter of ten years. I simply wanted to go somewhere where it was not too hot and where leaves rustled in the forest. I just wanted to creep away and vanish in the very heartland of Russia—if there were such a place.[1]

These lines heralded what would become a program of "village prose" for the next twenty years. The novels and stories of Valentin Rasputin and other "rural writers" of the 1960s and 1970s were invariably based on such themes as the earth's cyclic ecosystem, a home delimited by shared cultural and ethical traditions, humanity defined by spiritual memory and experience, and modernity's disruption of all of these. In Rasputin's story "Vasily and Vasilisa" (1966), for example, the days of the heroes, "divided not into hours but into samovars," are opposed to the chaotic time of the city, as introduced by strangers to the village. Ethnography becomes a literary genre in itself with Vasily Belov's *Harmony* (1979–81), a volume of essays on folk aesthetics which provides, according to an American scholar, "a remarkable description of daily life in northern Russian villages near Vologda."[2]

The fiftieth volume of the *Great Soviet Encyclopaedia* (1957) includes some remarkable data on the "class composition of the Soviet population" in 1955:

— workers and employees: 58.3 percent;
— collectivized (collective farm) peasants and "cooperativized" craftsmen: 41.2 percent;
— individual peasants and "non-cooperativized" craftsmen: 0.5 percent (no kulaks).[3]

Where have all the peasants gone? Here is what Soviet sociologist Pyotr Simush wrote in his 1980 book, *Who Is the Soviet Peasant?*: "The Soviet sociologists agree on the fact that [the collective farm population] does not include the workers from the state farms (the sovkhozes), who are part of the 'working class and of the employees'"; and "the [Soviet] countryside is losing its purely peasant character."[4] Some other passages of Simush's book, which is obviously a propaganda piece for the third world (it has also been published in French,

Spanish, and Hindi), are worth quoting as well. Simush has this to say about the "gendered division of labor," for example: "In the collective farm [known as] 'The Lenin Path' (Rostov region), combine harvesters are driven by couples: the husband is generally in control of the powerful machine, whereas his wife assists him"; and, about the collective–farm family: "The kolkhoz family is not merely a family unit, but also a family working group"; and, "the family of the collective farmer is composed of husband, wife, and their children." "The peasants," says Simush, "are residing in the countryside; this is where they are living, where they are working, where they rest, where they introduce themselves to culture and get instruction."[5]

Between the idealistic depiction of a long-since vanished "harmony" and the tautology-generating paralysis of official ideology, the identity of the village became confused. Soviet "village prose" eventually faded from public view in the mid-1980s with the publication of Rasputin's *Fire* (1985), Victor Astafiev's *Sad Detective* (1985), and Belov's "anti-urban" novel, *The Best Is Yet to Come* (1986), and with a subsequent turn to essayistic modes in which nostalgia yielded to nationalism and xenophobia. The small, closed world of the dying village was transformed into closure and the rejection of both the outer world and its own alien residents, primarily Jews. During the 1980s, the celebration of the old Russian communality was increasingly identified with the "Right," whereas the proponents of democracy and a market economy identified themselves with the "Left." Today, new and apparently paradoxical alliances are formed within a National Salvation Front, where imperial dreams of "Holy Russia" confront conservative Communist nostalgia, with their respective adherents disagreeing on everything except a common Great Time of the past and its corruption by alien (Western, Jewish, etc.) forces. These are the people who defended the "White House" (the Russian Parliament in Moscow) in September 1993, united under the strange amalgamation of the sign of the cross and the red flag's hammer and sickle. A related question is how the rise of ethnic and nationalist movements within the Russian Federation and the successor states of the former Soviet Union are to be explained. Did the organization of socialism "freeze" national consciousness in the former USSR, or did it enhance it?

Katherine Verdery claims, in "Nationalism and National Sentiment in Post-Socialist Romania," that socialism did not suppress national conflict, but enhanced national consciousness, and that the supposed "exit" to democratic politics and market economies aggravated it further:

> In [the former USSR and Yugoslavia] the main national groups each had their own republics: the principle of national difference was constitutionally enshrined. . . . Precisely because the Soviet regime had destroyed all other bases for political organization while constitutionally enshrining the national basis, national sentiment emerged to overwhelm federal politics.[6]

What remains to be explained, however, is the very concept of "national sentiment," which is taken here, it seems, as a given. Before we can answer the question of whether the regime encouraged, enhanced, or destroyed the feeling of belonging to such-and-such a group, we have to come to terms with what it means and *meant* to be Russian, Ukrainian, Tadjik, Chechen, or Soviet—which brings us back to the notions of *people* and *nation* in the Russian and Soviet historical contexts.

The Russian term *narod* is one of those "untranslatable" words that reveals a troubled content: in the Russian nineteenth-century context, and beyond, it could mean "the nation" as well as "the people," depending on who was using it and for what purpose. *Narodnost* was the second term in the official triad of "Autocracy, National Character (or Spirit), Orthodoxy" under Nicholas I, but the term did not denote an *ethnie*, or even a nation–state, because it could apply to non-Russian territories or even "foreign" kingdoms, a fact which was expressed in the official title of the ruler: "Tsar and Autocrat of Great, Little, and White Russia," followed by a long list including the Kingdom of Poland, the Dukedom of Lithuania, and the Khanate of Kazan, ending with "etcetera, etcetera, etcetera." Another meaning of narodnost, "popular spirit," could relate to an ethnic representation of Russianness, but proponents of Slavophilism and its glorification of the peasant tradition of communality (the *mir*), or populism, and later versions of both imagined the "narod" from their own alienated position. This time it was alienation from the state and from the people. As to the people, it kept virtually silent, at least within the realm of "print capitalism."[7] But silence is only another form of discourse, so when the Russian *narodniki* (populists) went "to the people," the people responded by handing them over to the Tsarist police. Could not this phenomenon be interpreted as one of the first manifestations of "popular" counter-discourse? The subsequent history comprises other "invented traditions" and the counter-discourses of its alleged subjects, even in the worst times of Soviet "totalitarianism" when the "nation" (the people?) allegedly became "atomized" and thus "disintegrated."

I believe that the shifting notions of "people" and "nation" in the Russian, Soviet, and post-Soviet contexts can be clarified by examining the various representations of Russia's traditional "silent majority," the peasant, or *muzhik*, and its mutations in Russian culture since the nineteenth century.

The peasants' "monarchist" response to the Russian populists of the 1870s was based on the vivid memory of their rebellions and upheavals in the seventeenth and eighteenth centuries, the dream of the righteous tsar and the tsar-deliverer. But it was also the result of a long tradition of utopian sectarianism, originating in the Great Schism and the first expression of mass "dissidence" in Russian history: that of the Old Believers and their later diverse embodiments. As Richard Stites observes in *Revolutionary Dreams*:

> Peasants of the 1870s failed to respond to the socialist utopias of the populist intelligentsia; those of the 1900s similarly failed to rise up to (or even understand) concrete Marxist visions of the future outlined to them by radical workers. Russian peasants were not socialists in any European or intellectual sense; nor were they conservative in the sense attributed to them by the ruling elite—they were peasants. Their dreams and aspirations, however cloudy the formulation, of land and freedom and order (their own order) resurfaced in 1905 with great force. In 1917 the peasants swept away an ancient social system and then stood puzzled and angry at the looming menace of a new order not of their making. The traditions of peasant utopia were based upon deep popular aspirations. How they behaved during the Russian

Revolution and what they wanted to create and sustain, before their civilization was destroyed by Stalin's collectivization, is a clear demonstration that the image of *pravda, volya* (= truth and freedom), and self-rule shone far brighter in the vastness of the Russian skies than the red star of Bolshevism, or any other political idea.[8]

The years of the revolution and the early 1920s were deeply marked by the peasant question. In what Katerina Clark has called the "duel of utopias," the anti-urbanists largely dominated the cultural scene. Scythianism, a movement of the Russian *moderne*, interpreted the revolution as the triumph of the organic forces of "deep Russia" over Western civilization.[9] "Beat the communists. We're for the revolution," say the peasant followers of Arkhipov, one of the Bolshevik "leather jackets" in Boris Pilnyak's novel *The Naked Year* (1922). "Peasant poetry" (i.e., by Esenin, Klyuev, and Klychkov, among others) coincided with an unprecedented interest in rural studies after 1917, with the "Agrarian Marxists" competing against the "Organization–Production" school of the Timiryazev Academy. Leading the latter was the famous agronomist Andrei Chayanov, a victim of the Great Terror in the late 1930s (his works were republished in the 1980s) and the author of a stunning "rural utopia," *The Journey of My Brother Aleksei into the Land of Peasant Utopia.*[10] Like Julian West in Edward Bellamy's *Looking Backward: 2000–1887,*[11] the hero of the *Journey* falls asleep and wakes up in . . . 1984, in a country where the village has conquered the city, where handicraft cooperatives have replaced industry. As in Evgeny Zamyatin's *We,* theosophical elements and contemporary allusions converge, but both novels address the same reality: the unresolvable war between the city and the country.[12] Chayanov's "rural utopia" was published in 1920, enjoying a print run of 20,000 copies, while Zamyatin's anti-utopia had to await the end of the century for publication in Russia. Chayanov predicted that state power would pass into peasant hands by 1932 and that the country would totally triumph over the city by 1937. It all came out differently, as we know.

Maxim Gorky wrote, in a well-known essay of 1922, about the "zoological naturalness of anarchism, particularly applicable to the mass of the Russian peasantry"; about the "darkness of the Russian sectarian's soul"; and about the "unconquerable conservatism of the village," concluding that "the boundless, flat country has a poisonous quality which devastates a man, and empties him of desire. When a peasant goes beyond the limits of his hamlet and looks at the emptiness around him, after a time he feels that this emptiness has filled his heart." For the author of *The Mother*, neither Ivan Bolotnikov's program of primitive communism during the Times of Troubles nor the massive peasant revolts of Stepan Razin (seventeenth century) or of Emelian Pugachev (eighteenth century) left any traces in peasant memory. "This people has no historical memory. It dies not knowing its past—and seems even not to want to know it." [13]

A good example of anti-ruralness in the times of the NEP is to be found in Leonid Leonov's novel *The Badgers* (1924). It is the story of a Russian Vendée, with the final victory of the urban forces of revolution illustrated by the fortunes of two brothers who, taken as children from their native village to the capital, lose touch with each other and meet again at the end of the story. One of them, after experiencing the hardship of proletarian existence, runs away, becomes a factory worker, raises his consciousness, and joins the Communists. The other, after fighting as a soldier in World War I, returns to his village and ends up as a peasant leader defying the Bolsheviks. He eventually surrenders to his brother, who returns as the commander of a punitive mission. The progressive Bolshevik subdues the backward and reactionary rural bandit; organization triumphs over organicity; the "thousand never-sleeping eyes of the city" overcome the badgers, those "wild beasts of the night"; and, "once again, virgin soil is upturned." One of the leitmotifs of the story is the resurgence of a century-old feud between two villages over a meadow. When the Soviet administration attempts to settle the conflict by giving more to the poor and less to the rich, the peasants respond with destruction and chaos, calculating "with a shrewd, narrowed eye the chances of that day when [their] wooden ploughs would creak over the vile places where the town had stood." [14]

In a letter to Leonov, Gorky expressed his opinion of the novel: On the one hand, the author did not idealize the peasantry; everything was true in his story. On the other hand, Gorky regretted that the style of the novel was not "simple enough." He stated that it "would be difficult to translate this text into foreign languages" and that "even the best translators could not cope with the *skaz* [i.e., the oral–popular] type of style."[15] Twenty-nine years later, the author of *The Badgers* was criticized again: His description of the visceral forces lacked a precise class character; he was not capable of clearly describing the historical reality of these years, that is, the presence of two camps in the village—the camp of the working poor or peasantry, and the camp of the kulaks, among others. But the main target of the critics' attack was again the style of the novel: the overuse of dialect and colloquial expressions; the neologisms; the "chaotic narration, lacking interior links," that recalled the Serapion Brothers, the LEF and its "factography," and other decadent trends.[16] Why was style such an issue? There was a precise reason for all this, namely, Stalin's contribution to linguistics in June 1950.[17]

The effect of the publication of "Marxism and Problems of Linguistics" had the character of a natural phenomenon: it was highly unpredictable. But the average Soviet scholar reacted to it with a consciousness of history: " 'Marxism and Problems of Linguistics' has become a powerful instrument for the artists of the word in their struggle for the national character [*narodnost*] of the language of Soviet literature. . . . The writers begin to be more conscious of the inaccuracies of their style," observed the critic A. S. Bushmin in an article of 1952. He also gave a painstaking account of the changes that Alexander Fadeev's well-known civil war novel, *The Rout*, underwent between 1927 and 1951. "The most profound changes"—wrote Bushmin—"were undertaken by the author in 1949," thus implying that Fadeev had literally anticipated Stalin's article. "During the entire 1940s"—continued Bushmin—"Fadeev made eighteen changes in the text, but solely for the novel's publication in 1951 he made sixteen changes, a fact which no doubt is related to those high standards set for writers by the seminal work of Comrade Stalin."[18] In June 1953, an article by Isai Lezhnev entitled "For the Purity of Language: The New Edition of *Virgin Soil Upturned*" revealed the heroic efforts of Mikhail Sholokhov to correct the style of the first volume of his *Virgin Soil Upturned*, published for the first time in 1932. Lezhnev estimated that Sholokhov had made about 1,200 corrections in a recent edition of the novel, "cleansing" the text of, above all, "local" or "dialectal" words and replacing these with "standard–literary" ones. For instance, the popular word for "women" (*baby*) was replaced by such standard terms as *zhenshchiny*, *kazachki*, and *krestianki* (women, Cossack women, and peasant women, respectively), "more suitable to depict the feeling of distinction and culture of the collective farmers."[19] (A few years later, Sholokhov would purge these changes and restore *baby*.) In Stalin's "contribution," dialect and jargon, the two linguistic manifestations of ethnicity and social class, were defined as substandard, as not belonging to the language "that the entire nation has in common." As a result, literary works with dialect or jargon that had been published, rewritten, and republished during the 1920s and 1930s—works that had already been "cleansed" and "standardized" over the years—were again purged of their ethnic and social roots.

The history of Soviet culture since the 1930s can therefore be characterized in terms of a double process: the "nationalization" of social class and the "de-ethnicization" of narodnost, coinciding with its folklorization. The concept of "proletarian internationalism" increasingly competed with the "All-Union" concept of the socialist motherland (*rodina*); the "rural alternative" was replaced by a new kind of syncretic folklore: Soviet folklore. This evolution was particularly visible in the stylistic and thematic transformations of works rewritten by their authors, but not exclusively so; it also affected other cultural expressions, such as film, fine arts, and "popular culture." The process had already started in the 1920s. Fyodor Gladkov's *Cement*, one of the first "production novels" of Soviet literature, was criticized by Gorky after its 1924 publication in the journal *Red Virgin Soil* for its overuse of dialect, its "ornamental" style, and its neologisms.[20] In the next edition of his novel, Gladkov replaced the regionalisms of Novorossiysk (a southern Russian port near Krasnodar) with standard–literary language, and the rest of it followed suit. The novel was rewritten over forty times by Gladkov. In the following samples from two editions, the first still reflects the typical features of the 1920s, while the second represents the rewritten, "socialist realist" (and therefore "ultimate") version. The passage is taken from Gleb Chumalov's speech at the funeral of a young worker who died during an attack by counter-revolutionary peasant bandits. Together, these excerpts could be entitled "From the Workers' Republic to Socialism":

> Again Gleb raised his arms on high.
>
> "Comrades, listen! A sacrifice to labour... With our united strength... No tears or sobs! The victory of our hands... the factory. We have won... We shall make ourselves heard with fire and machinery... The great work of building up the Workers' Republic... Ourselves, with our brains and bodies... The blood and suffering of the struggle—these are the weapons for winning the whole world. Let it go now, Brothers!"
>
> Cupping his hands round his mouth, Gleb shouted: "Comrades, this man is a sacrifice to our work, to our struggle . . . Should we weep and wail, when victory, joyful victory, is in our grasp? Soon the plant will roar aloud with fire and machinery. Together we're beginning the tremendous task of building socialism. Yes, blood has been spilled, the suffering has been great. Immense difficulties have stood—and will stand—in our path. But that path, that hard path, leads to happiness, to the final victory over the world with our own hands. With the name of Lenin in our hearts, with our faith in boundless happiness, we will redouble our strength and go on to conquer the future."[21]

One interesting "by-product" of Soviet socialist "nationalization" and "de-ethnicization" was what I am tempted to call the *nationalization of gender*. As we know, gender affects ethnic, national, and "race" relations, and *vice versa*.[22] The "woman question," heavily debated during the 1920s, was "resolved" in 1944 with the introduction of a new civil code abolishing "free love" and forbidding marriage between Soviet citizens and foreigners; abortion had already been outlawed in 1936.[23] Women were reintegrated in the Five-Year Plan and were eligible for their own production bonus: after the birth of her tenth child, a Soviet woman was entitled to the honorific "mother heroine" (*mat geroinia*).

What about "popular culture"? All visitors to Russia have seen, bought, or been given those beautiful little artifacts of Russian folk art called "Palekh lacquer boxes," horrible copies of which are also sold to tourists. Svetlana Boym describes the origin of these boxes in her recent book, *Common Places: Mythologies of Everyday Life in Russia*. In fact, the "traditional Russian" lacquer box is a recent invention. Inspired by the nineteenth-century "pseudo-Russian style" of "folk art" and designated for consumption outside the village (including at international exhibitions abroad), the lacquer boxes were first made after the revolution by craftsmen and icon painters who organized themselves into the "*Artel* of Proletarian Art" and began to use Russian icon-painting techniques to depict "revolutionary fairy tales" on traditional Japanese lacquer boxes. Maxim Gorky called them "a little miracle of the revolution" and praised Palekh painters for transforming "craft into true artistic mastery." [24] The Palekh box is just one of many examples of the folklorization of ethnicity. "Folk" art, "folk" music," "folk" dance, and "folk" carnivals were promoted in all the national republics and regions during the 1930s, shaping Soviet "national" (i.e., centralized) culture while also underlining the commitment to ethnic values for decades thereafter. [25]

We already know the rest of the story: Following the "thaw," which occurred shortly after Stalin's death, literature rediscovered social class and ethnicity. Sholokhov "re-ethnicized" his style (i.e., by restoring the words he had purged from *Virgin Soil Upturned*), and Solzhenitsyn returned from exile to "vanish in the very heartland of Russia," adding, "if there were such a place." I frankly think there was, but all depends on how we look at it or, rather, from which point of view. Remember what Richard Stites said in the passage quoted earlier about the Russian peasant and his inexplicable resistance during the 1920s: "Russian peasants were not socialists in any European or intellectual sense; nor were they conservative in the sense attributed to them by the ruling elite—they were peasants." [26] The problem with tautology ("Russian peasants were peasants") is that this rhetorical figure expresses not only "deeper," "inexpressible" meaning, but also what is "true" by definition, like, for instance: $2 \times 2 = 4$. Let us try to bypass the predefined but "inexplicable" peasant and give *him* (or *her*) the opportunity to speak for him/herself.

Two documents written during the Great Terror (1936–39) can help us measure the degree of the Soviet peasant's resistance to the state (or urban) construction of his or her identity. They are part of a collection of diaries of the 1930s, spanning a wide range of locations within the former Soviet Union.[27] The first series of excerpts is from the diary of Ignat Frolov. (All misspellings, as well as odd or missing punctuation, are intentional; they reflect the diarist's writing.)

> 22-nd of January [1937]. The weather in the morning was not too cold 10–8 below with a light Southeast wind. overcast. today at 5¾ in the morning the Cow calved she stuck it out the whole 287 days she had her fling on April 10 today manya went to Kolomna to get hay for the Collective Farm, and today the 22-nd of January Ivan Zakharovich Stepanov passed away at 5 o'clock in the morning at the age of 72 from a chronic digestive problem for a long time his stomach wouldn't take any food, just liquid.
> . . . .
> 13-th of March [1937]. Overcast weather foggy with a strong Southeast wind warm no frost the snow in the fields has just about all melted no more slay riding. Today a lot of people in the village and us sandbagged the Cellars. but in the Collective Farm the Potatoe in the storage cellar was flooded. the water went up to 1½ *arshins* [i.e., 42 inches] from the top from their carelessness they couldn't get the snow dug out and let the water run through in time. Today Mother left for Kolomna to get herself on the right track, she's fasting. because with the flooding the priest couldn't get here to Lukeryino and also because of his weak health Today they took everyone's passports for exchange and also took the meat supply contracts for checking.
> . . . .
> 16-th of April. Overcast weather with a North wind its chilly but there's no rain they're still replowing the land for potatoe and planting Potatoe.
> . . . .
> 25-th of April. Overcast weather with a mild east wind and scattered showers all day long. but late in the afternoon and at night it started raining good and heavy but not warm at night with a strong east wind, they're still planting Potatoe.[28]

The second series of excerpts is from the diary of Andrei Arzhilovsky.

10/29 [1936] . . . We eat soup made from pig heads and count our blessings for it. I was at my brother Mikhail's recently. He's still keeping up appearances, with his valuable dog and his mistress. A modern Mazepa. . . .[29] Just now Galina piped up, "If I can get a neckerchief I'll join the Pioneers."[30] So all it takes is a neckerchief. She's not too bright. Every once in a while she'll spout such nonsense, you wouldn't even believe it. They study geometry and algebra, but they're utterly empty, spiritually. And they're going to feed us in our old age?

. . . .

11/8 [1936] I went into town yesterday. It was a bright, cheerful day. The parades [i.e., celebrating the anniversary of the October Revolution] were a great success. It seemed as though the entire city had come out onto the streets: not so much to march in the parades as just to gawk. Lots of people and noise, everyone all decked out in their best. Enormous achievements. Life has become easy. People sing songs that say this is the only place in the world where a man can breathe free. It's a fact. A foreigner would get a most unlikely impression: you sure live well, God grant everyone such a life. It would be interesting to calculate the amount of vodka and beer drunk to celebrate the anniversary. That seems to be the general tendency: in the morning there's the show; after the parade, the juices start to flow. Take your choice. History will figure it out; what we do goes by the wayside. I'll go out myself today and do my part.

. . . .

12/18 [1936] You may call it nonsense, but still, dreams are a fact of life. I want to write down an interesting dream I had. Someone told me I could see Stalin. A historical figure, it would be interesting to get to see him. And so. . . . A small room, simple and ordinary. Stalin is drunk as a skunk, as they say. There are only men in the room, and just two of us peasants, me and one other guy with a black beard. Without a word, Vissarionovich[31] knocks the guy with the black beard down, covers him with a sheet and rapes him brutally. "I'm next," I think in despair, recalling the way he used to carry on in Tiflis,[32] and I'm thinking, how can I escape, but after his session Stalin seems to come to his senses somewhat, and he starts up a conversation, "Why were you so eager to see me personally?" "Well, why wouldn't I be? Portraits are just portraits, but a living man, and a great one at that, is something else altogether," said I. Overall, things worked out fairly well for me and they even gave me some dinner. . . . I've had two dreams about Stalin: once before my release and now this time. And in fact, before the revolution I dreamed about Nicholas II. At the time I thought: what is this all about? I had never seen him and wasn't really interested in him. But then during the revolution and after his execution, I found myself often recalling this strange, doomed man, the last and weakest of his kind. I suppose there is some reason for my Stalin dream. One way or another, this huge comet is destined to leave an especially bright trail across the universe, but it will do so as a comet, not a planet. In any case, I didn't make it up, I'm just writing down facts, demented though they may seem.[33]

We know nothing about Ignat Frolov except that he was a collective farmer in the village of Verkhnee Khoroshevo, district of Kolomna, region of Moscow. Andrei Arzhilovsky's diary was given to Konstantin Lagunov (editor of a version published recently in a Russian journal) by an employee of the Tiumen regional KGB, who "works a lot and stubbornly to liquidate the 'white spots' of our region's history."[34] Arzhilovsky, a peasant from the Chervishev district of the Tiumen region, was arrested in 1919 for being a member of a politically incorrect committee and was convicted and sentenced to eight years in a labor camp. He was released in 1923, however, thanks to an amnesty related to the creation of the USSR. In 1929, he was arrested for being a kulak (he was living in his own house and had two horses, two cows, some poultry, and about eight acres of cultivated land) and for "anti–collective farm activities." This time he was sentenced to ten years in a labor camp, but in early 1936 Arzhilovsky was granted a medical release so that he could die at home. A year later he was arrested again, for participating in a "counter-revolutionary wrecker's kulak organization," and his diary served as evidence for his conviction. Arzhilovsky was executed on 5 September 1937. A few months later his brother, Mikhail, was also executed, for being the relative of an "enemy of the people."

These two diaries make me think of two prominent figures of the 1930s: Georg Lukács and Mikhail Bakhtin. Lukács dreamed of the great epic of the future, in which the feeling of totality would be restored by classless society. But collective farmer Ignat Frolov's chronicle, devoted almost exclusively to the current weather, could have been written (barring a few details) during, say, the seventeenth century: southeast wind, the calving of a cow, the passing away of a neighbor, a flood, fasting, and "planting Potatoe," the very flow of discourse that never seems to stop and that does not repeat itself despite endless repetitions of the "same" events; all this belongs to the same epic chronotope in which the world is whole and man still feels "at home," not yet alienated by these later times of "transcendental homelessness." Bakhtin evoked this peasant in his "Discourse in the Novel," speaking of the "illiterate peasant, miles away from any urban center, naively immersed in an unmoving and for him unshakable everyday world."[35]

Frolov's epic is of this past: he dates most of his diary entries by the "old" (Julian, i.e., prerevolutionary) calendar. But we find nothing of this sort in our second "peasant diary"—because Arzhilovsky experiences the "necessity of having to choose a language." Bakhtin again:

> As soon as a critical interanimation of languages began to occur in the consciousness of our peasant, as soon as it became clear that these were not only various different languages but even internally variegated languages, that the ideological systems and approaches to the world that were indissolubly connected with these languages contradicted each other and in no way could live in peace and quiet with one another—then the inviolability and pretermined quality of these languages came to an end, and the necessity of actively choosing one's orientation among them began.[36]

What is so fascinating in these diaries is that they testify to the simultaneous coexistence of two types of consciousness or identity: on one hand, a totality made of the epic, the religious, the peasant, the ethnic; and on the other, its rupture, its transformation, generating irony and anger against "spiritual emptiness," in Arzhilovsky's words.

"At Soviet Russia's point of entry into the NEP, the country was still saddled with a version of the agrarian nexus. No court, no gentry anymore, but an agrarian economy and a huge muzhik ocean," observes Moshe Lewin in *The Gorbachev Phenomenon*.[37] Later, when the movement toward proletarian internationalism was replaced by efforts to construct a Soviet nation, and when class struggle gave way to the struggle against the internal and external enemy (the wrecker, the spy), the People began to be represented as One, always implying an alien Other. This representation, however, became increasingly inadequate in the face of the enormous social changes that have affected Soviet society since the 1930s. How could collectivization, industrialization, economic planning coupled with disorganization, the creation of new borders and the displacement of populations, and powerful social processes, such as the urbanization of the village and the ruralization of cities—all this centrifugal diversification—create one nation?

And how could it create one identity? At the very end of *The End of History and the Last Man*, Francis Fukuyama uses the image of a long wagon train as some sort of parable for his homogenized and liberalized "last man." This train is strung out along a road, bound for the city. "Some wagons will be pulling into town sharply and crisply, while others will be bivouacked back in the desert . . . [I skip the mountains, the Indians, etc.]. But the great majority of wagons will be making the slow journey into town, and most will eventually arrive there."[38]

Vasily Shukshin, one of the more interesting "village writers" of the "era of stagnation," tells us another story in "Moving to the Country." It is the story of a man, Nikolay, who, once upon a time, that is, at the beginning of the 1930s, was "swept out of his village and deposited in the city." Every Saturday, he would go to the railway station and start to discuss his plans for "leaving the city forever" with the folks, most of them country folks, who hung around in a place next to the lavatories that was set aside for smoking. And there Nikolay would ask about places—living conditions, prices—and collect addresses:

"That's just why I want to leave—I can't stand it any longer! I suppose you think I'm poor. No, I do fine. Nobody could ask for better! I've got a two-room flat, for just me and the old woman, but I can't stand it any longer! Turns my insides, it does!" And at that moment, as he was shouting into the villager's face, he was really suffering, beating his breast with his fist, almost in tears. But, most surprising of all, he'd quite genuinely forgotten how he himself swore at the drivers and the loaders and was the last man you could approach with a question. Suddenly, he forgot all that, and his heart smoldered with resentment at all the rudeness, swearing, shouting and insults. This was no life, he thought, to hell with it and to hell with his two-room flat. He longed for a little house in a village to live out his days in peace and dignity, like a human being. He'd no desire to turn into an animal here, along with all the rest of them. Oh no, he was a man! And Nikolay loved it all, loved all the talk about human dignity and peace, felt compelled to shout at the top of his voice, his heart filled with exultation and pain. Sometimes the men around him fell silent and he went on alone—in all that smoke and stench— talking and shouting. They strongly sympathized with him and were anxious to help.

And so Nikolay would set off home, having had his say, with a pocketful of addresses. . . .

He wasn't going to move anywhere. Nothing was further from his mind, but by now he couldn't live without those visits to the station. They'd become a real need. If someone were to try to shame him out of them, if his elder son, for instance, were to tell him flatly to stop going to the station and taking down addresses and talking to the villagers . . . but what would be the point? He'd still slip away there when no-one was lookin'. He couldn't do without it, now.[39]

Anthony Smith has recently pointed out that "even if elements of ethnicity are 'constructed' and 'reconstructed' and sometimes plainly 'invented,' the fact that such activities have been operating for centuries, even millennia, and that several ethnie while changing their cultural character have nevertheless persisted as identifiable communities over long periods, suggests that we ignore the presence and influence exerted by such communities on the formation of modern nations at our peril."[40] The present "ethnicization of nations" does not confirm the "end of history," in Fukuyama's terms, but announces the rise of the social, at least in that part of the world. For the time being, it wears ethnic, provincial, or national clothes, but it is the rise of what was once the "muzhik ocean," which resurges with a vengeance.

Notes

1   A. Solzhenitsyn, *Stories and Prose Poems*, trans. Michael Glenny (New York, 1971), 3.
2   Kathleen F. Parthé, *Russian Village Prose: The Radiant Past* (Princeton, 1992), 54.
3   *Bol'shaia Sovetskaia Entsiklopediia* (Moscow, 1957), 50: 106. All translations are my own unless otherwise indicated.
4   I am quoting from a French translation: Petr Simouch, *Le Paysan soviétique, qui est-il?* (Moscow, 1980), 45.
5   Ibid.
6   Katherine Verdery, "Nationalism and National Sentiment in Post-Socialist Romania," *Slavic Review* 52 (1993): 182.
7   See Benedict Anderson, *Imagined Communities: Reflections on the Origin and Spread of Nationalism*, 2d ed. (London and New York, 1991 [1983]).
8   Richard Stites, *Revolutionary Dreams: Utopian Vision and Experimental Life in the Russian Revolution* (New York, 1989), 18–19.
9   Katerina Clark, "Political History and Literary Chronotope: Some Soviet Case Studies," in *Literature and History: Theoretical Problems and Russian Case Studies*, ed. Gary Saul Morson (Stanford, 1986), 235.
10 A. V. Chaianov, *Puteshestvie moego brata Alekseia v stranu krest'ianskoi utopii* (Moscow, 1920).
11 Edward Bellamy, *Looking Backward: 2000–1887*, edited and introduced by Cecelia Tichi (New York, 1987).
12 E. I. Zamiatin, *Sochineniia* (Works) (Moscow, 1988).
13 Maxim Gorky, "On the Russian Peasantry," *Journal of Peasant Studies* 4 (1976): 12–13.
14 Leonid Leonov, *The Badgers*, trans. Hilda Kazanina (Westport, CT, 1973), 230.
15 As quoted in V. A. Kovalev, *Romany Leonida Leonova* (The Novels of Leonid Leonov) (Moscow/Leningrad, 1954), 32–33.
16 Ibid., 54. The "Serapion Brothers" was the name of a literary movement of the early 1920s that included such writers as Lev Lunts, Mikhail Zoshchenko, Venia-

min Kaverin, Vsevolod Ivanov, Mikhail Slonimsky, Konstantin Fedin, and Viktor Shklovsky, among others. Their poetic name was inspired by E. T. H. Hoffmann's hermit, Serapion. They used to meet at the Petrograd House of the Arts, where they had the opportunity to hear Zamyatin's lectures on literary craftsmanship. The LEF (Left Front of the Arts) was an avant-garde movement (and journal) of the 1920s which united Russian Futurists, Constructivists, and Formalists; "factography" was propagated by the LEF and meant the "bare" representation of extraliterary facts for agitational purposes.

17 I. V. Stalin, "Marksizm i voprosy iazykoznaniia," *Pravda*, 20 June 1950.

18 A. S. Bushmin, "Rabota A. Fadeeva nad romanom *Razgrom*: Avtorskaia pravka izdanii 1927–1951 godov" (A. Fadeev's Work on the Novel *The Rout*: The Author's Corrections of the 1927–1951 Editions), in *Voprosy sovetskoi literatury*, ed. A. S. Bushmin and K. D. Muratova (Moscow/Leningrad, 1953), 309–30.

19 I. Lezhnev, "Za chistotu iazyka: Novaia redaktsiia *Podniatoi tseliny*," *Zvezda*, No. 6 (1953): 156–70.

20 See I. P. Ukhanov, *Tvorcheskii put' F. Gladkova: Posobie dlia uchitelei srednei shkoly* (The Creative Path of F. Glakov: A Manual for High School Teachers) (Moscow, 1953), 47.

21 Feodor Vasilievich Gladkov, *Cement*, trans. A. S. Arthur and C. Ashleigh (London, 1929), 149; Fyodor Gladkov, *Cement*, trans. Liv Tadge (Moscow, 1981), 205–6.

22 See Sylvia Walby, "Woman and Nation," in *Ethnicity and Nationalism*, ed. Anthony D. Smith, Vol. 50 of *International Studies in Sociology and Social Anthropology* (Leiden, 1992), 81–100.

23 For a recent presentation of these issues, see Mary Buckley, *Women and Ideology in the Soviet Union* (Ann Arbor, 1989), 128–37.

24 Svetlana Boym, *Common Places: Mythologies of Everyday Life in Russia* (Cambridge, MA, 1994), 106–7.

25 See Richard Stites, *Russian Popular Culture: Entertainment and Society Since 1900* (New York, 1992), 94–97; Rosalinde Sartori, "Stalinism and Carnival: Organisation and Aesthetics of Political Holidays," in *The Culture of the Stalin Period*, ed. Hans Günther (New York, 1990), 41–77.

26 Stites, *Revolutionary Dreams*, 19.

27 *Intimacy and Terror: Soviet Diaries of the 1930s*, ed. Véronique Garros, Natalia Korenevskaya, and Thomas Lahusen; Eng. ed. directed by Thomas Lahusen, trans. Carol Flath (New York, 1995).

28 Ibid., 14, 19, 22, 23.

29 Ukrainian Cossack leader of the seventeenth century who betrayed Peter the Great when he joined Charles XII at the Battle of Poltava. The author is no doubt referring to Pushkin's poem "Poltava," in a double allusion to the preparations for the 1937 Pushkin commemorative celebrations and to the image of Mazepa as a national traitor.

30 The Young Pioneers, a youth movement and organization founded in 1922 as a junior branch of the Komsomol and guided by the Communist Party, was open to

children aged ten to fifteen. Although membership was not officially compulsory, almost all children of those ages were members. The organization, which adopted some features of the Scouts, sponsored camps, festivals, sporting events, and so forth. The red neckerchief was worn by Young Pioneers as part of their uniform.

31 Joseph Stalin's patronymic.

32 A reference to Stalin's involvement in plotting a spectacular holdup in Tiflis (Tbilisi), on 25 June 1907, in order to "expropriate" funds for the Party.

33 Ibid., 113, 120, 132–33.

34 Konstantin Lagunov, "Gody i sud'by: Andrei Arzhilovskii. Dnevnik 36–37-go godov" (Years and Fates: Andrei Arzhilovsky. Diary of the Years 1936–37), *Ural* (Ekaterinburg), No. 3 (1992): 138–60.

35 M. M. Bakhtin, "Discourse in the Novel," in *The Dialogic Imagination*, ed. Michael Holquist, trans. Caryl Emerson and Michael Holquist (Austin, 1981), 295.

36 Ibid., 296.

37 Moshe Lewin, *The Gorbachev Phenomenon: A Historical Interpretation*, expanded ed. (Berkeley, 1991), 20.

38 Francis Fukuyama, *The End of History and the Last Man* (New York, 1992), 338–39.

39 Vasily Shukshin, *Roubles in Words, Kopeks in Figures and Other Stories*, trans. Natasha Ward and David Iliffe (London, 1985), 81–82.

40 Anthony D. Smith, "Nationalisms and the Historians," in Smith, ed., *Ethnicity and Nationalism*, 75.

Anders Linde-Laursen

Small Differences—Large Issues: The Making and Remaking of a National Border

The nation has increasingly been a subject of discussion during the last ten years. It has steadily gained more public attention with the developments toward integration in Western Europe and the disintegration of the former Eastern bloc, and it has garnered more attention lately from academia as well.

We have seen many books and articles published on what the nation was or is, including a group of now classic texts by such scholars as Benedict Anderson, Ernest Gellner, Eric Hobsbawm, and Anthony D. Smith.[1] What is surprising, then, given that so much work has been done on the nation's real character, is that so few convincing conclusions have been reached. All that has been agreed on so far is that the nation cannot be separated from the invention of a people and language— or of their representation through a state— and thus from politics and power, as well as the fact that these connections have consequences for the outcome of different nation-building processes. But we have to realize that we still know very little about how and

The *South Atlantic Quarterly* 94:4, Fall 1995.
Copyright © 1995 by Duke University Press.
CCC 0038-2876/95/$1.50.

why these connections among nation, state, people, and language were made in different times and under different circumstances. And we know even less about how these imagined communities[2] have been perceived and integrated into people's everyday lives.

Most researchers studying the nation have either concentrated on single cases or produced general discussions about when this imaginary was invented (in the late eighteenth century), by whom (the middle class or the intelligentsia), and how it has been represented—and pretended—through different media. A list was developed (and is still being extended) of everything which a *proper* nation *must* have: a language; a common past and destiny; heroes (to whom it can build monuments) and villains; exhibitions and museums; a folk culture; sacred lands; a national bird and flower; a flag and an anthem—a *national do-it-yourself kit*, as it has been called by Orvar Löfgren.[3] Nations thus present themselves in ways that are in fact highly transnational, which may seem like a paradox but is not. If a nation is to be recognized as such, among all the others, it has to make itself visible as such to all the others. It is therefore not surprising that micro-nationalistic movements all over Europe are able to express themselves through representations that other nations can recognize, if not always appreciate or even tolerate. Once such movements are recognized, then other nations have to deal with the political, geographical, historical, and economic effects of a newborn nation and its subsequent struggles for recognition as an independent state.[4]

Most analysts of nation-building processes are able to deconstruct these modern creations, pinpointing their historical emergence and the forces (or persons) at work endowing them with feelings and meanings. They can show how nations become culturally marked, often very heavily. Such deconstructionists, however, fail to realize that nations formed in the era after the French Revolution not only had a tremendous political and economic effect, but also really meant something to people—in short, that nations could be experienced as part of everyday life.

Clearly, experiences of real difference are meaningful, and such experiences can be wrapped in national colors. The study of the nationalization of everyday life, as I will show, is closely related to cultural studies and to the study of national identities. The making of the border between Denmark and Sweden (as well as the narratives on differences between Danes and Swedes) exemplifies both the experience of nationalized life and its value as a focus of research.

≡≡≡≡≡

Wars were often fought over the border between the territories of the Swedish king (which included Finland) and the Danish–Norwegian king up to the early eighteenth century (see Figure 1 and Table 1). The border in Øresund (the Sound) was established in 1660 with the Peace of Copenhagen, when the Danish–Norwegian king had to withdraw from the provinces of what is today the southernmost area of Sweden. This peace treaty was the final step in the Swedish king's protracted efforts to fight his way out of a position as a minor power in the Baltic and to break the Danish–Norwegian king's hold over the lands surrounding his territory. The Swedish king had been especially eager to cut a swath all the way through to the west coast, which would open up new opportunities for international trade. Thus was Göteborg (Gothenburg) founded on the Swedish king's only piece of the west coast in the early years of the seventeenth century.

The border in Øresund would not be altered by any of the hostilities that flared up after 1660. This was not necessarily because the Swedish and Danish–Norwegian kings agreed to maintain it, but because the major powers in Northern Europe—the Netherlands, France, England, and Russia—found it more convenient not to have the coast on both sides of the entry to the Baltic, a major area of world trade since the early Middle Ages, under the control of the same king. Øresund thus became a strategic key to world trade. Paradoxically, it continued to be of major importance for the economy of the Danish king and state even after 1660, since ships passing Helsingør (Elsinore) were charged a tribute to the Crown (until 1857). In 1835, for example, this Øresund tribute accounted for about two million of the fourteen million–*rigsdaler* state budget.

In the period after 1660, the Swedish king succeeded in gaining the loyalty of the newly captured provinces through a policy of replacing their gentry and priests with persons loyal to him. This policy secured

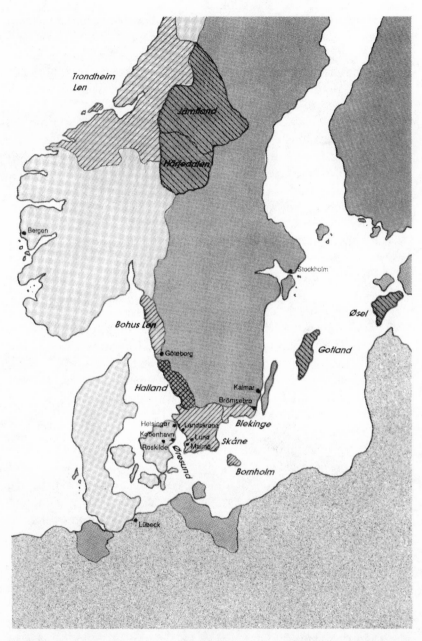

Figure 1. A Dane's-eye view of the shifting Swedish/Danish borders from 1563 to 1720 (see Table 1).

Table 1. Wars between the Danish–Norwegian King and the
Swedish (–Finnish) King, as Seen from a Dane's Point of View

Year(s)	War	Borders
1563–70	Nordic Seven Years	No change of borders.
1611–13	Kalmar	No change of borders.
1643–45	Torstensson's	At the Peace of Brömsebro, the Danish king ceded Gotland, Øsel, Jämtland, and Härjedalen for good, and Halland for 30 years (indicated by hatching [\\\] on map in Figure 1).
1657–58	First Carl Gustav	At the Peace of Roskilde, the Danish king ceded Skåne, Halland (this time for good), Blekinge, Bornholm, Bohus Len, and Trondheim Len (indicated by hatching [///] on map).
1658–60	Second Carl Gustav	At the Peace of Copenhagen, the Swedish king returned Trondheim Len and Bornholm to the Danish king.
1675–79	War of Skåne/Scanian	No change of borders.
1709–20	Great Nordic	No change of borders.

Note: Shaded areas on the map indicate the territories of the Danish–Norwegian (light) and Swedish (dark) kings just before the Peace of Roskilde in 1658. Only one war involving the Danish king between 1563 and 1720 did not include hostilities with the Swedish king: the War of the Emperor (1625–29). This war, which did not lead to any border changes, dramatically shifted the balance of power in the Nordic region: the Danish king, Christian IV, was defeated at the Battle of Lutter am Barenberg (in what is Germany today) on 18 August 1626 and lost his military potential. The Swedish king, Gustav II Adolf, fared much better in the Thirty Years War (which was basically a war between Protestants and Catholics), securing his kingdom's position as a major power in the Baltic until his successor, Carl XII, was defeated in the 1709 Battle of Poltava (in what is Ukraine today).

the loyalty of the whole population, as the sociopolitical structure of the Lutheran feudal kingdom made the king the highest secular *and* religious power. It was as a consequence of this policy that the University of Lund was founded in 1666 with the specific mission of educating priests to be employed in the conquered provinces of Skåne, Halland, and Blekinge.

The history of the province of Bornholm illustrates how arbitrary the Swedish/Danish–Norwegian border came to be and yet what striking political logic it had.[5] The provinces of Skåne, Halland, Blekinge, and Bornholm had been a legal and administrative unit since the Middle Ages, and Bornholm had been transferred along with the other provinces to the Swedish king after the First Carl Gustav War, at the Peace of Roskilde in 1658. And the people of Bornholm (gentry, citizens, priests, and peasants) had sworn their allegiance to the Swedish king, Carl X Gustav, at a ceremony in Malmö. (Actually, they swore the oath to an empty chair since Carl Gustav had no time to participate.)

When hostilities were renewed by the Swedish king in August 1658 (the Second Carl Gustav War) and his army surrounded København (Copenhagen), the Danish–Norwegian king, Fredrik III, needed help. He therefore urged people in the provinces so recently ceded to the Swedish king to revolt, and he asked Lübeck, a merchant–republic at the southwest corner of the Baltic, to send merchandise (food, ammunition, etc.) needed in København, offering Bornholm as security for a loan until he could pay for the supplies. The merchants in Lübeck sent the merchandise, but turned down the offer of Bornholm as security; instead, they were granted reduced customs rates on their trade with Bergen (in western Norway).

But a message from København to a leading figure in Bornholm, Peder Olsen, mayor of the tiny town of Hasle, had already been sent. Although he had sworn allegiance to Carl Gustav earlier that year in Malmö, in December 1658 Peder Olsen organized an uprising and gained control of the island. The medieval fortress of Hammershus in northern Bornholm, which was the administrative seat of the Swedish king, surrendered after a one-day siege and only a few lives were lost. When the rebel leaders arrived in København and announced that they were delivering the island into the hands of the Danish–

Norwegian king, he used them as game pieces in a coup d'état. Fredrik III wanted to institute an absolute monarchy in Denmark and Norway, and, with the support of the high bourgeoisie in København, he was able to do so in 1660. As a first step toward that goal, in December 1658 the king asked the people of Bornholm (as represented by the rebels) to declare him their absolute monarch, in return for which the leaders of the uprising were personally rewarded: Peder Olsen became the local judge; another leader gained the release of his brother, who was awaiting trial on a murder charge; and others obtained official positions in the royal administration. So when the war ended and a new peace treaty had to be negotiated in 1660, the Danish king needed Bornholm as a precedent on which to base his claim to absolute power—the only part of the kingdom where he already had it.

The Swedish Crown, on the other hand, had a certain interest in giving the island to the Danish. Since the leading figures there would be pro-Danish, if the Swedish Crown regained control of Bornholm, it would be forced to take action against them. Even more to the point, the Danish king would be forced to give the Swedes something in return, which was what he did. Fredrik III had to exchange about ten percent of all the land in Skåne for the island—land that he had to buy from the gentry. So he gave some landlords big estates in Jylland (Jutland) in return for their holdings in Skåne, which he ceded to the Swedish Crown. With this transaction, the Swedes were able to get rid of some Skåne landlords who had central positions as royal officials in København and were presumably loyal to the Danish king—and their manors could be given to persons loyal to the Swedish Crown, thereby strengthening its power base in Skåne. So both parties got what they wanted. And Bornholm, remaining a Danish island far away in the Baltic, functioned as a cornerstone in the process by which Skåne became Swedish. But only in political terms. Over the next two centuries, Bornholm and Blekinge, southwest Skåne and east–central Sjælland (Zealand), and northeast Skåne and Småland remained very close to each other in cultural terms, such as in regard to their house-building and food-making practices. The political borders did *not* coincide with the cultural ones.

It is obvious from this history that in the seventeenth century there was no connection between political loyalty and commitment to a people, a language, or a nation. And it is equally obvious that history could have taken a completely different course. If the greater powers in Northern Europe had not jointly insisted on maintaining the border in Øresund, wars could have continued to erupt far beyond 1720.

Now, what all this means is that the Swedish/Danish border in political terms was established well before the period when the nation —understood as a unit of and commitment to a people, a language, and a state—came into being. Thus when the people on either side of Øresund realized during the nineteenth century that they were *Swedes* and *Danes*, the border came to be seen as natural. So no national minorities do or ever did exist on either side of this border, but rather individuals—like myself—who have chosen for various reasons to move to the other side. Like other borders in the Scandinavian region, the Swedish/Danish border is perceived as so natural that Scandinavians sometimes look with irony or confusion on other parts of the world, such as the Balkans, where the topography of the border is still considered worth fighting, killing, and dying for. There is an evolutionary aspect to this perspective of irony and confusion, whereby "we," in the northwest, regard "others," in the south and east, as less developed because they have not yet organized themselves around natural borders. However, it is obvious that the Scandinavian merging of nation, state, language, and people is very unusual in the world—and that it is only relative. The course of history has meant that there is, for example, a German-speaking minority in southern Jylland and a Swedish-speaking population in western Finland. Moreover, at present a large number of immigrants and refugees can be found in both countries.

Because the border in Øresund has this undisputed and natural character, however, it is a very good place to study the *nature* of the *nation*. This border can be used to exemplify the ideal (relative to the general understanding of nations) relationship between two nation–states—and to analyze the border as both narrative and reality.

≣

The images and narratives of Sweden in Denmark, and vice versa, have been of major importance to the construction of national identities in both countries since the latter part of the nineteenth century. Each country has been more eager to compare itself with its neighbor across Øresund than with either nearby major powers, such as Germany and Russia, or the latter-day minor nation–states of Norway and Finland (with which Sweden and Denmark actually share some history). These images and narratives were, as they still are, disseminated in the usual ways, not least through the schools. They are taught, obviously, as *history*—but also, and importantly, as *geography*. In illustrating present-day borders, geography explains limitations on movement as well and thereby explains cultural space.[6] With the establishment of the nation–state, history became territorialized—and each territory became historicized.

These narratives about Sweden and Denmark were also disseminated through native contact with immigrants who had crossed the border. Until about the period of the First World War, people mainly went from Sweden to Denmark; since the late 1930s, however, emigration has been mostly in the other direction. These narratives have been changing over the last century and can therefore be used strategically as a scientific tool to investigate both nations' self-images.[7] Narratives about nationality are, after all, dependent on a mutual recognition of distinctiveness by the nations comparing themselves. This makes it impossible to investigate a single case when studying nationhood (as many researchers actually try to do). National identity has to be studied as a specific relation between a "self" and a "significant other." Being a Dane, for example, is perceived quite differently through American spectacles than through a Swedish lens. As a consequence of the relational character of the nation, both countries in a given case will share images of each other, as do Swedes and Danes.[8] Studying these narratives of the *significant Other* enables one to get a clear, concise picture of the imaginary of the *Self*—and of how, why, and by whom Self and Other are reshaped in different historical contexts.

Danishness was created in the second half of the nineteenth century on the basis of three central elements: *peasant, family enterprise,* and *democracy*. An imaginary that grew out of peasants' aspirations to economic and, later, political power, it was acquired through the folk high schools and was connected to the efforts of the followers of

Niels Frederik Severin Grundtvig, the ideological father of the Danish (and) peasant movement. This sense of Danishness drew strength from looking down on a poor, underdeveloped, and undemocratic Sweden, an image that was reinforced by the rather large group of Swedish immigrants in Denmark prior to the First World War, most of whom were too poor to emigrate to the United States. So Danes looked down on Swedes, who regarded Danes as superior. This is the background to the book and Oscar-winning film *Pelle Erobreren* (*Pelle the Conqueror*). The author, Martin Andersen Nexø, spent part of his childhood on Bornholm among poor Swedish immigrants.

The relationship of Swedishness and Danishness did not change until the 1930s, when the Swedes, through a rapid modernization of their society, took the lead among the Nordic countries. But this did not cause any changes in Danishness; looking across Øresund, the Danes saw only huge industries and the "totalitarian" government of the Social Democrats in Sweden. The Social Democrats stayed in power from 1932 until 1992—sixty years—with only one break in the 1970s. And during this period, the Social Democrats were closely allied with Swedish intellectuals. Architects of the modernizing movement created what would later be seen as the foremost symbol of the aspiration to modernity in Scandinavia: a large exhibition on housing and style in Stockholm in 1930. And still the Danes, looking across Øresund, were able to emphasize their own Danishness: peasant, family enterprise, and democracy. In Sweden, however, the narrative of Denmark changed: Danishness was no longer superior, but rather Continental, petit-bourgeois, and cozy.

These modern narratives have remained stable so far. Nevertheless, with developments in contemporary society—rather positive prospects for the economy and a long period of political stability in Denmark, but an economic crisis and an unstable minority government in Sweden—things are changing again. It is still too soon to predict how these developments will affect the Swedish and Danish narratives in the long run.

These narratives, however inaccurately they may paint the picture of historical or present-day society, have been very useful as metaphors. In politics, for example, the image of Sweden as *modern* has been successfully used in Denmark to paint a picture of Swedish social fragmentation, mainly by right-wing Danish politicians in attacks on the Danish Social Democrats, who in this way had to bear the burden of their Swedish counterparts' success. Given the important role played by these narratives, not least when they are manipulated or exploited by different political groups, it comes as no surprise that they also affect the way people perceive *difference*. The existence of this kind of narrative implies that it serves a function as a way of explaining and coping with any kind of experienced difference. One could even say that we are equipped with a *nationalizing eye*. When we must, or feel it appropriate to, explain differences, we know a proper and acceptable way to do so: by nation (as well as by class, gender, ethnic origin, etc.).

This argument can be made more concrete through the example of doing the dishes.[9] Since the nineteenth century, we have become more knowledgeable about cleanliness, which has been intimately related to the creation of the modern society and the revision of the order of things. The development of the microscope in the late nineteenth century led to the discovery that specific living organisms caused specific diseases, and three modern strategies were developed to counteract the spread of diseases:

(1) Medicine shifted from the provision of general treatment to aggressive efforts to combat specific causes of disease.
(2) Fresh air and exercise were recommended as a means of fostering healthy, disease-resistant bodies.
(3) To prevent the spread of organisms that cause disease, society endeavored to control the physical environment such that no unsafe contact between different elements could occur. There was to be a functional division in everyday life, a division intended to prevent contamination and reduce the risk of epidemics. For example, to prevent the spread of cholera, graveyards were moved out of major cities all over Europe; with the dead thus separated from the living, a new order was established.

These strategies were all part of a public health or hygiene movement, which transformed purity into an aesthetic as well as a moral value.

With the development of better living conditions and housing standards in the latter part of the nineteenth century, more and more spheres of everyday life became subject to this process of modern reorganization. And the work connected with this reorganization was primarily the responsibility of a single person: the housewife. During the late nineteenth and early twentieth century, several new *national* organizations were formed by and for housewives, disseminating information through pamphlets, members' newsletters, and, later, via radio and television, on the conduct and practices of a proper housewife. The work of the housewife, or home economics, was also introduced as a subject in elementary schools.

This was, indeed, a *transnational* phenomenon, with similar national organizations established and funded by state subsidies, created and supported by roughly the same kinds of people at roughly the same time, all over (at least northwest) Europe. We can trace the process by which national organizations merged to form international (in this case, Nordic) organizations as they adopted each other's methods for dealing with their task: to educate the housewife so that she could make her family and home—her life—proper and clean in the most rational and economical way.

With the development of indoor plumbing, many homes had running water and drains by the 1920s and, subsequently, water heaters. The availability of hot tap water then gave rise to debates over the proper way to wash dishes and the optimum design and construction of the kitchen sink and worktop. From the 1930s on, this discussion, like many similar ones, was conducted in the housewives' organizations, with various studies made and a number of specific methods identified, recommended, and enforced. By the early 1950s, the issue of dishwashing practices had been settled and the recommended methods had become established in both Sweden and Denmark (see Figures 2a, 2b).

In *Sweden*, dishwashing is done at a sinktop made entirely of stainless steel with two sinks in it—a large one to the right and a smaller one to the left. The Swedish practice is to begin by rinsing all of the dishes and stacking them on the sinktop to the right of the sinks (step

Dishwashing process from right to left:

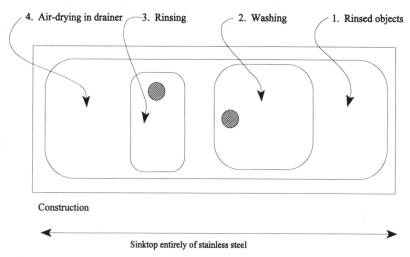

Figure 2a. Sweden.

1, Figure 2a). Then they are washed in the larger sink on the right (2); the detergent is rinsed off in the smaller sink on the left (3); and the dishes are air-dried in a drainer standing on the sinktop to the left of both sinks (4).

This is the most rational and hygienic way of doing the dishes— according to a 1946 scientific report issued by the Swedish Domestic Research Institute.[10] This detailed report covered virtually all aspects of dishwashing: the length of time required, the price and quality of different detergents and brushes, the size of the sinks, the height of the sinktops, and so on. Clearly, dishwashing was seen as an activity to be regulated so that the most rational, hygienic, and economical methods would be recommended and then practiced in thousands of homes throughout Sweden. These recommendations were disseminated both in pamphlets for housewives and through the schools. (A colleague told me that in Landskrona, a medium-sized town in Skåne, children in the fifth grade still have to pass an examination that tests their ability to wash dishes properly.) Moreover, the specific design and construction material of the worktop (stainless steel

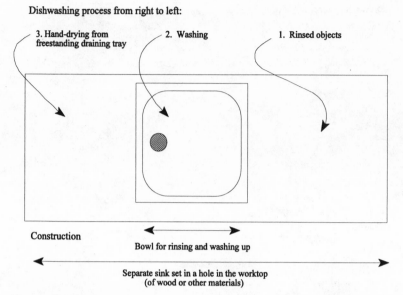

Dishwashing process from right to left:

3. Hand-drying from freestanding draining tray   2. Washing   1. Rinsed objects

Construction

Bowl for rinsing and washing up

Separate sink set in a hole in the worktop
(of wood or other materials)

Figure 2b. Denmark.

with two sinks) is likewise regulated through the terms under which state subsidies for new housing construction are granted.

In *Denmark*, a different design and construction material, as well as a different method, are recommended, taught, and practiced—on the basis of the *very same report* by the Swedish Domestic Research Institute. Dishwashing in Denmark can be done with only one sink, set into a worktop that can be made of wood or some other material. One starts by rinsing all the dishes and stacking them to the right of the sink (step 1, Figure 2b). Then they are washed in a bowl within the sink (2), transferred to a draining tray on the left (3), and then immediately picked up and dried with a tea towel. Two sinks are recommended if there is enough space, but in that case the smaller one has to be to the *right* of the sink in which the washing bowl is placed (rather than to the left, as in Sweden) so that the rinsing and washing can be done in one continuous process from right to left.

Obviously, there is a functional relationship between the differences in design and construction material and the two different bodily practices of dishwashing. The Swedish worktop has to be made out of a material which can withstand the moisture from dishes left to air-dry in the drainer, so stainless steel is recommended. The Danish worktop, on the other hand, can be protected from moisture as a result of both a freestanding draining tray and the practice of drying the dishes by hand, after which the draining tray is removed and the sink-top wiped.[11] Since there is no moisture problem, the Danish sinktop can be made out of any material.

It is worth noting that identical rationales pertaining to economy, ergonomy, and efficiency (i.e., time/productivity) are used in both Sweden and Denmark to argue for the practice in each country as the best and proper way to do the dishes. It is also worth noting that neither Swedish nor Danish experts have been able to explain these different national dishwashing practices. One of the women behind the 1946 Swedish report suggested that they could be due to differing amounts of calcium in the water of the two countries (i.e., the harder Danish water would leave calcium stains if not wiped off the washed plates, glasses, etc.). And a Danish kitchen-design consultant thought that the different practices might be due to the fact that hot water was—and still is—more expensive in Denmark than in Sweden. But my concern here is not with the causes of these differences, but rather with the differences per se.

We can draw three conclusions from these differences between Swedish and Danish dishwashing practices. First, while the problems of the modern world are transnational, as are discussions about them and the institutions dealing with them, the solutions are created within the cultural space of the individual nation–states. In this case, a transnational problem—*public health or hygiene*—and its discussion as a question of the housewife's role in maintaining household *cleanliness* led to a new expression of national diversity along the Swedish/Danish border. This conclusion by no means entails any claim that there is a Swedish way and a Danish way of doing the dishes, but rather that the Swedish/Danish border is what signifies the difference; in other words, *the political border is turned into a cultural one*. If Germans wash dishes as Danes do, the Danish way is no less non-Swedish for all that. As I noted earlier, one has to think in terms of a *specific Other* when investigating cultural identities, for little can be inferred from a study of the relations between the *Self* and *all the rest*. Only by analyzing specific relations of contrast between a Self and an Other can the whole cultural organization of the issue in question be clarified. The Other has to be approached as much more than just exotic if we are really to come to terms with the processes of cultural identity.

Second, modernity represents both emancipation *and* new constraints. Modernity has emancipated us from a great many laborious and time-consuming tasks, due to better living conditions, including better housing (from which women have perhaps benefited the most). But modernity has also spawned an insidious exercise of power over mass, undifferentiated bodies, since every-body must be "normal" if this modern project is to work. The "average," or "mean," is a central concept here: nobody too high, nobody too low—and, of course, every-body right-handed; left-handed people only cause trouble!

Third, this difference illuminates an unusual relationship between nation and gender. The nation is often seen as a male construction, with national prominence the exclusive preserve of historical (or legendary) war heroes,[12] of (male) explorers and great writers at the turn of the century, or of (mostly male) sports and popular music celebrities today. In the case of doing the dishes, as in a lot of other aspects of everyday life, the issues and practices are defined by women (together with men) and the activity is nationalized as a predominantly female task.

Such nationalizations of everyday practices can lead to highly concrete personal experiences of national identity, as in the following anecdote:

> It is October 1988. I have been living in Lund for ten months, and I am visiting some of my Swedish friends. It is rather late in the evening and Sune—the host—goes into the kitchen to clean up; I follow him and start doing the dishes. I put the first washed things in the dish drainer. Suddenly, Sune turns to me and says: "You're not washing up properly, you're doing it the Danish way. Let me show you." There is no doubt that Sune is unpleasantly affected by my way of washing up, so I let myself be taught how to rinse off the detergent before the dishes are left to air-dry—

not to be dried by hand with a tea towel. As I continue to wash up, I feel singled out for being Danish. It is perfectly clear that I have breached the local—Swedish—code of decent dishwashing.

In this concrete situation, the host clearly chose to express his disgust with something in national terms, having learned from the narratives that nationality was a legitimate way to explain difference, having learned to perceive with a nationalizing eye. Therefore, he tried to *avoid* embarrassing his guest by *not* accusing him of being *unhygienic*—a very serious accusation in the modern world, where cleanliness is a central theme of identity.

From the 1930s through the 1950s, the right way of doing the dishes was intensely and *publicly* discussed. Since then the respective methods endorsed and adopted in both Sweden and Denmark have been reconstructed as natural: the cultural has been naturalized, put beyond question, and made morally loaded. This is what Mary Douglas's discussion of pollution and taboo is all about.[13] (Actually, most people today do not like to discuss their ways of doing the dishes!) Nevertheless, such differences can be experienced concretely, evoking feelings of national identity, and such experiences of national culture are very real aspects of our everyday lives when crossing borders.

Keeping both the narratives and the nationalized cultural practices in mind, we can draw some conclusions about *national culture* on (at least) two different levels: (1) national culture as something *remembered* (*husket*), and (2) national culture as something *recollected* (*erindret*), to borrow and apply Kierkegaard's distinction.[14]

What is *remembered* can always be discussed and shared with others—and its truth can be questioned or considered subject to revision. Remembering is a temporal process in which one moves the *then* to the *now* in order to deal with it. This level corresponds to the culturally loaded narratives of nations, supported by the empirical work done in history, art history, literature, folklore, and ethnology since the late nineteenth century, when all of these disciplines were (as they still are) engaged in collecting and related conservation activities to save some national heritage.

On another level we have what is *recollected*, which is personal, emotional, and *not* something that can be shared with others. It will always be experienced as *the* reality—*now* shifted to *then*—as déjà vu. This level corresponds to the individual experience of difference in such contexts of everyday life as dishwashing practices—and to individual strategies for coping with such expressions of difference. As an experience, recollection seems much more *authentic*: something so personal that it remains closed to debate or contestation by others, yet something that generates interpersonal tension, such as when others are perceived as not maintaining "natural" standards of cleanliness and one needs to explain this lapse.

What this distinction reveals is that the national is not authentic on the level of the *narrative*—all of the elements associated with such loaded concepts as national pride and other emotional identifications since the nineteenth century can be readily deconstructed as the invention of an imagined community. But what we must realize is that this metaphorical way of explaining difference is so deeply entrenched in modern society that it is readily available to us when we really do *experience* difference—and we must accept this experience as *personal* and *true*, or authentic. Thus the national experience occurs in the most unexpected places and under the most unexpected circumstances, namely, in the routines of our everyday lives. Small differences can become large issues; Selves become Selves through experiencing Others.

We can, naturally, also find examples of difference where the *nationalizing eye* does *not* capture the "reality" of the feature, although the people involved may have the *same* sense of authenticity when they perceive such differences on the level of the recollected. When I asked some high school classes of Swedish and Danish students (15–18 years old) to write a paper on what they knew of one another, quite a few remarked on each other's hairstyle. Danish students saw Swedish hairstyles as distinct from their own. *Swedish intellectuals*, however, perceived the very same styles not as *Swedish*, but as *working-class*. When analyzing this difference, then, some Swedes used the *classifying eye*—another appropriate way of explaining difference—instead of the nationalizing eye.

Although these ways of explaining difference seem to be—and are—much alike, there is one factor that distinguishes them: their relation to power. When Danes conclude that Swedish working-class hairstyles are different because Swedes are different, a *symmetrical* relation obtains between nation and nation: no Dane would like Swedes to become Danish. When Swedes attribute some (Swedish) hairstyles to class differences, however, they establish an *asymmetrical* intranational relation: nobody but a working-class person would get a haircut like that. This relation has the potential to be transformed into a normalizing execution of power.

Such an understanding of the nation and of authenticity can enable us to recognize that when we study national identity on the level of everyday life, we are not only studying the nationalization (or the ethnification, classification, or genderization) of more and more differences—that is to say, supporting the view that these imagined communities and borders really do exist—but also shifting real experiences of difference from the *recollected* and the *authentic* to the *remembered*. We are thereby making it possible to deal with and discuss these experiences, but at the same time we are depriving them of their authenticity: How many Danes or Swedes do or do not wash their dishes in the recommended way?[15] When studying national identities in these terms, we are in effect endorsing and subscribing to the *reality* of the *imagined* community and at the same time underlining its very character as a *modern invention* and a *cultural process*.

As a result of the comments I've received on my U.S. talks about small differences and large issues (see my acknowledgments note), it has become clear to me that many Americans are unable—or unwilling—to see these same processes of homogenization as occurring in everyday life in the United States. In this context, there seem to be two narratives, both of which deny the reality of elements that constitute "an American way of life." One narrative, on multiculturalism, denies that all Americans can live or behave in the same way. The underlying assumption here, which emerges particularly in discussions about American culture, is that Americans are different, and behave differently, from one another. The second narrative, on the American people's relationship to the state—which everybody is apparently against—denies that the state has any means whatsoever of intervening in and influencing the everyday life of Americans.

Homogenization can occur, however, not only through the intervention of the state, but also by means of other vehicles of cultural flow, such as the market or movements.[16] To give just one example of the concrete way in which everyday life in North America is really homogenized and differs from life in the Nordic countries, I saw something while visiting Laval University in Quebec that will be part of my recollected knowledge of difference from now on. Although I had experienced the same thing earlier during visits to the United States and Canada, I had never applied the nationalizing eye to it.

Before giving a lecture, I went to the toilet, where I noticed that many surfaces (the toilet itself, the tap, the paper-towel dispenser, etc.) were stamped with the words "American Standard." At first, I thought that some kind of government committee had studied all the aspects of such facilities (e.g., their dimensions, water-flow rates, etc.) and had developed a specific "American standard," which would explain the fact that North American and Nordic toilets are constructed differently. But, of course, I was wrong: "American Standard" is nothing but a trademark! (Though a rather impressive one nonetheless.)

Notes

Different versions of this article have been given as lectures at Laval University, in a series organized by Professors Bogumil Jewsiewicki and Jocelyn Létourneau called "Mondialité, Nationalité, Identité," and in a seminar organized by Professors Richard Wilk and Henry Glassie at Indiana University, both in November 1993. I thank all the organizers and participants in these seminars for their comments and reflections. I also thank my colleagues Gunnar Alsmark, Tom O'Dell, and Orvar Löfgren for inspiring points of view, and Alan Crozier for kindly helping me with the language.

1 It would be far too simple to see the current interest in the nation as just a result of the developments in Eastern and Western Europe. Nevertheless, it is obvious that the discussion is still very much a European one, with the "classics" written by Europeans and most research being carried out in Europe. See, for example, Benedict Anderson, *Imagined Communities: Reflections on the Origin and Spread of Nationalism* (London, 1983); Ernest Gellner, *Nations and Nationalism* (Oxford, 1983); E. J. Hobsbawm, *Nations and Nationalism since 1780: Programme, Myth, Reality* (Cambridge, 1990); and Anthony D. Smith, *The Ethnic Origins of Nations* (New York, 1986); and *National Identity* (London, 1991).

2 "Imagined communities" is, of course, Benedict Anderson's term. I think that his is still the best work on this kind of imagi-*nation*, although a lot of readers (at

least anthropologists and ethnologists) are so enthusiastic about his provocative separation of *community* from *interaction* on page 15 of *Imagined Communities* that they lose sight of many other useful thoughts in the rest of the book. Here is the passage from page 15 that is most often quoted in discussions of the nation: "It is *imagined* because the members of even the smallest nation will never know most of their fellow-members, meet them, or even hear of them, yet in the minds of each lives the image of their communion."

3 Orvar Löfgren, "The Nationalization of Culture," *Ethnologia Europaea* 19 (1989): 5–23 (a special issue on National Culture as Process, ed. Orvar Löfgren).

4 The Danish social anthropologist Anne Knudsen provides a good assessment of how micro-nationalistic (or regional) movements use all of the conventional expressions of nationhood to legitimize themselves; see "Mikronationalismens Dannelseshistorie," in *Nationella identiteter i Norden—ett fullbordat projekt?*, ed. Anders Linde-Laursen and Jan Olof Nilsson (Stockholm, 1991), 19–38.

5 For a more detailed history of Bornholm, see Ebbe Gert Rasmussen, "Dette gave-brev: Det politiske spil omkring den bornholmske opstand og Peder Olsens indsats i løsrivelsesværket 1658–59," *Bornholmske Samlinger* 15/16 (1982). See also Anders Linde-Laursen, "Skåne: Danskt, svenskt—eller skånskt?" in *Spelet om Skåne*, ed. Erik Osvalds (Malmö, 1993), 104–14; and "Skåne på skillevejen," *Skalk*, No. 2 (1993): 18–27.

6 The relation between nation-building and spatial limits on geographical movement is one of the most central points of Anderson's *Imagined Communities*, although page 15 and his arguments on print capitalism are much better known. This may be because most researchers still look upon the nation as a primarily historical phenomenon and fail to see the basic spatial dimension of the problem.

7 This perspective is developed in Anders Linde-Laursen, "Er Sverige inter-essant . . . ?" in Linde-Laursen and Nilsson, eds., *Nationella identiteter i Norden*, 39–57.

8 This perspective on national identities is developed by Michael Harbsmeier, "Danmark: Nation, kultur og køn," *Stofskifte: Tidsskrift for Antropologi* (Copenhagen) 13 (1986): 47–73.

9 For a more detailed discussion of dishwashing in Sweden and Denmark, see Anders Linde-Laursen, "The Nationalization of Trivialities," *Ethnos* (Stockholm) 58 (1993): 275–93.

10 *Diskning*, HFI Meddelanden 1 (Stockholm, 1946).

11 Water running back into the single sink from the draining tray would reduce the temperature of the water used for dishwashing, which is why Danes do their dishes in a plastic bowl placed in the sink. With the double sinktop used in Sweden, however, the water from the drainer runs down into the rinsing sink, so Swedes do their dishes in the sink itself.

12 Whenever the Danish nation's survival has been threatened (such as during Denmark's two wars with Germany, in 1848–50 and in 1864, over Slesvig–Holsten/Schleswig–Holstein, or during the Occupation in the Second World War, or in con-

nection with a referendum on Denmark's relationship to the European Union in 1992), persons and events from the seventeenth- and eighteenth-century wars between the Swedish and Danish–Norwegian kings have become prominent again. Old books have been reprinted and new ones written, films have been made and plays produced, about the history of Bornholm, say, or Admiral Tordenskjold, or the guerrilla leader Gøngehøvdingen.

13 See Mary Douglas, *Purity and Danger: An Analysis of the Concepts of Pollution and Taboo* (London, 1966).

14 See the preface to Søren Kierkegaard, "In Vino Veritas," in *Stages on Life's Way: Studies by Various Persons*, ed. and trans. Howard V. Hong and Edna H. Hong (Princeton, 1988), 9–19.

15 In response to this question, we say that *over 90 percent* of the kitchens sold in Sweden and Denmark are constructed as respectively recommended. So despite the fact that not all Swedes and Danes follow the recommended bodily practices, doing the dishes is one concrete activity of everyday life in which many people, Swedes and Danes alike, would experience difference in the kitchens of the Other.

16 For further discussion, see Ulf Hannerz, *Cultural Complexity: Studies in the Social Organization of Meaning* (New York, 1992).

John McCumber

Dialectical Identity in a "Post-Critical" Era: A Hegelian Reading

In the wake of Kant, philosophy became critique; this is as true of the logical positivists as it is of Marxists, phenomenologists, and Habermassians. In every case, philosophers undertook to judge the realities of social life (including those of philosophical discourse itself) against standards—verifiability, dialecticality, apodicticity, communicative action. Often enough, philosophy found those realities wanting, and that was valuable. But the overall project of critique has ultimately, I think, been unable to find a way out of its site of origin: to swim against the current flowing from the wake of Kant.

The problem seems to be epistemological. In order to judge reality against a set of standards, we have to know what those standards are. We must also know what entitles them to be standards—which is the question of why, when reality diverges from our model, it is reality itself and not the model that is found wanting. The nature of our knowledge of critical standards, including the question of whether it is to be had at all,

The *South Atlantic Quarterly* 94:4, Fall 1995.
Copyright © 1995 by Duke University Press.
CCC 0038-2876/95/$1.50.

has preoccupied much of twentieth-century philosophy. Recent inabilities to justify it in terms of anything more than pragmatic usefulness[1] perhaps warrant calling the present era "post-critical" as well as "postmodern." Certainly, thinkers from Foucault to Rorty would underwrite this.[2]

I believe that the fatality of critique, the site of its demise and, perhaps, its wake, is indeed epistemological. But I do not think that the terminally problematic knowledge in question is knowledge of our standards of evaluation, while I do think that once the deeper difficulty is isolated, we will find the resources to carry on, if not "critique," then a related project under a different name.

On the above, explicitly Kantian model of critique, reawakened most spectacularly by Habermas, knowledge of critical standards is distinct from knowledge of actual states of affairs, and so must be justified distinctively. Christa Bürger has argued that this "rationalist" version of critique is not really "critique" at all. As she puts it, "Within the [rationalist] tradition, critics are in possession of some yardsticks which assure them superiority over the object of criticism." Opposed to such superior and objectifying critique, for Bürger, is the tradition of "immanent critique . . . which does not dogmatically conclude that because it [critique] is true the other is untrue, but which gets inside the theory being criticized and derives an impetus to thinking from its lacunae and contradictions."[3] Immanent critique derives its critical standards from the very object criticized. It attributes to that object not failure with respect to some external model, but the object's own "lacunae and contradictions."

But this does not really solve the problem. Marx and thousands of others after him fought their way heroically to the "inside" of the proletariat, and of competing theories about the proletariat, exposing numerous lacunae and contradictions in both—only to have it become clear, in 1989, that "the proletariat" had in a sense never existed at all. On the contrary, even in "socialist" countries workers still, beneath the surface, thought of themselves in terms of religion and ethnicity rather than class. In this the workers explicitly confirmed the judgment of Adorno and Horkheimer that classical Marxism had falsely imputed truly emancipatory potential to the proletariat, having failed to understand the social reality of the very people who were its object.[4] What this suggests is that critique has a problem with its knowledge not merely of its own standards, but also of the realities to which those standards (whether externally derived or "immanent") are applied.

In fact, as I will argue here, critique entails a very special sort of knowledge of social realities—what in his *Logic* Hegel called "judgment"[5]—which must claim to know not merely the facts about a given reality, but its *essence* or *nature* as well. Marx, for example, knew plenty of facts about workers. However, his detailed knowledge of their oppression notwithstanding, he did not understand their "true nature"—their *essential* ideology—or that, despite their class oppression, they would see themselves, even after decades of socialist consciousness-raising, in different terms. It is here, I suggest, in such *imputation of essence* that problems arise both for external or "rationalist" critique and for the immanent or "dialectical" variety.

The matter can be put as follows. In addition to its knowledge of critical norms, critique also requires knowledge of the social realities to be judged against those norms. It must know the nature of the object to be judged so as to permit either its external comparison with a norm or standard or the generation from it of a new object.[6] Critique thus entails a nonempirical claim about its object, for it must claim not only factual knowledge of it, but also that this factual knowledge is *constitutive* of the object's "true" nature or essence—its basic set of properties from which all other socially relevant ones follow and without which that object would not exist. No one ever doubted, for example, that many capitalists oppress their workers. It is quite possible, in fact, to see such oppression as endemic to capitalism and still defend capitalism as an idealized social order (à la that hoary "defense" of Christianity—its never having been tried). In order to constitute a critique of capitalism itself, there must be a claim that such oppression is not merely an accidental, contingent failing of capitalists, but one that is intrinsic to them, that their basic nature, as capitalists, is to oppress workers.

The object thus criticized, however (and we would-be critics must not forget this), is a human reality—not *just* a theory or a practice, but a person who holds a theory or engages in a practice.[7] A theory which nobody held or a practice in which no one engaged would hardly be a fit object for critique; it would be a fantasy. Hence critique—whether immanent or external—always contains a component of dialogical *address*, and discourse in such address is not cast in the third-person voice but the second. So understood, critical procedure looks—in a general and oversimplified way—like this:

(1) This (predicates a . . . h) is your reality.
(2) These (i . . . z) are the normative predicates which ought to apply to your reality.
(3) Your reality thus does not match the applicable normative predicates.

Many people, like Bürger, see the problem with critique in the wake of Kant as residing in (2), or as one of stating and justifying critical norms, which is why Bürger thinks that it can be resolved by deriving those standards internally rather than by justifying them externally. But the problem really resides, I suggest, in (1), and we owe its exposure (in one of history's many ironies) to the man who is often credited with the paternity, or at least the grandsiring, of immanent critique: Hegel.

In the section of his *Phenomenology* entitled "The Struggle of Enlightenment with Superstition," Hegel successively treats two forms of enlightened discourse which can be approximated, respectively, to what Bürger calls "rationalist" and "dialectical" critique. In the first discursive form, or "rationalist" critique, Enlightenment attributes all sorts of superstitions (i.e., defective knowledge and practice) to religious Faith.[8] But Enlightenment is thereby operating from a different conceptual repertoire than that of Faith. It is describing Faith's reality from the standpoint of its own enlightened standards, so its imputations all sound false to Faith.[9] In order to depict Faith in a way that is acceptable to Faith itself, Enlightenment must do so in terms which it shares with Faith: "immanently," as a result of "getting inside" Faith. But then its critique can only consist in reminding Faith of truths about itself that Faith would like to forget, to "put away somewhere."[10] Enlightenment thus points out lacunae in Faith—truths that should be claimed, but that Faith refuses to acknowledge. This refusal to acknowledge reality can be construed as a "contradiction" with it, so this approach by Enlightenment accords with Bürger's "dialectical" critique.

If Faith and Enlightenment really share the same terms of debate, however, then this practice of hiding unpleasant truths must also be a characteristic of Enlightenment. It, too, must be "putting away" such truths about itself, or else it would be operating from a standpoint of courageous self-awareness which Faith could not share. In Hegel's words: "To Faith, Enlightenment [still] seems to be a perversion and a lie because it points out the *otherness* of its moments; in doing so, it seems directly to make something else out of them than they are in their separateness."[11] In other words, even when Enlightenment *correctly* points out these "other," unpleasant truths about Faith, it remains untrue to one of the important characteristics that those truths had for Faith: that they were hidden away or "separate" from it. By violating that characteristic, Enlightenment once again renders itself foreign—and its analyses unacceptable—to Faith.

In order to reach Faith with a truly immanent imputation that Faith will accept, Enlightenment must go one step further and not only adopt the same overall structure as Faith, that of "putting away" unpleasant truths, but also put away the *very same* truths that Faith does. With this move, however, Enlightenment loses all of its capacity to critique Faith; it can do nothing for Faith that Faith cannot do for itself. The "truth of Enlightenment," therefore, is that it is exactly the same as superstition.[12]

It is tempting to wonder what would have happened if philosophers had paid more attention to Hegel's account of critique here as a matter of "dialogical address." The important lesson is that a critic is not in a position to properly describe the reality that he or she wishes to critique. For that description will be made either in terms of external standards already known and justified on their own account or in terms of a dialectical move to the next level, motivated by "lacunae and contradictions" to be discovered in (or imputed to) the object. In neither case can the imputations of critique actually be true to its object. That can only happen when critique adopts exactly the same overall conceptual scheme as the (human) reality that is its object, in which case it cannot criticize that object.

And so we see that critique, both immanent and external, is still bobbing in the wake of Kant—and of modernity in general. For it partakes of the general prejudice of modernity toward assertions —toward propositions that actually tell us about the world—and against the kinds of generative or "poetic" thought that produce not truth, but concepts or parameters. I will not go into the problems of what I call "assertionism" here.[13] Nor will I pursue what might seem to be another promising strategy: tracing the rest of the *Phenomenology*'s dialectics—all the way to Absolute Knowing, if need be—in hopes of finding a solution somewhere along the line.

I propose instead to make an end run around this entire set of problems by viewing my job as a philosopher not as "critique," but as "presentation."[14] What I will present here are concepts—two concepts of identity. My presentation will be "philosophical" in that it will be *restricted* to (a) giving a clear account of the concepts in question, (b) exposing certain problems with them, and (c) contrasting them to one another. So understood, my job is not to prove a proposition (critical or otherwise), but neither is it to say that the concepts I am presenting capture other peoples' experiences, nor to recommend either that they replace any other concepts or that one concept replace the other. Still less is it to make a "judgment," claiming that my concepts capture not merely the experiences of others, but their very nature. I will, in short, skip step (1) above altogether, which means that step (2) will also be avoided; I will simply compare each concept I formulate with competing concepts and isolate what can be—for whatever reasons my readers may have—regarded as its strengths and weaknesses. When and whether such a presentation attains "critical" force is thus a matter to be decided not by me, but by those whom I address here. It is *up to the reader* to decide whether any concept thus presented actually captures certain features of her experience, just as it is *up to the reader* to decide whether or not she considers that to be a bad thing. In short, the concept of "presentation" I am seeking to formulate here has affinities with the concept of "poetic interaction" I explored in detail elsewhere.[15] In this way, I hope to go beyond modernity *and* its epigones, perhaps to allow Kant—that distinguished gentleman, so often (rudely) awakened—his final wake.

Hegel might seem a strange place to start if you want to give a clear presentation of anything, but something in his *Philosophy of Right* is intriguing enough to provide material for reflection. As Emil Fackenheim has noted, Hegel's text suggests that the French Revolutionary government did the right thing with regard to the Jews (i.e., granting them full civil rights), but for the wrong reasons—because Jews are human beings rather than because they are Jews.[16] What could Hegel have been thinking of with this sort of paradox? *Les droits de l'homme*, the civil rights afforded to Jews, were universal in nature, so how could membership in a particular group qualify anyone for universal rights? What sort of interplay between being Jewish and being human allowed Hegel to make this criticism of the French Revolution?

The first concept I wish to present is that of "essential identity," and my first task is to liberate some of Hegel's views on essence from the intensely personal jargon in which he expressed them. But a further preliminary explanation is in order here. For Hegel, any concept which can even hope to apply to human beings as such—insofar as they are not merely physical objects or animals—must be narrative in nature. Human beings are distinct from nature, in Hegel's view, because they are Spirit; and the term "Spirit" designates a set not of states of affairs, but of transformations. When such a narrative concept is philosophical, the transformations it designates will be necessary. So any philosophical concept of human identity will in effect be the basic theme of a story, each of whose stages leads inexorably to the next. My presentation of both essential identity and—my second concept—dialectical identity, then, will amount to the telling of two contrasting stories. According to Hegel,

— Essence is a truth, that is, it is what something else "really" is;
— Essence as the truth of something else is reached from something else, that is, in Hegel's jargon, from "Being";
— Essence is a "simple equality with itself" which "preserves and maintains itself";
— in this unity, specific properties or "determinations" develop that remain "self-subsistent, but only in their association with each other in this unity."[17]

We see in the first and second of these that "Essence" for Hegel is what I am calling a narrative concept: it is part of a story which begins with Essence itself being somehow reached from something else, namely, Being. Since Being is thus the other of Essence, we can say that it will lack the features which Essence has. It will not be a "truth," in the above sense—it will not be what anything "really" is. It will not be reached from anything else, but simply given—in some sort of experience, though obviously of a rather confused sort. And it will not be a simple self-preserving unity, but will change polymorphously, indeed chaotically: it will be a dynamic flow about which no rational story can be told.

Essence can be reached from Being, we are told, in two ways. One is by an "external negation" of, or movement on from, Being.[18] In this "external negation," something outside the experiences that constitute Being—perhaps another person or group who has not had those experiences—makes the negating move. The resulting Essence is imposed from outside, by an other, and is "only a product, and artefact." Such an Essence—what Edward Said calls "Orientalism" provides a paradigm[19]—I will call "inauthentic." The other way of reaching Essence from Being is by "internalization," or "recollection." Here the manifold experiences of Being *themselves* collect *themselves* by exhibiting determinations which preserve and maintain *themselves*.[20] I will call this second sort "authentic" Essence, and now we can see what it is. Authentic Essence is a set of characteristics which maintain themselves as a group through a series of otherwise chaotic experiences from which they are reached. As authentic, the group maintains itself against those others who would define it, and it defines—or internalizes—its own nature.

———

Departing now from Hegel's text and jargon, we can regard essence as a sort of identity: it is what a set of experiences "really" is, and it is those characteristics which persist through that entire set and are never found apart from one another in it. Thus my individual identity is those features of me that I myself find in all my experiences. To "internalize" them is in this case to become explicitly aware of them, to see them as the "self-equal unity" which they are. Similarly for the identity of a group—a class, a nation, a society, or an ethnic group—its essential identity is the set of characteristics that can always be empirically observed in individual members of that group and that make those individuals "a" group as such.

Individual Subscription Request

Please enter my subscription to *South Atlantic Quarterly*, at the rate of $26.00 for four issues. (Add $12.00 for postage outside the U.S.; Canadian subscribers add 7% GST.) My subscription will begin with the Fall 1996 issue (volume 95, number 4).

_____Please bill me. (No issue can be sent until payment is received.)

_____My check or money order, payable to Duke University Press, is enclosed in an envelope with this card.

_____Please charge my credit card:

Card Number	Exp. Date
Signature	Daytime Phone

Name

Address

City/State/Zip Code

HSE

For fastest service, please call (919) 687-3617 Monday-Friday between 8:00 a.m. and 4:30 p.m. EST with credit card information.

Institutional Subscription Request

Please enter our subscription to *South Atlantic Quarterly* (to begin with volume 95, number 4 Fall 1996]) at the annual institutional rate of $66.00 (4 issues). (Add $12.00 for postage outside the U.S.; Canadian subscribers add 7% GST.)

_____Please bill us at the address below. (No issue can be sent until payment is received.)

_____An institutional check or purchase order, payable to Duke University Press, is enclosed. (No issues can be sent until payment is received.).

_____Please bill our agent: _____

Name

Address

City/State/Zip Code

HSE

BUSINESS REPLY MAIL
FIRST CLASS PERMIT NO. 1000 DURHAM NC

POSTAGE WILL BE PAID BY ADDRESSEE

South Atlantic Quarterly
c/o Duke University Press
Journals Fulfillment
Box 90660
Durham, NC   27708-0660

BUSINESS REPLY MAIL
FIRST CLASS PERMIT NO. 1000 DURHAM NC

POSTAGE WILL BE PAID BY ADDRESSEE

South Atlantic Quarterly
c/o Duke University Press
Journals Fulfillment
Box 90660
Durham, NC   27708-0660

Such identity, even though authentic, is going to run into problems, in Hegel's view, because it contains a certain incoherence at its core. While such essence can exist only by virtue of being derived from a chaotic and changing experience, it claims to be determinate and self-maintaining—static. This, of course, contradicts what I earlier suggested was a basic characteristic of humanly applicable concepts for Hegel, namely, that they be narrative in character. The concept of essential identity *arises* narratively, to be sure—as people attempt to discern the common characteristics exhibited in all their experiences. But there the story ends: with a set of static properties, persisting unchanged ever after, and a chaotic set of experiences by which those properties will remain untouched.

But everything human, for Hegel, is subject to change, so we can get a better view of authentic essence by continuing the story beyond the point where it is supposed to stop. Let us suppose that a certain domain of being—call it a group of people—has a number of experiences. They recognize that in all those experiences certain characteristics are to be found. When they view those omnipresent characteristics as their essence, they grant that set of characteristics the right to maintain itself, without change, in all of their further experiences. But time is what it is, and experience is chaotic. There will eventually—inexorably—be experiences of that group in which at least some of those characteristics are not found and through which new characteristics can be seen to persist. These new experiences, like those from which the group essence was originally reached, are given—are being. And as such, it would seem, they have the same right as the original set of experiences to be regarded as that from which essence is reached. The new set of characteristics thus has an equal claim with the old to be constituted as the essential identity of the group. Yet if the original set is to be maintained, the new experiences, and their new characteristics, must be excluded. By what right?

The answer is *by no right at all*. The original essence was justified *only* by, and with respect to, the experiences from which it was internalized. The new experiences are just as much "experiences" as the old, so, with no *reason* to exclude them, essence can do so— and maintain itself—only by *force*. The very strength with which it resisted the imposition of inauthentic essence by an other is now directed against the experience of the group itself. In its struggle to persist unchanged, the group reduces its new experiences to the status of illusion—what Hegel's translator, A. V. Miller, calls "illusory being"—refusing to allow them to constitute a new essence.

Essential identity, we see, turns on a denial of time itself. It denies, first of all, the future: it insists that the future is not radically indeterminable, but rather that it will *essentially* be just like the present. In order to justify this denial of the future, essential identity must deny the past as well, for the past of any essence is just the being from which it was reached. And, as we have seen, to admit that its legitimacy was thus derived is to admit that it can be thus removed. The legitimacy of essence thereby changes, inexorably; it is no longer a matter of what was derived in a particular way in the past, but simply of what exists right now.[21] We could follow this process through the usual Hegelian moves: the new set of determinations would constitute a second essence, despite efforts to exclude it, and would be in "contradiction" with the original set; then we would have the dynamic opposition of contradictions that Hegel calls "dialectic." But I will stop here.

We could say, at this point, that essential identity has demonstrated an inconsistency: while it has no other legitimacy than that of being derived from certain chaotic experiences, this is the very legitimacy that it now denies to the new characteristics which have emerged from the new experiences of the group. Am I making a normative, critical judgment here, appealing to "consistency" as an overall critical norm? I think not. I am not saying that consistency is a standard to which something else ought to conform; for one thing, I am not talking about reality at all (still less about a human reality), but only about concepts and the stories they structure. With regard to the concept of essential identity, again, I am not advancing consistency as a standard to which *it* ought to conform. On the contrary, the concept of essence cannot conform to such a standard because it is *defined* in terms of its inconsistency, that is, as the attempt to formulate an identity beyond time, which contradicts all things. It can no more become consistent than a triangle can become four-sided.

It is possible, however, to present a concept of identity that avoids the inconsistency inherent to the notion of essential identity. In doing so, I present an alternative concept—I tell a different philosophical story.

═══════

Suppose that the members of the group embrace their new experiences. Suppose they recognize as they go through their lives, building their common history, that not all of their seemingly permanent characteristics will endure and that new ones will arise. Their group identity is to be equated not with any single set of determinations, but with the movement by which new determinations are added to, and old ones subtracted from, their essence. The identity of the group is no longer a static set of essential determinations, but something which transforms itself over time—changing to meet new challenges. What belonging to the group means is not a matter of having a certain set of characteristics, but of fitting yourself into a certain story, taking on a particular identity and helping to transform it over time. It is to have what I will call "dialectical" identity.

This second sort of identity differs from the first kind. In the first place, while at any stage it is perfectly determinate, its determination is only temporary: "what we are right now" versus "what we always were and will be." The unity of the identity here is thus only relative. Moreover, such identity is only aspectual: it does not embrace the entire nature of the individuals so identified because part of their activity *as members of the group* now consists in confronting new experiences which are foreign to that group. Over and above the set of characteristics that constitutes their present identity, each of them is also something else: constitutive of the activity of transforming their identity in light of new experiences. Their current identity, then, is only one aspect of that which they truly are—not "what we are right now," but "an aspect of what each of us is right now."

This kind of identity clearly cannot stand on its own. Because it is temporary and aspectual, it is understood to be a particular case of something more general—of the whole story of this group, a story which in part remains to be told. Dialectical identity is then understood to be dynamically related to something larger than itself: to the whole story of the group. It is merely one phase of that ongoing temporal dynamic. How, then, are we to understand that story as a whole? In fact, we cannot "understand" it because we do not know what its future components will be. The whole story, the entire dialectical identity, must be conceived of as a space which is only partially filled, and whose future contents are unknown. This means that dialectical identity cannot exclude its other, as essential identity can. Given any determinate other, future experiences may someday give our group characteristics which it shares with that other, so that a new identity—fully authentic for both groups—may come to characterize both. Nothing can be excluded from this identity, except the static nature of essentiality. Hence we must recognize that in the course of our unique history we may come to identify ourselves—in certain aspects—with any other group that experiences a sufficiently similar history. To have a history is, for Hegel, to be Spirit—to be human. And so the presently unfilled space of future identities can be understood as "universal humanity" itself.

Humanity so understood is not a present given, but an always future construct: it is the ultimate name for everything that *may* come to be identified with us in our history. Humanism of this sort is not an exclusionary game, for definitive exclusion can only be justified on the basis of permanent essence. Rather, as a dialectical process, it is an inherently inclusionary project.

It thus seems that any group with a dialectical identity must face the fact that it may lose its identity altogether, that its defining characteristics will come to be shared not just by the members of that group, but by all humankind. This is not necessarily the case, however, for even if my group—say, philosophy professors—eventually comes to lose all of its distinctive characteristics and to merge with a larger whole—say, intellectuals—our identity will not be entirely determined by that larger whole. Rather, it will include the story of how we philosophers came to identify ourselves with that larger set of intellectuals. Within that set, philosophers will not have any distinguishing characteristics; you will not be able to look at an intellectual and tell that she is a philosopher. What will distinguish her from other intellectuals will be only the story of how she came to be an intellectual. This will give philosophers a particular *trajectory* within that whole identity; having come into it by a particular route, they will enlarge it, and if they leave it, also by a particular route, they will diminish it as well. Being an intellectual—or being human—is thus, like all identities, a phase through which people pass, not a fixed or static identity.

There is another way in which humankind operates on the basis of dialectical identity. The strategies for coping with new experiences are, *to some degree*, proper to the group whose experiences they are. Catholics encountered the new technologies of birth control differently than did many Protestants, for example; those technologies had an impact on Catholicism that they did not have on other religions. But the ways in which that impact was gauged and determined were not entirely unique to Catholics. They involved practices of argumentation and decision-making which were not set out in advance by the religion because the new technologies themselves could not have been anticipated by Catholicism. Any unanticipated experience by the group, in other words, calls for the employment of strategies of integration that cannot be dictated in advance, let alone derived entirely from the present identity of the group. These strategies cannot, then, be immanent in the present identity of the group; they must come, like the experiences which call for them, from outside—from that empty space I am calling "humankind." On the most general level, these strategies for coping with the unanticipated—Hegel's *Logic* comprises, I believe, a set of them—belong to all of us rather than merely to any one group.

We can now see why it was that Hegel thought Jews should have civil rights as *Jews*. For to be a "Jew" (or anything else) is not to have a unique set of properties, but to have a history in the course of which various properties are added and subtracted at various times. And while this history may be unique and "particular" to a group's identity, it is also always in constant interplay with a larger history, ultimately that of unrealized humanity. Our *universal* rights, as humans, amount to the right to play our own role in the constitution of that larger history. But we can have such universal rights only by virtue of our particular identities, that is, only by virtue of the specific contribution that our past has readied us to make.

The moral of my presentation is that essential identities will ultimately be required, by their own conceptual incoherence in the face of the unpredictable nature of experience, to maintain themselves by exercising force against the very individuals whose identities they constitute. Dialectical identities, on the other hand, are not subject to this particular incoherence, for while they are based on a set of experiences, and an internalization of what is common to those experiences, they do not exclude the possibility that future experiences will subvert present identities. This concept of identity does not attempt to draw a distinction between the chaotic experiences that are the bases of one's identity and the equally chaotic experiences that are mere "illusory being." To the extent that my readers view these exclusions and attempted distinctions as defects, my presentation of dialectical identity gains critical force over and against that of essential identity: these readers will think that dialectical identity is the better sort to have.

On the other hand, dialectical identity brings with it a certain loss of security. For if it is nothing more than a series of transformations, the individuals and groups who adopt it as "their kind of identity" must face the fact that they may eventually cease to exist as distinct individuals in a distinct group. There is no other group with which they may not find themselves identified at some later stage, and this loss of separateness may be viewed, in the end, as a kind of communal death. Dialectical identity thus constitutes a mortal community. The only way to avoid the discomfort of this identity is to presume certain characteristics of such a community to be permanent and so beyond time itself: to embrace, once again and perhaps unwisely, essential identity. In which case, we philosophers (and other intellectuals) must accept, perhaps more wisely, the essential imputations of traditional critique.

Notes

1 I have argued that pragmatic justification in terms of "learning processes" is basic to Habermas's project; see John McCumber, *Poetic Interaction* (Chicago, 1989), 351–57. The issue of the pragmatic usefulness of any paradigm or project is always decided in advance, to some extent, because implicit to *any* paradigm is at least one sort of "pragmatic usefulness"—that of keeping its practitioners employed. A "pragmatic" justification of anything, it would seem, consists in a judgment of its relative usefulness vis-à-vis others of its kind—other beliefs, practices, or projects. But beliefs, practices, and projects—to stay with just these three—are very dif-

ferent sorts of things, so arguments about their usefulness will be correspondingly heterogeneous. The "practice" of critique, for example, would need to be measured against other practices to see if it is more deserving of resources than they. But against which "other practices"? Those of empirical research? Art? Religion? And do not these other practices also embody elements of "critique"? How can we justify allocating resources to critique without formulating a global overview of its relation to other practices that compete for our time and energy—indeed, to *all* such other practices? The ghost of Hegel, pragmatism's dark progenitor, is twitching already.

2   See Michel Foucault, "Intellectuals and Power," in *Language, Counter-Memory, Practice*, trans. D. F. Bouchard and S. Simon (Ithaca, 1977), 205–17; and Richard Rorty, "Postmodernist Bourgeois Liberalism," in *Objectivity, Relativism, and Truth* (Cambridge, 1991), 197–202.

3   Christa Bürger, "Modernity as Postmodernity: Lyotard," in *Modernity and Identity*, ed. Scott Lash and Jonathan Friedman (Oxford, 1992), 75.

4   See Max Horkheimer and Theodor W. Adorno, *Dialectics of Enlightenment*, trans. John Cumming (New York, 1972).

5   For a discussion of this, see John McCumber, *The Company of Words* (Evanston, 1993), 37ff.

6   A generation which itself, to be sure, comes about in accordance with a norm or standard, such as having no "lacunae or contradictions."

7   Cf. the remarkable *cris du coeur* of two "objects" of Habermassian critique, Derrida and Lyotard. Derrida complains that "Habermas goes on to intervene in, interpret, arbitrate, conclude my debate with Searle without making the slightest reference to my text"; Jacques Derrida, *Limited Inc.*, ed. Gerald Graff (Evanston, 1988), 156 n. 9. With similar bitterness, Lyotard writes of himself as one of those "thinkers . . . who have not had the honor of being read by Professor Habermas"; Jean-François Lyotard, *The Postmodern Explained*, trans. Don Barry et al. (Minneapolis, 1992), 4. Habermas, it appears, believed that he could criticize their authorial practices without addressing Derrida and Lyotard themselves as partners in a dialogue.

8   Capitalized terms are used in their strictly Hegelian senses.

9   See G. W. F. Hegel, *Phenomenology of Spirit*, trans. A. V. Miller (Cambridge, 1977), 337ff.

10 Ibid., 344.

11 Ibid.

12 Ibid., 350.

13 See McCumber, *Company of Words*, chap. 2, for an account of this.

14 This amounts to a direct leap to the end of the *Phenomenology*; ibid., 19n.

15 See McCumber, *Poetic Interaction*.

16 Emil Fackenheim, *Encounters between Judaism and Modern Philosophy* (New York, 1973), 126.

17 G. W. F. Hegel, *Science of Logic*, trans. A. V. Miller (New York, 1976), 389, 394, 390.

18 Ibid., 390.

19 Edward Said, *Orientalism* (New York, 1978).

20 The distinction between these two sorts of Essence is, perhaps, that between the "essence of woman" asserted by such Great White Males as Aristotle, Thomas Aquinas, and Hegel himself, and the "essence of woman" formulated and agreed upon by a group of women.

21 This denial of past and future in favor of the present—what postmodern thinkers like to call the "privileging" of the present—is a basic theme of Hegel's *Phenomenology*, for the "certainty" with which each stage of that book begins is precisely such a denial. In "certainty," consciousness is always sure that it has reached the Absolute—that it will not have to undergo any future transformations and that the future can therefore be just like the present. And consciousness can only do this, at each stage, by "forgetting" the past—the previous stages whose outcome it is, and which thus afford it precisely the kind of situated and temporary legitimacy against which Essence struggles in the *Logic*.

Immanuel Wallerstein

The Insurmountable Contradictions of Liberalism: Human Rights and the Rights of Peoples in the Geoculture of the Modern World–System

On 26 August 1789, the French National Assembly adopted the Declaration of the Rights of Man and the Citizen.[1] It has remained the symbolic assertion of what we today call human rights. It was in effect reaffirmed and updated in the Universal Declaration of Human Rights and adopted with few abstentions and no negative votes by the United Nations on 10 December 1948.[2] There was, however, no parallel emblematic assertion of the rights of "peoples" until 14 December 1960, when the United Nations adopted the Declaration on the Granting of Independence to Colonial Countries and Peoples.[3]

The Preamble to the 1789 Declaration opens by stating "that ignorance, neglect, and scorn of the rights of man are the sole causes of public misfortune and of the corruption of governments." It thus begins with the problem of ignorance, as befits a document of the Enlightenment, and the immediate implication is that once ignorance has been overcome, there will no longer be "public misfortune." Why did the French Revo-

The South Atlantic Quarterly 94:4, Fall 1995.
Copyright © 1995 by Duke University Press.
CCC 0038-2876/95/$1.50.

lution not produce a similar declaration on the rights of peoples? In fact, Abbé Grégoire did suggest to the Convention in 1793 that it seek to codify the laws relating to "the rights and reciprocal duties of nations, the rights of peoples [*gens*]." But Merlin de Douai argued that such a proposal "should not be addressed to the Convention of the French people, but rather to a general congress of the peoples of Europe,"[4] and this suggestion was tabled.

However pertinent the distinction may have been, there was of course no such "general congress" at that time. And when it did eventually emerge, more or less, first as the League of Nations and then as the United Nations, such a declaration was not immediately forthcoming. In 1945 the colonial powers, victorious in the war waged for their own freedom, were still not ready to admit the illegitimacy of colonialism. It was only in the 1960 Declaration, after much of the colonized world had already won its independence, that the United Nations, reaffirming its "faith in fundamental human rights, in the dignity and worth of the human person, in the equal rights of men and women and of nations large and small," therefore "solemnly proclaim[ed] the necessity of bringing to a speedy and unconditional end colonialism in all its forms and manifestations."

My focus here is neither on the debate over whether or not human rights, or the rights of peoples, are inscribed in natural law nor on the history of these ideas as intellectual constructs, but rather on their role as key elements in liberal ideology, insofar as that ideology became the geoculture of the modern world–system in the nineteenth and twentieth centuries. Moreover, as I will show, this geocultural construct is not only logically self-contradictory, but the insurmountable contradiction it presents is itself an essential part of the geoculture.

World–systems all have geocultures, although it may take some time for one to settle into place in a given historical system. I use the word "culture" here in the sense traditionally used by anthropologists, that is, as the set of values and basic rules which, both consciously and subconsciously, governs rewards within the system and creates a set of illusions that tends to persuade members of the system's legitimacy. There are always persons and groups within any world–system who reject the geocultural values in whole or in part, and who even struggle against them. But as long as most of the system's cadres accept these values actively, and as long as most of the ordinary people within the system are not overtly skeptical, the geoculture can be said to exist and its values to be prevailing.

Furthermore, it is important to distinguish between fundamental values, cosmology, and teleology, on the one hand, and the politics of implementing them, on the other. The fact that groups are in active political revolt does not necessarily mean that they do not subscribe, if only subconsciously, to the fundamental values, cosmology, and teleology of the system. It may just mean that they feel these values are not being implemented fairly. And finally, we must keep historical process in mind. Geocultures come into existence at one moment and, at a later moment, may cease to hold sway. In the case of the modern world–system, it seems to me that its geoculture emerged with the French Revolution and then began to lose its widespread acceptance with the world revolution of 1968. The capitalist world–economy has been operating since the long sixteenth century. It functioned for three centuries, however, without any firmly established geoculture. That is to say, from the sixteenth to the eighteenth century, no one set of values and basic rules prevailed within the capitalist world–economy, actively endorsed by the majority of the cadres and passively accepted by the majority of the ordinary people. The French Revolution, *latō sensō*, changed that. It established two new principles: (1) the normality of political change, and (2) the sovereignty of the people.[5] These principles quickly became so deeply rooted in popular consciousness that neither Thermidor nor Waterloo could dislodge them. As a result, the so-called Restoration in France (and indeed throughout the world–system) was at no point and in no sense a true restoration of the ancien régime.

The key point to note about these two principles is that they were, in and of themselves, quite revolutionary in their implications for the world–system. Far from ensuring the legitimacy of the capitalist world–economy, they threatened to delegitimate it in the long run. It is in this sense that I have argued elsewhere that "the French Revolution represented the first of the antisystemic revolutions of the capitalist world–economy—in small part a success, in larger part a failure."[6] It was therefore in order to contain these ideas, by drowning them in a larger whole, that the cadres of the world–system felt an urgent need to elaborate and impose a larger geoculture. The elaboration of this larger geoculture became the debate about ideologies. I am using the term "ideology" here in a quite specific sense. What we usually call the trinity of ideologies that developed in the nineteenth century—conservatism, liberalism, and socialism—represented, I believe, three responses to a single question: Given the widespread acceptance of the two concepts of the normality of change and the sovereignty of the people, what political program would be most likely to ensure the good society?

The answers to this question were extraordinarily simple. Conservatives, horrified by these concepts and basically abhorring them, were those who advocated the utmost caution in public action. Political changes, they said, should be enacted only when the claims in their favor were overwhelming, and even then the changes should be undertaken with the least possible disruption. As for popular sovereignty, they argued that it was most wisely utilized when power was effectively turned over to those who traditionally exercised it and who represented the wisdom of continuous tradition.

The opposite view was taken by the socialists (or radicals). They welcomed change and called upon the people to exercise their sovereignty fully and directly in the interest of maximizing the speed with which changes that would lead to a more egalitarian society could be effected.

The conservative and socialist positions were clear-cut and easy to understand: As slow versus as fast as possible! As much resistance to equalizing measures versus as much dismantling of inegalitarian structures as possible! The belief that very little real change is possible versus the belief that anything can be done—if only the existing (and purposeful) social obstacles are overcome! These are the familiar contours of Right versus Left, a pair of terms that were themselves derived directly from the French Revolution. But what then of liberalism, which claimed to stand opposed to conservatism on the one side and to socialism on the other? The answer was formally clear but substantively ambiguous. In formal terms, liberalism was the via media, or the "vital center" (to use a self-description of the twentieth century).[7] Neither too fast nor too slow, but change at just the right speed! In substantive terms, however, what did this mean? Here liberals could in fact seldom agree among themselves, not even those within the confines of a specific place at a specific time, and certainly not liberals of different places and different periods.

Consequently, what has defined liberalism as an ideology has not been the clarity of its program, but rather its emphasis on process. To be sure, liberals believed that political change was inevitable, but they also believed that it would lead to the good society only insofar as the process was rational, that is, if social decisions were the product of careful intellectual analysis. It was therefore crucial that the actual policies be conceived and implemented by those who had the greatest capacity for making such rational decisions, that is, by the technicians or specialists. It was they who could best elaborate the necessary reforms that could and would perfect the system in which they lived. For liberals were by definition not at all radical. They sought to perfect the system, not to transform it, because in their view the world of the nineteenth century was already the culmination of human progress—or, in a phrase that has recently been revived, "the end of history." If we are living in the last epoch of human history, then naturally our primary (indeed our only possible) task is to perfect the system, that is, to engage in rational reformism.

The three ideologies of modern times have been, then, three political strategies to cope with the popular beliefs that have dominated our modern world since 1789. What is most interesting about this trinity of ideologies is that, first, although all three were formally antistate, in practice they all worked to reinforce state structures; second, among the three, liberalism swiftly and clearly emerged triumphant, which can be seen from a pair of political developments. Over time, both conservatives and socialists moved their actual programs toward the liberal center rather than away from it. And it was the conservatives and the socialists, acting separately but in complementary ways, who were in fact largely responsible for implementing the liberal political program, far more so than the capital-L Liberals themselves. This is why, as liberal ideology triumphed, Liberal political parties tended to disappear.[8]

Within the framework of triumphant liberal ideology, what are human rights and on what basis are they claimed? While there have been diverse answers to this question, in general the answer for liberals has been that human rights inhere in natural law. Such an answer gives human rights a powerful base with which to resist opposing claims. However, once this has been asserted and a specific list of human rights enumerated, many questions still remain open: Who has the moral (and legal) right to enumerate these rights? If one set of rights conflicts with another set, which set prevails, and who decides this? Are rights absolute or are they limited by some rational appreciation of the consequences of their exercise? (This last dilemma is reflected in the famous declaration by Justice Oliver Wendell Holmes that freedom of speech does not include the right to shout "Fire!" in a crowded theater.) And above all, who has the right to exercise human rights?

The last question may seem surprising, for is it not obvious that the correct answer is *everyone*? Not at all. In fact, absolutely no one has ever said this. For example, it is almost universally agreed that an infant does not have these rights, or at least not all of them, on the obvious grounds that an infant does not have the mental capacity to exercise them wisely, if at all, for himself or others. But if we agree about infants, then what about, successively, the senile aged, small children, sociopaths, or felons? And from there the list may be extended ad infinitum: What about the young, the neurotic, the soldiers, the aliens, the uneducated, the poor, the women? Where is the self-evident line that distinguishes capacity from incapacity? There is, of course, no such self-evident line, and surely not one that can be deduced from natural law. Thus it is that the definition of the persons to whom these human rights apply is inevitably a recurrent—and always current—political question.

The question of who has human rights is closely connected with the issue of who may claim to exercise the rights of the people. And here another concept deriving from the French Revolution enters the picture, namely, the citizen. For those who were most clearly authorized to exercise the sovereignty of the people were the "citizens." But who were the "citizens"? Although no doubt meant to be a group larger than the "king" or the "nobility" or even "persons of property," this group was also far smaller than "everyone" or even "everyone resident within the geographic bounds of a given sovereign state."

And therein lies a tale. Over whom is a sovereign's authority exercised? Within the feudal system, authority was parcellized among several overlords, none of whom could therefore count on undisputed authority over his subjects. The modern world–system created a legal and moral structure that was radically different, one in which the sovereign states, located within and constrained by an interstate system, asserted *exclusive* jurisdiction over all persons falling within their territory. Furthermore, all these territories were bounded geographically, that is, by surveyors' measurements, and were thus rendered distinct from other territories; in addition, no area within the interstate system was left unassigned to some particular state. Thus when "subjects" were transformed into "citizens," the current inhabitants of an area were immediately divided into "citizens" and "noncitizens" (or aliens). Aliens came in many guises, ranging from long-term (even lifelong) migrants, at one extreme, to visitors passing through, at the other. But in no case were such aliens considered citizens. On the other hand, since the early nineteenth-century states were congeries of "regions" and "localities," the actual citizens, however defined, were themselves usually representative of quite varied backgrounds, with different languages, different customs, and different historical memories. Once subjects became citizens, these citizens in turn had to be actively transformed into "nationals," that is, persons whose loyalty to their state would take priority over other social loyalties. This transformation was not easy, but it was essential if the exercise of popular sovereignty were not to result in presumably irrational intergroup conflict.

Hence while such states as Great Britain, France, and the United States were fostering a sense of nationalism amongst their citizens,[9] pre-state nationalists in other places, such as Germany and Italy, were struggling to create states that would foster such nationalism. Two institutions were given the main responsibility of promoting such a sense of national identity in most nineteenth-century states: the primary schools and the army. Those countries that accomplished this task best flourished the most. As William McNeill notes:

Under these circumstances, the fiction of ethnic uniformity within separate national jurisdictions took root in recent centuries, as some of the leading nations of Europe harked back to suitably idealized and arbitrarily selected barbarian predecessors. (It is surely amusing to note that the French and British chose Gauls and Britons as their putative national ancestors, in cheerful disregard of subsequent conquerors and invaders from whom they inherited their respective national languages.) The fiction of ethnic uniformity flourished, especially after 1789, when the practical advantages of a neo-barbarian polity in which all adult males, trained to the use of arms, united by a sense of national solidarity, and willingly obedient to chosen leaders, demonstrated its power against governments that limited their mobilization for war to smaller segments of the population.[10]

If you reflect upon it, neither primary schools nor armies have been notorious in their practice of human rights. They are both top-down, quite authoritarian structures. Transforming ordinary people into citizen–voters and citizen–soldiers may be very effective ways of ensuring state cohesion, both vis-à-vis other states and in terms of minimizing internal civil violence or class struggle, but what does it really do for the promotion and realization of human rights?

The political project of nineteenth-century liberalism in the core countries of the capitalist world–economy was to tame the "dangerous classes" by offering a triple program of rational reform: suffrage, the welfare state, and national identity. The hope or assumption was that ordinary people would be content with this limited devolution of reward and would therefore not press for full recognition of their "human rights." The propagation of such slogans as "human rights" or "freedom" or "democracy" was itself part of the process of taming the "dangerous classes." The thinness of the social concessions made to these classes might have become more salient if not for two factors: the overall living standards of the core countries were benefiting from the effective transfer of surplus from the peripheral zones; and the local nationalism of each of these states was complemented by the collective nationalism of the "civilized" nations vis-à-vis the "barbarians." Today, we call this racism, a doctrine explicitly codified during just this period in just these states and one which came to permeate all social institutions and all public discourse profoundly. At least, that is, until the Nazis brought racism to its logical conclusion, its ne plus ultra, and thereby shamed the Western world into a formal, but only partial, theoretical repudiation of racism.

Who were the "barbarians"? The colonial peoples, to be sure; to Whites, the Blacks and Yellows; to the West, the East; to the "historic" nations of Western Europe, the "nonhistoric" nations of Eastern Europe; to the Christians, the Jews. From the beginning, the human rights of "civilized" nations were predicated on the assumption that they were indeed "civilized." The discourse of imperialism was the other side of the coin. The duty of the countries that claimed to respect human rights was therefore to "civilize" those that did not—those with "barbarous" customs that made it necessary to take them in tow and teach them, as children might be taught. It followed that any "rights of peoples" were reserved to a few specific peoples and were by no means the rights of all the other peoples. Indeed, granting "barbarians" their rights as peoples was thought to result in the effective denial of the "human rights" of their peoples. The two sets of rights were therefore placed in direct conflict with one another in the nineteenth century; there was no way that the world could have both.

———

Liberalism in the nineteenth century solved the problem it had set out to solve. Given a world–system in which the doctrines of the normality of change and the sovereignty of the people had come to prevail, how could an upper stratum of men of reason, goodwill, competence, and property keep the "dangerous classes" from upsetting the applecart? Liberalism's answer to this question had been rational reforms—in appropriate doses. In practice, this meant strictly limiting the group of those who could exercise their human rights to *some* of the people as well as limiting the peoples who could exercise sovereignty at all *even more strictly*. Since, however, in the logic of liberalism, these rights were theoretically universal, limiting them had to be justified on convoluted grounds and speciously. In theory, then, the rights were asserted to be universal, but the last thing liberals wanted was for these liberal principles to be taken literally, that is, to be truly applied universally. In order to avoid any literal interpretation of these principles, liberalism needed a constraining force. That force was racism, combined with sexism. But, of course, this could never be avowed by liberals, since both racism and sexism were by definition anti-universal and antiliberal. Edward Said captured the spirit of this second face of liberalism and its consequences in *Orientalism*:

> Along with other peoples variously designated as backward, degenerate, uncivilized, and retarded, the Orientals were viewed in a framework constructed out of biological determinism and moral-political admonishment. The Oriental was linked thus to elements in Western society (delinquents, the insane, women, the poor) having in common an identity best described as lamentably alien. Orientals were rarely seen or looked at; they were seen through, analyzed not as citizens, or even people, but as problems to be solved or confined or, as the colonial powers openly coveted their territory, taken over.
>
> . . . .
>
> My point is that the metamorphosis of a relatively innocuous philological subspecialty [Orientalism] into a capacity for managing political movements, administering colonies, making nearly apocalyptic statements representing the White Man's difficult civilizing mission, all this is something at work within a purportedly liberal culture, one full of concern for its vaunted norms of catholicity, plurality, and open-mindedness. In fact, what took place was the very opposite of liberal: the hardening of doctrine and meaning, imparted by "science," into "truth." For if such truth reserved for itself the right to judge the Orient as immutably Oriental in the ways I have indicated, then liberality was no more than a form of oppression and mentalistic prejudice.[11]

What happened in the twentieth century was that those oppressed by racism and sexism insisted on claiming the rights which liberals had said that they theoretically had, in the form of both human rights and rights of peoples. The First World War marked a political caesura,

1914 - 1945 → legitimacy of rights
new of people +
national liberation

Liberalism in the Modern World–System   **1171**

and the subsequent breakdown of order among the core states (the "thirty years war" from 1914 to 1945) created an opening for the new movements. Since the most immediate problem on the world scene was colonialism/imperialism, that is, the juridical control of large parts of Asia, Africa, and the Caribbean by European states (but also by the United States and Japan), the most immediate claim was for the rights of peoples, not for human rights. The legitimacy of this demand was recognized most spectacularly by Woodrow Wilson when he made the theme of the "self-determination of nations" the centerpiece of global liberalism. Of course, Wilson intended self-determination to be doled out judiciously, methodically, rationally, when nations were ready. Until then, these nations could be held "in trust" (to use the language of the U.N. Charter of 1945).

Conservatives tended to be even more cautious than liberals, as might be expected, and to consider that any such "readiness" was likely to be attained only in the far distant future, if ever. Conservatives often fell back on the theme of human rights to argue against the rights of peoples during the first half of the twentieth century. They argued that these colonized populations were not true "peoples," but simply congeries of individuals whose human rights might be recognized when an individual had acquired sufficient education and had adopted a sufficiently Western lifestyle to have shown himself— rarely herself—to be a "civilized person." This was the logic of the formal assimilationist doctrines of a number of colonial powers (e.g., France, Belgium, and Portugal), but the others also practiced a similar, though informal, mode of categorization and of doling out human rights.

Those socialists who were radically antisystemic and antiliberal at the time of the First World War, namely, the Bolsheviks (or Leninists) and the Third International, were initially quite suspicious of all the talk about the rights of peoples, which they associated with European, middle-class, nationalist movements. For a long time, they had been openly hostile to the concept. Then, rather suddenly in 1920, they shifted course quite radically. At the Baku Congress of the Peoples of the East,[12] the tactical priority of the class struggle within Europe/North America was quietly shelved and a new tactical priority, anti-imperialism, was declared. The Third International hoped to build a political alliance on the basis of anti-imperialism between mainly European Communist parties and at least the more radical national liberation movements of Asia (and of other peripheral zones). But, by making anti-imperialism their new priority, the Leninists were in fact joining the liberals in their pursuit of the Wilsonian agenda of the self-determination of nations. And when, after the Second World War, the USSR pursued an active policy of fostering "socialist construction" in a series of countries that were politically linked to it more or less closely, the USSR was de facto pursuing the world liberal agenda of the economic development of underdeveloped countries.

Hence, we can say that between 1945 and 1970, liberalism had a second apotheosis. If, in the decades just prior to 1914, liberalism had seemed to triumph in Europe, from 1945 to 1970 it seemed to triumph throughout the world. The United States, world spokesman for liberalism, was the hegemonic power. Its only theoretical opponent, the USSR, was pursuing a substantively similar tactical agenda, at least in terms of the rights of peoples. The USSR was thereby effectively assisting the United States in taming the "dangerous classes" of the world–system. Furthermore, this liberal policy seemed to be actually paying off for these classes. The national liberation movements had come or were coming to power throughout the third world. And they seemed to have achieved power (at least partial power) elsewhere as well, that is, not only via Communist regimes in the Soviet bloc, but also through the strong role played by Social-Democratic parties in Western Europe and in the White Commonwealth nations. And, as part of the incredibly rapid global economic expansion that occurred between 1945 and 1970, the growth rates in virtually all peripheral countries were reasonably high. These were years of optimism, even where (as in Vietnam) the struggle seemed quite ferocious and destructive.

Looking back on what seems in retrospect to have been almost a Golden Age, what is striking is the absence from that period of any concern for human rights, which were conspicuous by their absence or diminished role everywhere. From the purge trials in Eastern Europe to various forms of dictatorship in third world countries—but also, let us not forget, from McCarthyism in the United States to the *Berufsverbot* in the Federal Republic of Germany—it was scarcely an era of triumph for human rights. But more significantly, it was not a period in which there was even much rhetorical attention paid to human rights by the world's political movements. Advocates of human rights causes everywhere were seen as threatening national unity in the Cold War struggle. And there was no greater degree of observance of human rights among those third world states most closely linked to the West than among those most closely linked to the Soviet bloc. Furthermore, U. S./Soviet-expressed concern with human rights in each other's sphere was limited to propaganda broadcasts and had no serious impact on actual policy.

What has happened since then? Two things, principally: the annunciatory and denunciatory world revolution of 1968, which challenged the liberal geoculture; and the mounting evidence, beginning in the 1970s, that the liberal package of rights concessions was empty. In 1968, the students and their allies in the Western countries, the Communist bloc, and the peripheral zones were charging that liberal ideology (including the verbally distinct but substantively similar Soviet variant) consisted of a set of fraudulent promises and that the reality for the great majority of the world's population was largely negative. Of course, the revolutionaries, wherever they were, tended to address the specifics of their countries, which varied between, say, the United States and Germany, Czechoslovakia and China, Mexico and Portugal, or India and Japan, but the same themes recurred.[13]

The world revolution of 1968 did not dismantle the world–system. Far from it. But it did dislodge liberalism from its place as the defining ideology of the world–system. Both conservatism and radicalism moved away from the liberal center and more or less back to their relative topographies of the first half of the nineteenth century, thereby upsetting the delicate balance that liberalism had sought to maintain by limiting the revolutionary implications of human rights and the rights of peoples. How much this balance was upset is evident from the impact of the second major change, the socioeconomic structuring of the world–system. Since circa 1967/1973, the world–economy has been in a Kondratieff B–phase, a period of stagnation. This stagnation has effectively nullified the economic gains of most peripheral zones, with the exception of an East Asian corner which has been the locus for the kind of production relocation to a limited segment of the world–economy that is a normal feature of Kondratieff B–periods. It has also resulted in various rates of decline in the real income of the working classes of the North. The bloom is off the rose. And the enormity of the deception has become visible. The hoped-for steady, orderly improvement of life prospects held out by world liberal forces (and their de facto ally, the world Communist movement) has not been realized, and, as hope was lost, questions about the degree to which the rights of peoples had in fact been meaningfully achieved were raised by the presumed beneficiaries themselves.

This questioning of the meaningfulness of what had previously been considered the successful achievement of the rights of peoples in the post-1945 era had two political consequences. On the one hand, many groups and individuals began to champion the rights of new "peoples," some perhaps because they thought that the rights of their "people" had not been recognized. Hence new and more militant ethnicities, secessionist movements, and demands by "minority" peoples within existing states arose, which corresponded to claims made for or by other groups or quasi-peoples, such as women, gays and lesbians, the disabled, and the aged. On the other hand, questions were raised about the rationale of suppressing concern for human rights in order to achieve the rights of peoples, given that the emphasis on peoples' rights had not paid off. As a result, within the Soviet bloc and within third world one-party states or military dictatorships, there was a sudden upsurge in demands for the immediate implementation of human rights (i.e., the so-called democratization movement). Within the Western world, this was also a time for dismantling structures that had seriously limited the expression of human rights as well as a time for creating new rights, such as the "right to privacy" in the United States.

Furthermore, not only did everyone seem to start talking about human rights in their own countries, but they also started expressing concern about other countries' policies: President Carter's proclamation of human rights as a U.S. foreign policy matter, the Helsinki Accords, the spread of such movements as Amnesty International and Médecins du Monde, and the willingness of intellectuals in the third world to discuss human rights as a general issue, indeed as a priority issue, all testified to this resurgence of concern.

The two movements of the last ten to twenty years—the search for new "peoples" whose rights needed to be affirmed, and the intensified demands for or concern with "human rights"—were both reactions to the perceived deceptions of the post-1945 era, culminating in the world revolution of 1968. This revolution had centered precisely on the theme of the false hopes generated by global liberalism and the nefarious motives behind its program of rational reformism. The two responses seemed at first to be a single one, with the same people who were asserting the rights of the "new" peoples also demanding human rights. However, by the late 1980s, and particularly with the geopolitical upheaval of the erstwhile U.S. hegemonic system marked by the collapse of the Communisms, what seemed like a single movement began to divide into two separate, even opposite, movements. By the early 1990s, there were distinct movements to counter (once again) the rights of the "new" peoples by using the theme of human rights. An obvious example was the U.S. neo-conservative/anti-PC campaign, but just as salient in this regard was the proclamation by Médecins du Monde and allied French intellectuals of the *droit d'ingérance*[14] (the right to interfere)—to interfere, that is, in Bosnia and Somalia today, in China and Iran tomorrow, and (why not?) in Black-dominated U.S. municipal governments the day after tomorrow.

Liberalism today is cornered by its own logic. It continues to assert the legitimacy of human rights and, a bit less loudly, the rights of peoples. It still doesn't mean it. These rights are asserted in order to *avoid* their full implementation. But this is getting more difficult to avoid. And liberals, caught, as they say, between a rock and a hard place, are showing their true colors by transforming themselves into conservatives, even occasionally into radicals.

Let us take a simple, very important, and immediately relevant issue: migration. The political economy of the migration issue is extremely simple. The world–economy is more polarized than ever, both socioeconomically and demographically. The yawning gap between North and South shows every sign of widening in the next few decades. As a consequence, there is obviously a great South–North migratory pressure. Now, let us look at this from the perspective of liberal ideology. The concept of human rights obviously includes the right to move about. In the logic of liberalism, there should be no passports or visas. Everyone should be allowed to work or to settle anywhere, as is the case, for example, in the United States and in most sovereign states today, certainly in any with pretensions to being a liberal state.

In practice, of course, most people in the North are literally aghast at the idea of open frontiers. The political shifts of the last twenty-five years have been in exactly the opposite direction to liberalism. The United Kingdom was an early erector of new barriers against its erstwhile colonial subjects, but in 1993 alone similar barriers were erected in three other northern countries. The German Parliament severely curtailed its open-door policy toward "refugees"—just when the peoples of Eastern Europe could actually emigrate. (It was a good show to denounce the evil Communists for not letting their peoples go, but now we are seeing what happens when these evil Communists are no longer in power and in a position to restrict emigration.) In France, the government has passed laws which not only limit immigration from former French colonies, but even make it more difficult for children born of immigrants in France to become citizens. And in the United States, the governor of California, the largest state and one that, significantly, anticipates having a non-White majority soon, called for amending the U.S. Constitution to end one of our most revered traditions, the *jus soli* that endows anyone born on U.S. soil with U.S. citizenship.

What was the justification for these actions by the United Kingdom, Germany, France, and the United States? That we (the North) could not assume the burdens (i.e., the economic burdens) of the whole world. Well, why not? Only a century ago, the North was assuming the "White Man's burden" of a "civilizing mission" among the barbarians. Now the barbarians (the "dangerous classes") are saying: Thank you very much, but forget about civilizing us; just let us have some human rights—the right to move about freely, say, and to take jobs where we can find them.

The self-contradiction of liberal ideology is total. If all humans have equal rights, and all peoples have equal rights, then we cannot maintain the kind of inegalitarian system that the capitalist world–

economy has been and always will be. But if this is openly admitted, then the capitalist world–economy will have no legitimacy in the eyes of the "dangerous" (i.e., the dispossessed) classes. And if this system has no legitimacy, it will not survive. The crisis is total; the dilemma is total. We shall live out its consequences in the next half-century. However we collectively resolve this crisis, whatever kind of new historical system we build and whether it is better or worse, whether we have more or fewer human rights and more or fewer rights of peoples, one thing is certain: it will not be a system based on liberal ideology as we have known it for two centuries now.

Notes

1   For a discussion of the debates surrounding the adoption of this text, see Marcel Gauchet, "Rights of Man," in *A Critical Dictionary of the French Revolution*, ed. F. Furet and M. Ozouf (Cambridge, MA, 1989), 818–28. For the original text, see "Droits des gens," in *Histoire et dictionnaire de la Révolution française, 1789–1799*, ed. J. Tulard et al. (Paris, 1987), 770–71. The English text is reprinted (without the Preamble) in *Basic Documents on Human Rights*, ed. I. Brownlie (Oxford, 1971), 8–10.

2   United Nations General Assembly Resolution 217A (III), 1948.

3   United Nations General Assembly Resolution 1514 (XV), 1960. On the development of a "decolonization norm" in the post-1945 world–system, see the brief comments of G. Goertz and P. F. Diehl, "Towards a Theory of International Norms," *Journal of Conflict Resolution* 26 (1992): 648–51.

4   Tulard et al., eds., "Droit des gens," 770.

5   I have elaborated this argument elsewhere; on the normality of political change, see Immanuel Wallerstein, "The French Revolution as a World-Historical Event," in *Unthinking Social Science* (Cambridge, 1991), 7–22; on the sovereignty of the people, see Immanuel Wallerstein, "Liberalism and the Legitimation of Nation States: An Historical Interpretation," *Social Justice* 19 (1992): 22–33.

6   Immanuel Wallerstein, *The Modern World–System, Vol. 3, The Second Era of Great Expansion of the Capitalist World–Economy, 1730–1840s* (San Diego, 1989), 52.

7   See Arthur Schlesinger, Jr., *The Vital Center: The Politics of Freedom* (Boston, 1949).

8   I have developed these themes, too, at length elsewhere, but only summarize them briefly here in the context of the role of human rights and the rights of peoples as ideas in the politics of the modern world; see Immanuel Wallerstein, "Trois idéologies ou une seule? La Problématique de la modernité," *Genèses*, No. 9 (1992): 7–24.

9   The literature is voluminous. For a sample, see *Patriotism: The Making and Un-*

making of British National Identity, 3 vols., ed. Raphael Samuel (London, 1989);
Eugen Weber, *Peasants into Frenchmen: The Modernization of Rural France, 1870–
1914* (Stanford, 1976); and Seymour Martin Lipset, *The First New Nation: The
United States in Historical and Comparative Perspective* (New York, 1963).

10 William McNeill, "Introductory Historical Commentary," in *The Fall of Great
Powers: Peace, Stability, and Legitimacy*, ed. Geir Lundestad (Oslo, 1994), 3–21.

11 Edward Said, *Orientalism* (New York, 1978), 207, 254.

12 See *The Congress of the Peoples of the East*, ed. and trans. Brian Pearce (London, 1977).

13 For a discussion of six main theses that were common to all or almost all of
the events, see Immanuel Wallerstein, "1968, Revolution in the World–System,"
in *Geopolitics and Geoculture: Essays on the Changing World–System* (Cambridge,
1991), 65–83.

14 Indeed, as of 1993, Médecins du Monde was publishing a political journal entitled
Ingérances: Le Désir d'Humanitaire.

Kenneth Surin

On Producing the Concept
of a Global Culture

> Tears: a global enterprise.
> —John Cage, *A Year from Monday*, 1969

> When intuitionism opposed axiomatics, it was not only in the name of intuition, of construction and creation, but also in the name of a calculus of problems, a problematic conception of science that was not less abstract but implied an entirely different abstract machine, one working in the undecidable and the fugitive. It is the real characteristics of axiomatics that lead us to say that capitalism and present-day politics are an axiomatic in the literal sense. But it is precisely for this reason that nothing is played out in advance.
> —Gilles Deleuze and Félix Guattari, *A Thousand Plateaus: Capitalism and Schizophrenia*, 1987

I want to begin by making a few remarks, or rather declarations, that have a somewhat indirect bearing on what I hope will unfold as the primary concerns of this paper.

First, it has become a commonplace of this culture that we are now living in a time that has witnessed, and is continuing to witness, the exponential growth not just in our theo-

The *South Atlantic Quarterly* 94:4, Fall 1995.
Copyright © 1995 by Duke University Press.
CCC 0038-2876/95/$1.50.

ries, but also in social life, of new modes of transformation, movement, and coexistence or convergence. Equally novel and distinctive subjectivities and potentialities have emerged as part of this development. This time has also seen the proliferation of new kinds of knowledge, "knowledges" which accord central and decisive roles to notions like "arrangement" or "apparatus" (perhaps more familiar to us as the French *agencement* and *dispositif*, respectively) and "interest" and "importance," rather than appealing to such traditional epistemological categories as the true, the false, the erroneous, and so forth.[1] "Knowledges" whose decisive mark is that they make no appeal to an unquestionable *arche* or beginning point because we (i.e., the so-far unspecified metatheorists of these knowledges—but more about the impetus to metatheory in a moment) regard them as the productions of what is in the end an irreducible fabulation (or what Nietzsche called "the power of the false").[2]

A particularly significant development here has been the creation of "nonstandard" logics and topologies of change and relations, typically formulated for contexts which have the character of the arbitrary, the irregular, the aleatory, and so on. These new logics and topologies deal not only with the structuration of change and process, but also, perhaps more significantly, with textures, surfaces, meshings, rhythms, and their fractalized characters. We may indeed be living in an age that is seeing the invention of a new kind of Baroque (as Gilles Deleuze has pointed out[3]), a Baroque not just of countless radical proliferations that have cumulatively brought about a recasting of the human sensorium and issued in yet another elaboration of our sensibilities, but also one in which these new logics and topologies are generating forms of integration that enable quite different mechanisms to function in concert. Computer and information technologies, manufacturing, the nervous system, speech and semiosis—domains hitherto constituted on the basis of separate and even incommensurate lexicons and logics—are now being orchestrated in terms of a language that renders them isomorphic, fundamentally "harmonious." (The "cyberspaces" of the fictions of William Gibson and Bruce Sterling in many ways constitute an apotheosis of the integrations or concerts that have been formed between hitherto disparate materials and mediums: it does not require too great a leap of imagination for the reader of such works to see that their "cyberspaces" have striking and exemplary affinities with "the fold" that Deleuze takes to be the defining feature of the Baroque.[4])

Second, these new logics, topologies, and epistemologies seem to coalesce around a principle that has increasingly come to pervade and define intellectual production in this culture: the notion, rapidly becoming axiomatic, that it is not enough (whatever *that* may entail or imply) to have theories capable of integrating highly diverse ranges of phenomena, but that it is now also necessary for us to seek higher-order theories which, among other things, are able to narrate the places and functions of their "basal" or first-order counterparts. It would seem that theories at this time have a built-in propensity for this or that form of metatheoretical supplementation, one which typically comes in versions of another kind of theory (usually called a "genealogy," an "archaeology," or a "logic of [theoretical] practice") that tells the story of our lower-order theories or stories. In this way the lower-order theories come to be endowed with a much desired and even necessary reflexivity. It is not sufficient (to mention an example I will return to later) for someone (Michel Foucault, in this particular case) to come along and delineate the conditions which subtend the various states and forms of visibility (as Foucault does in *Les Mots et les Choses*); there must also be an associated theory of the "knowledges" that this or that kind of "knower" could have of the conditions in question (what readers of Foucault have come to know as the theory—well, his theory—of the *episteme* as such). It is hard to know how one can go about providing a full-blown metatheoretical elaboration of this kind for the concept of a global culture, but it seems just as hard to deny that "the spirit of the age" calls for precisely this moment of reflexivity, this advertence to a self-consciously produced image of thought, in our theoretical undertakings. I need to let myself off the hook here, so let me say that although I cannot provide this desired metatheoretical gloss in these pages, it should be obvious from my references where I would be inclined to look for "metatheory" should I feel the pressure of needing to find some.

Third, and there is sometimes a place and time for such confessions, what is said here reflects, however problematically or inappropriately, my alignment with a practical and intellectual tradition that can suitably be called a political materialism. And, as Perry Anderson, Samir Amin, and others have reminded us, it is one of the basic axioms of such a materialism (which they prefer to call a "historical materialism") that the struggles between classes (struggles that are in the end inextricably bound up with the constitutive antagonism between labor and capital) are finally to be resolved at the political, and not the economic or cultural, level of what is now a worldwide system of production and accumulation.[5]

Fourth, regardless of the considerable and maybe even intractable difficulties that attend the project of describing and analyzing them, there are connections in principle to be made between what is called globalization or global development and the current configurations of the capitalist world–system.

Fifth, and this seems to me to be virtually a truism, the task of characterizing the relationships between globalization and the current dispositions of the capitalist world–system involves in whatever way or ways the production of the concept of a global culture. This concept is of course widely and generally available to us these days— it has an undeniable currency as what some call a discursive "object." When I talk about the production or invention of the concept of a global culture, however, I am not "positing" this concept as ("merely") an alternative to these available discursive forms—an alternative that you or I might perhaps find impressive because it happens to be new or different or tantalizing or whatever when compared to the usages already in circulation. Let me elaborate by saying something about conceptual practice.

A theory of culture is something which is produced or created no less than its putative object. It is a practice, just as cultures are multilinear ensembles of practices. A theory, to be more specific, is a practice of concepts. A theory of culture, in this case global culture, is not "about" culture/global culture, but about the concepts that culture generates, concepts that are themselves related in more or less complex ways to other concepts associated with other practices, and so on. A theory of culture does not impinge directly on culture, but on the concepts of culture, which are no less practical, actual, or effective than culture itself. (This is simply another means of registering in a way that is as unavoidable as it is problematic that scarcely deniable effectivity of "thought" with which the "idealist" philosophical traditions have always been impressed, but which their "materialist" counterparts have tended to find embarrassing or insusceptible of adequate description and analysis or else reducible in principle to something more fundamental and compelling, namely, "matter.") Culture's concepts are not given in the assemblages of practices that constitute it, and yet they are culture's concepts, not theories about culture. Every culture generates for itself its own "thinkability" (and concomitantly its own "unthinkability" as the obverse of this very "thinkability"), and its concepts are constitutive of that "thinkability." Another way of making this point would be to say that a culture has to secrete its myriad expressivities precisely in order to be what it is and that its concepts—in ways that are inevitably selective, limiting, and even arbitrary—are the thematizations or representations of these expressivities. Or, more generally, the concepts of a culture are its expressivities rendered in the form of that culture's "thinkability."

Theories of culture, by contrast, are theories produced by reflection on the natures, functions, and so on, of these expressivities. They operate on a culture's "thinkability." It is fine and salutary to ask the question "What is culture?" but there is another kind of question to be asked as well, in this case, "What is (a) theory (of culture)?" Culture itself is an immensely varied and complex practice of signs and images, whose theory philosophers of culture and others must produce, but produce precisely as conceptual practice. No theoretical determination, no matter how subtle or thorough, can on its own constitute the concepts of culture. As indicated, these concepts are expressed in advance and independently of theoretical practice. Theorists, qua theorists, can only create or traffic in theories of culture.

The concepts that theorists deal with can function in more than one field of thought, and even in a single domain it is always possible for a concept to fulfill more than one function. Each field of thought is of course defined by its own internal variables, variables which have a complex relation to their external counterparts (such as historical periods, political and social conditions and forces, even the sheer physical states of things). (It is tempting here to understand this complexity in terms that are akin to Althusser's sense of the "overdetermined" relation between formations.) It follows that a concept comes into being or ceases to be effective only when there is a change of function and/or field. Functions for concepts must be created or abolished for them to be generated or eliminated, and new fields must be brought into being in order for concepts to be rendered irrelevant or invalid.

I am not of course saying anything really new here—Foucault's *Les Mots et les Choses* contains a now famous account of visibility that conforms in outline to my somewhat perfunctory descriptions of function and field. There, Foucault discredits the age-old conception of visibility as something that has its origin in a general/generative source of light which casts itself upon and thereby "illuminates" pre-existing objects. For Foucault, visibility is determined by an apparatus (*dispositif*) that has its own particular way of structuring light, determining the way in which it falls, spreads, and obscures; an apparatus that demarcates the visible from the invisible, in this way bringing into being whole ranges of objects with this or that mode of visibility as their condition of possibility; an apparatus or scopic regime that also causes objects to be wholly or partially effaced, hidden. Hence even something so taken for granted and innocuous as the very visibility of things is created by an apparatus or regime, in this case a scopic regime, which provides "rules" that govern the very existence and operating conditions of visibility. (And these conditions, as Foucault himself never tired of pointing out, are always "political.") It seems obvious that the concept of culture—of a global culture, in this case—likewise conforms to such "rules" for the generation and perpetuation of concepts.[6]

Turning now to some of the primary external variables of the field in which the concept of a global culture is to be produced, as I have already suggested, there are connections in principle to be made between the phenomenon of globalization or global development and the world–system instituted by the current regimes of capitalist accumulation.[7] Capitalism today is becoming more abstract, more algorithmic, because only in this way can it ensure that every and any kind of production—even that of a precapitalist variety—is mediated by it and made to serve accumulation. This latest phase of capitalist development has been "theorized" under a variety of now familiar labels (by Ernest Mandel, Immanuel Wallerstein, David Harvey, Toni Negri, the members of the regulation school, and others): "late capitalism," "advanced capitalism," "disorganized capitalism," "globalized capitalism," "post-Fordism," and so on. The transition to this phase has been marked in a number of registers: the creation of an international division of labor, the rise of an international debt economy, the modulation of capital into the structures of transnational corporations, the introduction of flexible manufacturing systems and labor processes, the growth of decentralized and informal economies, the exponential growth (especially in the economies of the peripheral and semiperipheral nations) of standardized markets and patterns of consumption, the development of complex securities and credit systems, the inauguration of a new semiotics of value, and so forth.

In this new regime of accumulation, production—in the nineteenth-century sense of an activity that typically requires the factory's functioning as a "disciplinary" space of enclosure or concentration owned and regimented by the capitalist (interestingly, the term "magnate," once so easily applied to the Morgans, Carnegies, and Vanderbilts of this world, now has an increasingly quaint flavor)—is effectively (though not entirely) relegated to the peripheral and semiperipheral nations. What takes place in the capitalist centers today is something quite different, a kind of production that is akin to a production of production, a higher-order or metaproduction, with markets that deal not so much in goods or merchandise (a word that now parallels "magnate" in its fall into desuetude) as in stocks, services, and instruments for the telematic orchestration of images and spectacles. The domain in which these orchestrations take place is of course culture.

In this most recent phase of capitalist development, even exchange is effectively metaphorized—in systems of exchange like the futures market what is exchanged is generated by the projections (in something akin to the psychoanalytic sense) of those who happen to participate in such markets. The generative principle of the junk bond, for instance, is that nothing really need "change hands"; the mere "idea" or emblematic coding of a "change of hands" is all that is needed to ensure, to fabricate, commerce in such bonds. Except for the fact that the one and not the other happens to be a unit in an "actually existing" system of exchange, there is no ontologically marked difference between a unicorn (say) and a junk bond or a "hypothetical" currency like the Eurodollar, which does not circulate at all. Marx did of course perceive that the "mystery" of exchange had its roots in something ineluctably metaphorical—the establishing of an abstract equivalence between two unlike things being precisely and irreducibly metaphoric, as he pointed out. But nowadays even the notion of an "exchange" has become pervasively allegorized. Where Marx had seen the movement of metaphorization as the instituting condition for the somehow "real" movements of exchange, today it is this movement—exchange—that has itself become metaphorized. In Marx's scheme, metaphorization operates through the commodity principle, which uses "value" (expressed or embodied by money) as a way of establishing the abstract equivalence that can then function as the basis of exchange. Today, however, the difference between the commodity and the noncommodity has been effectively erased not because there are no more commodities, but (quite the reverse!) because in our time everything has become "commodity." "Exchange" itself can therefore be (and is) allegorized or simulated, so, for one thing, value (or money, in this case) can itself become a commodity. It is the agreement or consensus, secured through a kind of collective projection, that an "exchange" has taken place which enables "value" to be determined, not the other way around (as was the case in a previous phase of capitalist accumulation).

The kind of metaproduction I am describing here is essentially dispersive, and its primary site is the corporation or the new kind of "laboratory" located in a science or technology park where whatever production takes place can almost conceal or minimalize itself because it merges "naturally" into a setting of lawns, fountains, and atriums. (It has to be stressed that the development described here has the character of an emphasis or a relative tendency: the familiar adage that there is a third world in the first world holds only too well for capitalism, and the age-old phenomenon of sweatshop labor, say, is as readily found today in New York or London as in Manila or Mexico City.) The current phase of capitalist expansion, with its progressively more extensive systems of metaproduction, has created a social order in which all the conditions of production and reproduction have been directly absorbed by capital—as a result of abolishing the boundary between society and capital, capital has itself become social. In order to further enable the extraction of new forms of surplus value—new forms that must be invented to deal with the crisis of the current paradigm of accumulation—capital has to extend its logic of command over the entire domain of productive social cooperation, thus effectively enveloping the whole of society. Only in this way can capital insert itself into the flow of social power, the power it needs to be precisely what it is—capital. Capitalist command is now universal and diffused; no longer is it enclosed and concentrated, as it was in the nineteenth century.[8]

Capital in this world–system is thus an immense machine, a machine that endlessly proliferates deconstitution after deconstitution and, concomitantly, reconstitution after reconstitution. The power of this "megamachine" surpasses that of the nation–state, although this superiority on the part of capital does not necessitate the abolition of the state—at least, it has not done so up to now. Instead, the state has undergone yet another a mutation, one that places it in a relation of reciprocity with capital. Capitalism is now a globalized algorithm or axiomatic that functions like a single city, of which the states are neighborhoods or sectors.[9] Deleuze and Guattari suggestively view capital as a "worldwide ecumenical organization," one which despite its overdetermining and polynucleated character does not totally displace the state. The state in its modern mutation is required by the current regime of accumulation to be a "model of realization" for capital. Capitalism wards off the limits that confront it by harnessing itself to the state–project: it is the state (i.e., governmentality) which among other things organizes social power on behalf of capitalism and thereby enables it to fend off the limits that threaten it.[10] (A qualification is necessary here: The state–project may undertake the task of organizing and regulating social power on behalf of capital, but there is nothing intrinsic to this project which guarantees that it will actually promote capital accumulation. There has to be a specific and appropriate productive conjunction between this or that disposition of state power and particular models of accumulation for the state–project to be able to serve as a site for the effectuation of capital. The state–form is not and can never be "essentially" capitalist.[11])

The transnational algorithm that is capital can ensure the "iso-morphy" (a term I have taken from Deleuze and Guattari) of diverse formations. ("Isomorphy" is not to be confused with "homogeneity" because, unlike the latter, it is compatible with the prevalence of a real diversity of formations.) As a kind of "grid" or "diagram" whose "logic" is to secure the conditions of its own reproduction, capital is situated at the crossing point of all sorts of formations (commercial or economic, religious, artistic, etc.) and thus has the complementary capacity to integrate and recompose noncapitalist sectors or modes of production. A case in point here would be a country such as Brazil, in which there is every conceivable kind of production from the tribal production of the Amazonian Indians to computer technology that is as advanced as anything to be found in the United States. It would seem that any and every kind of production—even that of a precapitalist variety—can be mediated in countries like Brazil and placed at the "disposal" of capital.[12] In such an "isomorphic" world literally everything can yield surplus value for capital. In a milieu in which capital has become ubiquitous, productive labor (as always, the sine qua non of capital) is also positioned within every component of society. But then, equally, the whole of society has to be organized so that capital is able to continue to reproduce itself. The outcome of this twofold development is that the absolute spatial division between exploiters and exploited posited by a more conventional Marxism has effectively been eliminated—the exploiters are everywhere and so are the exploited.

This state of affairs raises an important question in regard to the problematics of the mode of production because it is now clearer than ever that there must be a prior organization of social power before production can even begin to take place. In its metaproductive mode, capital has bypassed a phase in which it needed only to concentrate exploitative power at this or that specific point of production. In order to be what they are today, the modes of production depend crucially on an enabling matrix of antecedent processes which organize power and desire so that production can become possible. Another way of saying this would be to view the modes of production as expressions of desire, as the outcomes or derivations of this ceaselessly generative desire (or phantasy). What enables each mode of production to be constituted is a specific aggregation of desires, forces, and powers: it is this antecedent assemblage that produces the mode (of production). A requisite organization of productive desire or phantasy has always preceded capitalist accumulation—today, however, the very existence and nature of this desire, the process of its composition into an economy, has to be permeated by capital itself. The upshot is that nowadays capital has started to do much of its work even before it becomes "visible." This may look rather deviant to some who belong to the tradition of political materialism with which I am aligned, but it is broadly congruent with what Marx himself said, namely, that it is necessary for society—in this case, the state—to exist before capital can attain its condition of possibility, that a society/state capable of generating stockpiles of labor power must already exist if the extraction of surplus value is to occur.

Returning to the subject of culture, if capitalism is an axiomatic which transcodes or rearticulates a particular space of accumulation, culture is the site where capital organizes and distributes the kind of generative desire or phantasy that enables production and accumulation to take place. Capital has to saturate the spaces in which culture is organized and produced. And here the transnationalization of the capitalist axiomatic has as its "necessary" complement the transnationalization of the processes involved in the organization of generative desire (the locus of which is culture, as I have already pointed out).

What are some of the more decisive implications for a theory of culture of this transnationalization of the processes and apparatuses involved in the organization of generative desire? It has to be said that there is an anodyne, though perhaps salutary, sense in which talk of a "global culture" is simply a way of acknowledging, (merely) rhetorically or otherwise, that this latest mutation of capitalism— integrated world capitalism—has placed cultures and nations into even closer, but of course still mediated, proximities and adjacencies to each other. (I should stress that I am not at all interested in this "the world as global village" theme, alas prevalent in a certain kind of cultural studies, which suggests that we ought to have an analytical perspective on globalization because, say, *Dallas* is the most popular television program in Nigeria.)

But what does it mean to live in such a world—"our" world? A world marked by an experience of an ever-shrinking and interconnected globe, but a world whose character is at the same time harder to visualize because these interconnections have as their determining conditions displacements and transformations whose very expressions often convey no apparent sense of order or congruence? A world in which the past of a certain people can become the future of another people, and vice versa? A world in which no point of view or object ever stays the same because figure and ground alike are no longer in this or that state of fixity or suspension, but are continually in motion in space? This growth and development of radically new scenographies based on novel compressions and contortions of the space–time continuum (just adverted to here) is paralleled by the emergence of models of figuration that are equally distinctive. For this is also a world in which a new kind of story has typically come to be told (at least in the West), one in which description (but what is it to describe?) supplants the object, the concept dissolves into narrative (while at the same time we do not know how to adequately account for the many textual forms and operations associated with narrative), and the subject becomes point of view or "locus of enunciation" (although we cannot be certain anymore that "enunciation" is coextensive with signification and representation). Radically different powers of figuration, whose basic form is that of the allegorical, are made available by this supersession of the triad object–concept–subject, by the amalgam description–narrative–point of view.[13] (I will return to the subject of figuration and the allegorical shortly.)

It is customary these days to say that these developments are manifestations, however direct or tangential, of a historical and cultural transformation that amounts to an epochal rupture, in this case a break that usually goes by the name of "the postmodern." I don't have much to say about "the postmodern" (although there is certainly a great deal to be said about what this concept encompasses and designates), but I do want to note here that the changes and shifts designated by "the postmodern" also have to be seen in the context of what is possibly a new way of understanding identity and community (whether the local community or that larger community, the nation–state).

How has the experience, the constitutive experience, of living in a world of the kind I have just described affected our possible ways of talking about who we are, of saying what it means to belong to this or that community? (This is posed as a "conceptual," not an "empirical," question.) To be impossibly brief: Cultural and social formations are constituted on the basis of accords or "concerts."[14] These accords are dynamisms which make possible the grouping of whole ranges of events, personages, processes, movements, institutions, and so on, such that the ensuing integrated assemblage becomes an integrated formation. Capitalism, as a global axiomatic, is an accord of accords, accords which may be quite heterogeneous in relation to each other, but which express the same world, albeit from the point of view of the accord in question. Thus, to return to our earlier example—Brazil— the accord (or set of accords) that constitutes the "hi-tech" world to be found in downtown São Paolo and the accord (or set of accords) that constitutes the world of Stone Age production to be found among the tribespeople of the Amazonian basin are not inter-translatable, but what the accord of accords created by capitalism does (among many other things) is to make it possible for the artifacts produced by the tribes of the Amazonian basin to appear on the tourist markets in downtown São Paolo, where they are sold alongside Macintosh Power Books, Magnavox camcorders, and so forth. The seemingly disparate and incompatible zones of accumulation and production represented by downtown São Paolo and the Amazon basin are rendered "harmonious" by a higher-level accord or concert established by capital, even though the lower-level accords remain (qua lower-level accords) disconnected from each other. Each lower-level accord retains its own "spontaneity" (as it were), even as it is brought into concert with other such accords by the meta- or mega-accord that is capital. The "concerto grosso" achieved by the meta-accord enables the lower-level accords to remain dissociated from each other while still expressing the same world, the world of the current paradigm of accumulation and production.

It is true of course that there has long been an economic world–

system. If we accept the arguments of Janet Abu-Lughod, for instance, it would appear that such a system existed before the rise of the European imperial powers.[15] My claim here is not about the world–system as such, but rather about its present mutation, that is, the way(s) in which the mega-accord that is capital gets to be established in something like its current disposition. Accords are formed on the basis of selection criteria, that is, inclusion and exclusion criteria for this or that accord; these criteria also determine with which other (possible or actual) accords a particular accord will be consonant (or dissonant). What is happening today is that such selection criteria (which may or may not be explicitly formulated or entertained) seem to be weakening and are in some cases even in the process of disappearing altogether. Since selection criteria tend to function by assigning privileges of rank and order, their loss makes dissonances and contradictions difficult or even impossible to resolve and, correlatively, makes divergences easier to affirm. Events, objects, and personages can now be assigned simultaneously to several divergent and even incompossible series. Thus, for example, Lautréamont's somewhat derisive definition of reality ("the chance encounter between a sewing-machine and an umbrella on a dissecting table"), a definition that would perhaps have prompted some bewilderment on the part of a Kant or Descartes (or perhaps impelled them to become surrealists "before their time"), is virtually a commonplace now after all the culturally sanctioned opportunities many of us have had to negotiate the several historical avant-gardes, Borges, cyberpunk, and so forth. One could also mention, more typically in this connection, the music of Stockhausen or John Cage, where tones are arranged in series that escape any kind of resolution provided by the diatonic scale,[16] or (and here I indulge in favoritism) the contemporary British band Nurse with Wound or the collaborations of the experimental free jazz drummer William Hooker with the guitarist Thurston Moore. Such examples can be multiplied according to one's taste.

These accords appear to have been fairly decisively inserted into this culture, and they have precipitated the collapse of a number of once widely entrenched distinctions; the demarcations between public and private, inside and outside, before and after, and so on, have all become difficult, if not impossible, to sustain. In the process, however, accords thus detached from any conditions capable of guaranteeing their stability likewise become "impossible." We may be living in worlds, or reading texts, that are no longer predicated on any need to secure and maintain accords; worlds characterized by sheer variation and multiplicity; worlds that partake of a neo-Baroque more "truly" Baroque than its predecessor (as Deleuze seems to be indicating). It is in this context that the new powers of figuration I referred to earlier have emerged. These powers pivot on the allegorical form, in which description displaces the object, the concept gives way to narrative, and the subject becomes point of view or locus of enunciation. Let me illustrate this form by adverting to a passage from T. E. Lawrence's *Seven Pillars of Wisdom*, the text that furnished the basis for the screenplay of David Lean's movie *Lawrence of Arabia*:

> The dead men [Turkish soldiers just massacred by the Arab militia led by Lawrence] looked wonderfully beautiful. The night was shining down, softening them into new ivory. Turks were white-skinned on their clothed parts, much whiter than the Arabs; and these soldiers had been very young. Close round them lapped the dark wormwood, now heavy with dew, in which the ends of the moonbeams sparkled like sea-spray. The corpses seemed flung so pitifully on the ground, huddled anyhow in low heaps. Surely if straightened they would look comfortable at last. So I put them all in order, one by one, very wearied myself, and longing to be one of these quiet ones, not of the restless, noisy, aching mob up the valley, quarreling over the plunder, boasting of their speed and strength to endure God knew how many toils and pains of this sort; with death, whether we won or lost, waiting to end history.[17]

This is an allegory of the demise of the British Empire (or at least it can be read as such): (Lawrence's) "wishing to be a dead enemy soldier" is a description–predicate applicable to Lawrence that can be extracted from this passage; he is its subject-as-point of view; and the "concept" contained in this point of view is "the demise of the British Empire," of which Lawrence's wishing to be a dead/defeated enemy soldier now becomes the allegorical signifier. Of course, the end of the British Empire is not something that Lawrence had explicitly in mind at this time (or any other, almost certainly), and it is fairly safe to assume that it was not the kind of reading Winston Churchill had in mind when he said of *Seven Pillars* that "it ranks with the greatest books ever written in the English language" (to quote from the jacket blurb on my Penguin edition). But this is precisely how allegory works, that is, by presupposing the possibility of locating the event whose name is "T. E. Lawrence" in a series that radically diverges from its placement in a former or preceding (I won't use the term "original") series. That is to say, once allegory is allowed, there is little or no place for any accord or protocol of reading which prohibits this kind of movement or evacuation/eviction into another, divergent series. The event "T. E. Lawrence" can be dispersed into a multiplicity of semiotic frames, some of which are incompossible with others. (It almost goes without saying that in this highly succinct invocation of the allegorical I have had to gloss over the complexities of the various modes of allegorical interpretation.)

I have another (to me, somewhat more important) reason for wanting to dwell on this passage: it is, like the rest of Lawrence's book, saturated with assumptions and convictions about the subject matters addressed by this issue of *SAQ*—namely, nations, ethnicities, races, cultures, and identities—which can also be read allegorically. For instance, Lawrence's emphatic "Englishness" (that he was born in Wales, but did not see himself as Welsh is another, quite interesting story) can be allegorized at precisely the point of his identification with the Turkish soldiers he has killed; after all, *Seven Pillars of Wisdom* gives every indication that Lawrence did not demur from the then stock English view of Turkey as the proverbial "sick man of Europe." However, to allegorize "Englishness" in the scheme of things adopted here is to place it in at least two divergent series, and, moreover, it is to affirm one's acquiescence in principle to the relativization or dissolution of any accord or accords which stand in the way of allocating "Englishness" to two or more divergent series yielded by this process of allegorization. Since any such "transcendental" accord would entail selection criteria by which to determine what did or did not count as "Englishness," discarding it would effectively eliminate or render irrelevant its selection criteria as well. An "Englishness" deriving its sense from an end of empire (which in my view is what this allegory delivers) would be very different from the robust and settled sense of "Englishness" explicitly purveyed by Lawrence himself in this narrative.

=======

The following is a huge and maybe tendentious generalization, but I shall make it nonetheless. Let me pose this generalization in the form of a question: What if, because of this "systemic" loss of "transcendental" accords, those who belong to this culture now experience the world (e.g., their communal affiliations) in terms of propensities that are shot through with allegory? What if our very criteria of belonging to this culture are inextricably bound up with such allegorizing propensities? So that to say "I belong" is to say and do something that is necessarily emblematic and inscriptive of something else, something very different from what would be the case if there were some kind of necessity or requirement that preempted my (or your) "belonging" from being placed in two or more series that diverged.

If what I have just said were plausible, then the matter of conceiving (let alone assigning or determining) identities would become highly problematic. For the conceiving of identities is an undertaking that hinges crucially on the retention of the *concept* (as opposed to the *description*, which can be more recognizably propelled into this or that divergent series). The specification of an identity requires that the identity in question be determinate with regard to a concept ("being English," "being a communist," "being an academic," or whatever), a concept whose range of applicability is regulated by certain criteria of belonging. And if such criteria have no ("transcendental") accords to motivate and underpin them, then identities can always be read emblematically and inscriptively, that is, allegorically. So where does this leave us?

It leaves us with another, very different notion, that of a *singularity*. Intrinsic to the notion of a singularity is the principle that a common or shared property cannot serve as the basis of the individuation of X from all that is *not-X*: if I share the property of being over six feet tall with someone else, then that property cannot, in and of itself, serve to individuate either me or that person from each other. A singularity, the *being-X* of X that makes X different from all that is *not*-X, cannot therefore unite X with anything else. Precisely the opposite: X is a singularity because it is not united to anything else by virtue of an essence or a common or shared nature. A singularity is a thing with all its properties, and although some commonality may still pertain to this thing, that commonality is indifferent to it qua singularity. So, of course, Lawrence of Arabia will have the property "being English" in common with other people, many millions of them in fact. But a singularity is determined only through its relation to the totality of its possibilities, and the totality of possibilities that constitutes Lawrence is the totality of an absolute singularity—if another being had each and every one of the possibilities whose totality constituted and thus individuated Lawrence, then he would perforce be indistinguishable from Lawrence. He would be the same being or person.

In a time when "transcendental" accords do not give us our worlds or our texts, we have to look for another kind of politics: a politics which starts from the realization that our criteria of belonging are always subject to a kind of chaotic motion, that our cultures have always told us an enabling lie when they denied this knowledge and, through the denial of this knowledge, have made possible the invention of nation–states, tribes, clans, political parties, churches, perhaps everything done up to now in the name of community. Some of us sense that that time—up to now—has passed. Of course, we desperately need our solidarities. They are indispensable. But what we need just as desperately is a new and different politics, the politics of new spaces of liberty (to paraphrase Negri and Guattari), a politics capable of acknowledging that a true solidarity and an absolute singularity, far from being mutually exclusive, are in fact conditioned on each other in a polytopian world. A global culture would exist only if it permitted—"systemically," as it were—the coming into being of communities of such absolute singularities.[18]

Notes

For John Hick.

1   Deleuze and Guattari's "introduction" to philosophy, a best-seller in France, says of this trend: "La philosophie ne consiste pas à savoir, et ce n'est pas la verité

qui inspire la philosophie, mais des categories comme celles d'Interresant, de Remarquable ou d'Important qui décident de la réussite ou de l'échec"; see Gilles Deleuze and Félix Guattari, *Qu'est-ce que la philosophie?* (Paris, 1991), 80.

2   I make it seem here as if all these developments are of a relatively recent provenance, associated, however justifiably or tendentiously, with the "contemporary" (or perhaps more appropriately, "postcontemporary") intellectual/academic stances named "poststructuralism," "antifoundationalism," and so forth. This, as my reference to Nietzsche indicates, is not really the case: the obvious instance of Nietzsche apart, it could also be argued (as my colleague Fredric Jameson has done) that Marx's dramatology of the emergence of "value" is productively to be viewed as a "postcontemporary" and "anti-Cartesian" (in Jameson's terms) narrative staging of the modulation between the universal and the particular which takes place—"systemically," as it were—each time abstract equivalence is established between different things (e.g., when the proverbial miller and weaver exchange ten bags of flour for five yards of spun wool). It is not possible to do justice to Jameson's fascinating and complex restaging of Marx's drama of the stages of "value" in so brief a space, but what matters here (to this reader, at any rate) is his convincing demonstration that Marx's notion of value is not implicated in considerations of truth or error; that for Marx and his followers, argues Jameson, the manifestations of value must be judged in other ways, ways that account for the abstract quality of the instances of value in terms that are historical and social, not epistemological in this Cartesian sense. See Fredric Jameson, *Postmodernism, or, The Cultural Logic of Late Capitalism* (Durham, 1991), 231ff.

3   Gilles Deleuze, *The Fold: Leibniz and the Baroque*, trans. Tom Conley (Minneapolis, 1993). In this work Deleuze links the rise of the Baroque with a specific crisis in capitalism (110) and argues that the "Baroque introduces a new kind of story . . . in which description replaces the object, the concept becomes narrative, and the subject becomes point of view or subject of expression" (127). The "moment" par excellence of the Baroque for someone like Deleuze is thus eminently transposable: given certain mutations in the "idea" of the Baroque ("an operative conception" and not "an essence"), it is precisely that of the late twentieth century (which, of course, is better viewed, if such periodizations mean anything, as the time of the twenty-first century, the "current" century having ended, as it were, in 1968).

4   For more on the fold, in addition to Deleuze's book on Leibniz (cited in n. 3), see Gilles Deleuze, *Foucault*, trans. Seán Hand (Minneapolis, 1986). The Deleuzian fold is perhaps best viewed as an allegory of "the always between," a ceaselessly mobile "between" which connects radically different entities and states. (On page 13 of *The Fold*, Deleuze draws from Leibniz's philosophical lexicon and gives as examples of such entities "inorganic bodies," "organisms," "animal souls," "reasonable souls," etc.) Cyberspace is perhaps most conveniently characterized as a computer-driven, interactive feedback loop enfolding immense numbers and types of biological and technological components or dimensions.

5 See Perry Anderson, *Lineages of the Absolutist State* (London, 1974), 11. See also Samir Amin, *Accumulation on a World Scale: A Critique of the Theory of Under-development*, trans. Brian Pearce (New York, 1974), 20ff.; and "*Accumulation on a World Scale*: Thirty Years Later," *Rethinking Marxism* 1 (1988): 59. Here I am mindful of Etienne Balibar's reminder that the writers of the *Communist Manifesto* are to be credited with "uncovering" or "recovering" a "materialism other than that of history or even practice: *a materialism of politics*"; see his "Vacillation of Ideology," trans. Andrew Ross and Constance Penley, in *Marxism and the Interpretation of Culture*, ed. Cary Nelson and Lawrence Grossberg (Urbana and Chicago, 1988), 171; his emphases.

6 I mention Foucault as an exemplary figure in the formulation of this new "theoretics" of knowledges, but Pierre Bourdieu has also done significant work in this area. The most important figure for me here, however, has been Gilles Deleuze (see his interpretations of Foucault in the work cited in n. 4). For a more detailed treatment of the notions of concept, function, and field, see Deleuze and Guattari, *Qu'est-ce que la philosophie?*. Deleuze has analyzed cinema as a "crystalline regime" in his two-volume work on the cinema; see also his "Sur le régime cristallin," *Hors Cadre* 4 (1966): 9–45. I am deeply indebted to Deleuze's accounts for many of my formulations regarding conceptual practice.

7 The next few paragraphs owe a great deal to my article " 'The Continued Relevance of Marxism' as a Question: Some Propositions," *Polygraph* 6/7 (1993): 39–71.

8 This development has been extensively analyzed by Toni Negri and other thinkers of the Italian *operaismo* tendency. I discuss Negri in " 'Reinventing a Physiology of Collective Liberation': Going 'Beyond Marx' in the Marxism(s) of Toni Negri, Félix Guattari, and Gilles Deleuze," *Rethinking Marxism* 7 (1994): 9–27.

The "crisis of the current paradigm of accumulation" is a product of the convergence or intersection of two other crises: (1) the failure of the Keynesian or New Deal paradigm in the 1970s, owing primarily to the "unacceptable" social costs and inflationary consequences of policies adopted by governments to ensure that consumption was somehow always in line with production; and (2) the failure of the "monetarist" response to this crisis of Keynesianism, specifically, the switch of emphasis from fiscal to monetary policy (allied to a range of supply-side instruments) turned out to be too deflationary, and monetarism was effectively abandoned in the early 1980s by its primary advocate, the British Conservative government. The present crisis is thus one in which there is no (theoretically or practically) viable system of national macroeconomic management capable of producing sustained, noninflationary growth.

9 I have taken this conception from Gilles Deleuze and Félix Guattari, *A Thousand Plateaus: Capitalism and Schizophrenia*, trans. Brian Massumi (Minneapolis, 1987), 434–35.

10 In terms of capital's relationship to its limits, the gist of what I would like to say is expressed by Deleuze and Guattari in the following passage from *A Thousand Plateaus (463)*:

> Capitalism . . . would like for us to believe that it confronts the limits of the Universe, the extreme limit of resources and energy. But all it confronts are its own limits (the periodic depreciation of existing capital); all it repels or displaces are its own limits (the formation of new capital, in new industries with a high rate of profit). This is the history of oil and nuclear power. And it does both at once: Capitalism confronts its own limits and simultaneously displaces them, setting them down further along.

11 This point is cogently argued for by Bob Jessop in *State Theory: Putting Capitalist States in Their Place* (Cambridge, 1990), 338ff.

 Clearly, a lot more can be said about the place of the state in the present phase of capitalist development than is ventured here. Some critics of the proposition of a globalized economy have maintained that there are no plausible grounds for holding to this proposition while nation–states still play a decisive part in international economic management; see, for example, Paul Hirst and Grahame Thompson, "The Problem of 'Globalization': International Economic Relations, National Economic Management and the Formation of Trading Blocs," *Economy and Society* 21 (1992): 357–96. The point here, however, is not whether there is a place for the nation–state in the international economy, but whether—the undeniable instrumentality of states notwithstanding—there is still a pervading "isomorphy" (as I define the term below) among sectors, blocs, formations, and so on. It is a mistake to think, as Hirst and Thompson seem to, that this "isomorphy" must be premised on the elimination of a real, effective state–project.

12 I owe the example of Brazil to Toni Negri, "Interview with Alice Jardine and Brian Massumi," *Copyright*, No. 1 (1988): 83.

13 See Deleuze, *The Fold*, 125–27.

14 Ibid., 130ff.

15 Janet Abu-Lughod, *Before European Hegemony: The World–System A.D. 1250–1350* (New York, 1989).

16 John Cage thus describes his work as "music without measurements, sound passing through circumstances"; see his "Diary: Emma Lake Music Workshop 1965," in *A Year From Monday: New Lectures and Writings* (Middletown, CT, 1969), 22.

17 T. E. Lawrence, *Seven Pillars of Wisdom* (London, 1962), 315.

18 The idea of the allegorical as the mode of figuration par excellence for a post-traditional world is to be found in Deleuze, *The Fold*, 125–27. The brief account of singularity given here is taken from the much more substantial treatment in Gorgio Agamben, *The Coming Community*, trans. Michael Hardt (Minneapolis, 1993). I am grateful to Michael Hardt for drawing this work to my attention and for discussions that have helped me in the writing of this article.

Notes on Contributors

MARTIN BERNAL is Professor of Government and Adjunct Professor of Near Eastern Studies at Cornell University. He is the author of *Black Athena*, Vol. 1 (1987) and Vol. 2 (1991), which won the A.N.C. Kwanzaa Prize (1987 and 1991), the *Socialist Review* Book Award (1987), and the American Book Award (1990).

DOMINIQUE COLAS, Professor of Political Science at the Université de Paris–Dauphine and the Paris Institut d'Etudes Politiques, is the editor of *La Pensée politique* (1992) and the author of *Le Glaive et le fléau* (1992), an English translation of which by Amy Jacobs, *Civil Society and Fanaticism, Conjoined Histories*, is forthcoming from Stanford University Press.

MIRIAM COOKE is Director of the Asian and African Languages Program, Duke University. The author of *War's Other Voices: Women Writers on the Lebanese Civil War* (1988), among other works, she is currently coediting (with Roshni Rustomji-Kerns) a volume entitled *Blood into Ink: 20th Century South Asian and Middle Eastern Women Write War*.

DAPHNA GOLAN is a researcher at the Harry S. Truman Institute for the Advancement of Peace, Hebrew University, Jerusalem, and the director of a women's center, Bat Shalom of the Jerusalem Link. She is the author of *Detained without Trial—Administrative Detention in the Occupied Territories* (1992).

THOMAS LAHUSEN, Associate Professor of Russian Literature at Duke University, has recently edited a special issue of *SAQ* (94:3, Summer 1995), *Socialist Realism without Shores*, as well as *Intimacy and Terror: Soviet Diaries of the 1930s* (coedited by Véronique Garros and Natalia Korenevskaya, 1995). He is also the coauthor (with Edna Andrews and Elena Maksimova) of *On Synthetism, Mathematics and Other Matters: Zamiatin's Novel We* (in Russian, 1994).

JOCELYN LÉTOURNEAU teaches Canadian history at Laval University and is a member of CÉLAT. His research interests include the political economy of Canada and the historical consciousness of its youth. He completed his *SAQ* article while a fellow at the Zentrum für Interdisziplinäre Forschung, Universität Bielefeld, Germany.

ANDERS LINDE-LAURSEN, who was born in Denmark and earned his Ph.D. at the University of Copenhagen, is now a member of the Department of European Ethnology at the University of Lund, Sweden. Currently a Visiting Fellow in the Department of Anthropology, Indiana University, his most recent publications are *Det nationales natur: Studier i dansk–svenske relationer* (1995) and *Nordic Landscopes: Cultural Studies of Place* (1995).

WYATT MACGAFFEY, John R. Coleman Professor of Social Sciences at Haverford College, is the author of *Art and Healing of the BaKongo* (1991) and *Astonishment and Power* (a 1993 Smithsonian exhibition catalogue), among other works. His recent work on translations of KiKongo texts has been supported by the National Endowment for the Humanities.

JOHN MCCUMBER, Professor of Philosophy and German, Northwestern University, is the author of *Poetic Interaction: Language, Freedom, Reason* (1989) and *The Company of Words: Hegel, Language, and Systematic Philosophy* (1993).

V. Y. MUDIMBE, William R. Kenan, Jr., Professor of French and Italian, Stanford University, was at the time of the international seminar on which this issue of *SAQ* is based Professor of Romance Studies, Comparative Literature, and Cultural Anthropology at Duke University. He is the author of the prize-winning *Invention of Africa* (1988) and *The Idea of Africa* (1994), among other works.

KENNETH SURIN is Professor of Comparative Literature at Duke University. In his previous career, he was a professor of religion.

IMMANUEL WALLERSTEIN is Distinguished Professor of Sociology and Director of the Fernand Braudel Center for the Study of Economies, Historical Systems, and Civilizations at Binghamton University (SUNY). His many publications include the three-volume *Modern World–System* (1974, 1980, 1989) and *Geopolitics and Geoculture: Essays on the Changing World–System* (1991).

The South Atlantic Quarterly

Volume 94
Copyright © 1995 by Duke University Press
Durham, North Carolina

Contents of Volume 94

No. 1, Winter, pp. 1–370; No. 2, Spring, pp. 371–656; No. 3, Summer, pp. 657–979; No. 4, Fall, pp. 981–1206

Theory & Image

MICHIGAN QUARTERLY REVIEW

PRESENTS A SPECIAL ISSUE
FALL 1995 / WINTER 1996

THE MOVIES: A CENTENNIAL ISSUE

EDITED BY LAURENCE GOLDSTEIN AND IRA KONIGSBERG

ESSAYS: Michael Anderegg on Orson Welles; Leo Braudy on method acting and 50s films; Alexander Cohen on future technology; Bonnie Friedman on *The Wizard of Oz*; Tom Gunning on technologies of vision; William Harrison on being a screenwriter in Hollywood; Diane Kirkpatrick on the use of movie materials in modern art, with a portfolio; Ira Konigsberg on psychoanalysis and film; Martin Marks on music in *Casablanca* and *The Maltese Falcon*; Arthur Miller: a memoir of the movies; William Paul on the changing screen; Andrew Sarris on sound film and the studios; Gaylyn Studlar on fan magazines and star persona; Alan West on film and opera.

REVIEWS: Thomas Doherty on animated film; Laurence Goldstein on new books about masculinity and the male body in film; Poonam Arora on multi-cultural cinema.

ARCHIVAL MATERIAL: "Success," a treatment in story form by Aldous Huxley; an essay by H.D. on Garbo; a defense of censorship by Vachel Lindsay; a memoir by Samuel Marx on producing at M-G-M the first film about the atomic bomb.

POETRY: Tom Andrews, Margaret Atwood, Daniela Crasnaru, Lynn Emmanuel, David Lehman, Mordechai Geldmann, Ira Sadoff, Diann Blakely Shoaf, Gisela von Wysocki, Charles Webb, S. L. Wisenberg, David Wojahn, and others.

FICTION: Kathleen de Azevedo, Laura Antillano, Jim Shepard, Eugene Stein, and others.

For the two volumes of "Movies" send a
check for $16 (includes postage and handling) to:
Michigan Quarterly Review, 3032 Rackham Building,
University of Michigan, Ann Arbor, MI 48109-1070

WRITING & RITUALS

Neither Cargo nor Cult: Ritual Politics and the Colonial Imagination in Fiji
Martha Kaplan
248 pages, paper $15.95, library cloth edition $49.95

Writing the Past, Inscribing the Future: History as Prophecy in Colonial Java
Nancy K. Florida
464 pages, 16 illustrations, paper $18.95, library cloth edition $49.95

Misers, Shrews, and Polygamists
Sexuality and Male-Female Relations in Eighteenth-Century Chinese Fiction
Keith McMahon
384 pages, 6 drawings, paper $19.95, library cloth edition $49.95

Asia/Pacific as Space of Cultural Production
Rob Wilson and Arif Dirlik, editors
384 pages, 3 maps,
paper $15.95, library cloth edition $39.95
a boundary 2 book

DUKE UNIVERSITY PRESS · · · · · · · · · · · · · · ·

Box 90660 Durham, NC 27708-0660

Faculty of Arts
UNIVERSITY COLLEGE GALWAY, IRELAND

MA

in

Culture & Colonialism

A one-year multi-disciplinary MA by examination and minor dissertation

Taught courses include:

- Colonialism in Twentieth-Century Cultural Theory
- Gender and Colonialism
- The Creation of Colonial Societies: Ancient, Medieval and Early Modern Times
- Imperialism in the Nineteenth and Twentieth Centuries: Theory and Practice
- Colonialism and Political Economy
- Decolonization and Neo-Colonialism : The Politics of 'Development'
- Literature and Colonialism
- Cinema and Colonialism

FURTHER INFORMATION & APPLICATION FORMS MAY BE OBTAINED FROM:

Dr Lionel Pilkington
Department of English
University College Galway
Ireland
Tel: 353-091-24411
Fax: 353-091-24102
e-mail: lionel.pilkington@ucg.ie

Inside
the Mouse

**Work and
Play
at Disney
World**

The Project on Disney

"This is riveting reading, a clever mixture of journalistic reportage and, in the main, lightly referenced theory."—Max Farrar, Times Higher Education Supplement

Post-Contemporary Interventions

288 pages, 52 b&w photographs, paper, $15.95, library cloth edition $47.95

Blending personal meditations, interviews, photographs, and cultural analysis, *Inside the Mouse* looks at Disney World's architecture and design, its consumer practices, and its use of Disney characters and themes. The authors consider the park as both private corporate enterprise and public urban environment, focusing on questions concerning the production and consumption of leisure.

"A very inviting combination of high theory and informal memoir, Inside the Mouse *reworks some of the ground rules for writing cultural studies. Concentrating on issues of family, work, consumption, pleasure, and representation, it is original, highly thoughtful, and very engaging."*— Eric Smoodin, editor of Disney Discourse

Duke University Press Box 90660 Durham, North Carolina 27708-0660